LETTERS FROM HOME

Letters from Home

The Creation of Diaspora in Jewish Antiquity

MALKA Z. SIMKOVICH

EISENBRAUNS | University Park, Pennsylvania

Library of Congress Cataloging-in-Publication Data

Names: Simkovich, Malka Z., author.
Title: Letters from home : the creation of diaspora in Jewish antiquity / Malka Z. Simkovich.
Other titles: Creation of diaspora in Jewish antiquity
Description: University Park, Pennsylvania : Eisenbrauns, [2024] | Includes bibliographical references and index.
Summary: "Investigates rhetorical strategies Egyptian and Judean Jews used in their writings about life outside the Land of Israel, charting the development of the contested idea of diaspora and the making and breaking of boundaries that took place within Jewish letters of the Hellenistic era"—Provided by publisher.
Identifiers: LCCN 2024006027 | ISBN 9781646022748 (hardback) | ISBN 9781646022755 (paperback)
Subjects: LCSH: Jewish diaspora. | Jews—Egypt—History—586 B.C.–70 A.D. | Jews—Judaea (Region)—History—586 B.C.–70 A.D. | Jewish letters—Egypt. | Jewish letters—Judaea (Region)
Classification: LCC DS135.E4 S59 2024 | DDC 909/.04924—dc23/eng/20240315
LC record available at https://lccn.loc.gov/2024006027

Copyright © 2024 Malka Z. Simkovich
All rights reserved
Printed in the United States of America
Published by The Pennsylvania State University Press,
University Park, PA 16802–1003

New English Translation of the Septuagint. Copyright © 2007 International Organization for Septuagint and Cognate Studies, Inc. Used by permission of Oxford University Press. All rights reserved.

New Revised Standard Version Bible. Copyright © 1989 National Council of the Churches of Christ in the United States of America. Used by permission. All rights reserved worldwide.

Eisenbrauns is an imprint of The Pennsylvania State University Press.

The Pennsylvania State University Press is a member of the Association of University Presses.

It is the policy of The Pennsylvania State University Press to use acid-free paper. Publications on uncoated stock satisfy the minimum requirements of American National Standard for Information Sciences—Permanence of Paper for Printed Library Material, ANSI Z39.48–1992.

For Saba

Thy letters have transported me beyond
This ignorant present, and I feel now
The future in the instant.
Macbeth, *1.5*

(Immigrants disembarking at Ellis Island)
Customs official: Step up! Please confirm your origins and religion!
Man 1: I'm from Poland. Catholic.
Official: Got it. Next.
Man 2: Italy. I'm Catholic too.
Official: Right. Next!
Man 3: Why do you need to know my religion? How is that relevant? And where I'm from? I'm a citizen of the world!
Official: Ah, another Jew.

CONTENTS

List of Abbreviations xi
Map... xiv

INTRODUCTION 1

PART 1: ORIGINS OF DIASPORA

CHAPTER 1. Sacred Writings and the Question of Exile 17

CHAPTER 2. "A Letter They Did Not Send Us": An Early Case Study of Judea-Diaspora Relations.. 34

CHAPTER 3. The Judean Invention of the Diaspora................... 46

CHAPTER 4. The Hellenistic Strategies of Jewish Letter Writers.........61

PART 2: THE CONSTRUCTION OF DIASPORA IN JUDEAN LETTERS

CHAPTER 5. "Open Your Heart to His Law": Judean Letters to Egypt in 2 Maccabees 1:1–2:18 71

CHAPTER 6. "For Those Living Abroad Who Wish to Gain Learning": The Transformations of Esther and Ben Sira into Judean Correspondence 92

CHAPTER 7. "There Is Open Shame upon Us": Fantasies of Exile in the Letter of Baruch..110

PART 3: THE DISSOLUTION OF DIASPORA IN DIASPORIC LETTERS

CHAPTER 8. "A Sign of Friendship and Love": Fantasies of Judea in the Letter of Aristeas 129

CHAPTER 9. "Boundless and Immeasurable Earth": The Prayers of 3 Maccabees 153

CONCLUSION 172

Acknowledgments 179
Bibliography 183
Subject Index 201
Ancient Source Index 207

ABBREVIATIONS

Translations of the Hebrew Bible and New Testament in this book adhere to the New Revised Standard Version. With the exception of 2 Maccabees, translations of the books of the Apocrypha adhere to the New Revised Standard Version. Translations of the Septuagint adhere to the New English Translation of the Septuagint. Unless otherwise stated, translations of other texts are my own. Abbreviations of ancient sources follow those provided in the *SBL Handbook of Style*, 2nd ed.

Ancient Sources

1QM	War Scroll
Add Esth	Additions to Esther
b.	Babylonian Talmud
Bar	Baruch
1 Esd	1 Esdras
2 Esd	2 Esdras
Esth. Rab.	Esther Rabbah
Herodotus	
Hist.	*Histories*
Jdt	Judith
Josephus	
Ag. Ap.	*Against Apion*
Ant.	*Jewish Antiquities*
J.W.	*Jewish War*
Let. Aris.	Letter of Aristeas
1 Macc	1 Maccabees
2 Macc	2 Maccabees
3 Macc	3 Maccabees

Philo
    Alleg. Interp.   *Allegorical Interpretation*
    Cherubim   *On the Cherubim*
    Confusion   *On the Confusion of Tongues*
    Contempl. Life   *On the Contemplative Life*
    Creation   *On the Creation of the World*
    Decalogue   *On the Decalogue*
    Drunkenness   *On Drunkenness*
    Embassy   *On the Embassy to Gaius*
    Flaccus   *Against Flaccus*
    Flight   *On Flight and Finding*
    Heir   *Who Is the Heir?*
    Hypothetica   *Hypothetica*
    Migration   *On the Migration of Abraham*
    Moses   *On the Life of Moses*
    Prelim. Studies   *On the Preliminary Studies*
    QE   *Questions and Answers in Exodus*
    QG   *Questions and Answers in Genesis*
    Rewards   *On Rewards and Punishments*
    Spec. Laws   *On the Special Laws*
    Virtues   *On the Virtues*
Pss. Sol.   Psalms of Solomon
Sanh.   Sanhedrin
Sib. Or.   Sibylline Oracles
Sir   Sirach (Ecclesiasticus)
S. 'Olam Rab.   Seder 'Olam Rabbah
t.   Tosefta
T. Ash.   Testament of Asher
T. Benj.   Testament of Benjamin
T. Dan   Testament of Dan
Tg.   Targum
T. Jos.   Testament of Joseph
T. Levi   Testament of Levi
T. Naph.   Testament of Naphtali
Tob   Tobit
Wis   Wisdom of Solomon

Secondary Sources
AB   Anchor Bible
AJEC   Ancient Judaism and Early Christianity
BJS   Brown Judaic Studies

BZAW	Beihefte zur Zeitschrift für die alttestamentliche Wissenschaft
DCLS	Deuterocanonical and Cognate Literature
JAJ	*Journal of Ancient Judaism*
JAOS	*Journal of the American Oriental Society*
JBL	*Journal of Biblical Literature*
JQR	*Jewish Quarterly Review*
JSJ	*Journal for the Study of Judaism*
JSJSup	Journal for the Study of Judaism Supplements
JSP	*Journal for the Study of the Pseudepigrapha*
TAD	Textbook of Aramaic Documents from Ancient Egypt
TSAJ	Texts and Studies in Ancient Judaism
WUNT	Wissenschaftliche Untersuchungen zum Neuen Testament

Map of Ptolemaic Egypt circa 240 BCE. Map by Simeon Netchev (CC BY-NC-SA 4.0).

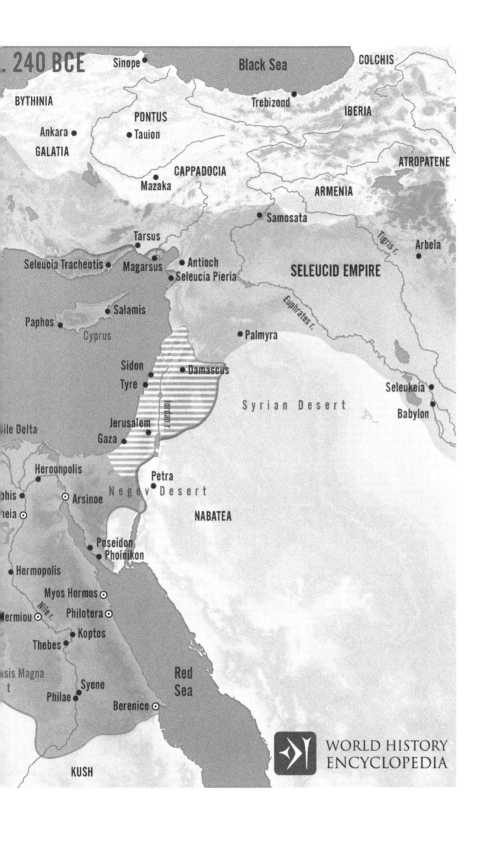

Introduction

IN THE YEAR 407 BCE, a man living on a small stretch of land in the Nile River dispatched a letter to an official of the Persian Empire stationed in the province of Yehud. The man, whose name was Jedaniah, described a dramatic crisis that had unfolded on the island, known at the time as Yeb. Egyptian priests living alongside Jedaniah's Judean community had desecrated and vandalized the temple that local Judeans had built to worship their god. The Judeans responded to this desecration with communal mourning. They wore sackcloth, fasted, and prayed for their temple to be restored. But they also needed guidance. They needed to know whether officials in Yehud, a region that included the city of Jerusalem, would permit the rebuilding and restoration of their temple as a place where meal offerings, animal burnt offerings, and incense could be presented to their god. This question lay at the heart of Jedaniah's letter, which was recorded in two versions by scribes working on the island. Sometime later, perhaps in early 406 BCE, Jedaniah and his community received a response. The Judeans of Yeb were granted formal permission to rebuild their temple, but they were to use the building only for meal offerings and incense. Animal sacrifices on the altar of Yeb would not be permitted.

Jedaniah's correspondence with authorities in Yehud raises intriguing questions. Did Judean and Persian officials in or near Jerusalem view themselves as wielding authority over the Judean community of Yeb? What was the nature of this perceived authority? How did Judeans living in Yeb and elsewhere outside the land of Israel understand their relationship with their kin living near Jerusalem? How can correspondences between these communities shed light on their relationships, their lives, and their sense of identity?

Only a few generations ago, it was commonplace for scholars to dismiss diasporic Jewish life as marginal to the "authentic" Jewish experiences that took place in the land of Israel. Underlying this scholarship was the presumption that Jews living outside the land of Israel were collectively guilty of sin and were suffering consequent estrangement from their god. Yet from a demographic perspective, life outside the land of Israel was a massive success.

After the deportations to Babylonia in 597–586 BCE, most Judahites and their descendants lived outside of the land of Israel, where they established robust communities. Even after Persian authorities vanquished Babylon and granted Judahites permission to return to their homeland around 538 BCE, most of them decided to remain outside their homeland. Over time, they scattered throughout the Persian world. Some settled locally in communities along the Tigris and Euphrates Rivers, and others moved west to regions lying along the Mediterranean Levant. Despite literary and material evidence suggesting that the descendants of these Judahites embraced their ancestral identities regardless of where they lived, scholars of early Judaism working in the late nineteenth and early twentieth centuries focused primarily on literature produced in the land of Israel to answer the question of how the "Judean-ism" of the early Second Temple era transitioned into the "Judaism" of the late Second Temple era, which the early rabbis inherited.

Over the past century, the discovery and publication of additional Jewish texts from the Second Temple era has prompted scholars to reassess prevailing assumptions about early Jewish self-understanding in the diaspora. The varied outlooks expressed in this literature testify to the countless ways that Jews outside the land of Israel creatively assimilated cultural ideas that circulated in their host communities. These Jews also retained ancestral practices such as circumcision, dietary laws, and the Sabbath. References to synagogues in Egyptian Jewish literature indicate that Jews in the Hellenistic world gathered regularly to read their scriptures, a practice that bound them in common memory and contributed to their sense of connection to Jews who lived elsewhere. The recollection of a shared past served to close the geographic gaps among Jews who were spread throughout the world.

The present consensus that most Jews in the Second Temple period held a positive attitude toward life outside the land of Israel marks a welcome turn from the anti-diaspora bias that once pervaded scholarship. And yet, academics who study the Jewish diaspora overcorrect this earlier scholarship, which privileged the study of Jewish life in the land of Israel. Analyzing material evidence from outside the land of Israel, these academics presume that the "diaspora" was a self-evident reality rather than a discursive category. Judean literature produced within the land of Israel that engages with the category of diaspora, meanwhile, is often ignored.

This book intends to fill this gap. It considers how Jewish writers working in the Second Temple period constructed their self-understandings in relation to other Jews who lived outside their communities. These writers accomplished this task by composing letters to one another and by producing documents about one another. All of these texts respond to new political realities in the late second century BCE. It was during this time that the political failures of the Hasmonean monarchy were coming into focus after decades of optimism that the victory over the Seleucid Greeks would herald a period of stability marked by the return of diasporic Jews to the land of Israel. This did not happen. Instead, conflict with the Seleucids continued, and Jews in Judea found themselves impacted by civil conflict occurring in the Ptolemaic Kingdom as well. At one point, Judea was nearly attacked by the Ptolemaic queen Cleopatra III, but this plan was abandoned at the last minute thanks to the intervention of Cleopatra's Jewish generals.

Judeans had good reason to assume that their Jewish kin in Egypt would negatively compare their own relatively successful experiences with the Ptolemies to the Judeans' diplomatic failures. The contrast between Egyptian Jewish and Judean Jewish roles in the military campaigns of their host and neighboring governments would have been especially stark. While Egyptian Jews enjoyed representation at high levels of the Ptolemaic government and military, Jews in Judea were forced to accept a humbling truce following their conflict with the Seleucids. The terms included a mandate that the Judean king John Hyrcanus accompany the Seleucid king Antiochus VII on his military excursions. For Judeans, such participation was not a sign of their exceptional political power. It was a sign of their political humiliation.

The Judeans' truce with the Seleucid Kingdom and their dependence upon Jewish diplomacy in Egypt may have been cause for concern among Judeans who worried that Egyptian Jews would note these setbacks and choose not to celebrate the newly established Judean holiday commemorating the Hasmonean reclamation of the Jerusalem Temple. After all, this holiday marked the defeat of the Seleucid Empire, and such a celebration may have rung hollow during these turbulent years.

In the face of these disappointments, Judeans wanted to show their kin who lived abroad, particularly those living in Egypt, that they were far from powerless. In the early decades of the Hasmonean monarchy, the Judean Kingdom had achieved remarkable political expansion. More importantly, Judeans perceived themselves as conservators of Jewish tradition amid this political turmoil. They believed that Jews in Egypt should neither pity nor condescend to them. Instead, Egyptian Jews were to admire them as authorities.

Judean Jews shaped their identities in ways that defined themselves against Jews who lived elsewhere. They developed the idea that the diaspora was a space on one side of an invisible boundary line, a space where Judeans were not meant to be, a space that they defined in relation to their homeland. Jews living in Egypt, however, shaped their identities in ways that bonded them to Judean Jews. Rather than enforcing an invisible boundary, these Jews expressed devotion to both their host government and their ancestral homeland. Given that the diaspora was drawn by those who lived outside of it and ignored by those who lived within it, any study of diasporic identity must chart the push and pull of boundary making and boundary breaking by engaging with both Judean and non-Judean texts.

The argument at the heart of this book is that Jewish writers in the Second Temple period expressed ideas about the relationship between Jews within and without the land of Israel by speaking in one another's voices. Judean Jewish texts purport to quote biblical heroes and religious leaders who bemoan that Jewish suffering outside Judea is a divinely wrought consequence of sin. Jewish texts produced in Egypt, on the other hand, purport to quote Judean Jewish leaders who embrace life outside the homeland as legitimate and long-lasting. As a fragile social category, the idea of diaspora became a flexible template upon which early Jews developed competing cosmologies that addressed the question of how the land of Israel figured into God's relationship with the covenantal people.

Judean and Egyptian Jews who wrote about these issues used letter writing as their primary mode of expression. By addressing their texts to real and imagined interlocutors, these Jews framed their cases as expressions of the personal and unshakable bond that connected them to Jews across the diasporic line. They also exhorted their audiences to change their attitudes by using epistolary strategies common in Hellenistic letter writing. These strategies include pseudepigraphy, the attribution of texts to older and more well-known authoritative figures, and ventriloquy, the use of embedded prayers, dispatches, and speeches that speak in the voices of Jews living outside the authors' communities. Both techniques represent a wish-fulfillment strategy that incorporates ideas about Judea's role into the construction of Jewish identity and intra-Jewish relations.[1]

Egyptian and Judean Jewish writers also used layering techniques in their letters. One such technique, known as mirroring, features diverse characters who all express a consistent attitude that reflects the opinion of the author. An example of such mirroring is known today as *mise en abyme*. In literature, this technique features a person engaging in a particular action that mirrors an identical action that took place in the past. This past action parallels yet another identical action that took place earlier. Such layering produces the effect of continuous motion and implies that the author's position is ancient and unrefuted. All of these strategies produce a "surround-sound" system that amplifies the writers' voices and subdues dissenting ones.

---

1. As Goldstein puts it, "A propagandist perpetrates a fiction only if it is useful in his own time" ("Baruch," 202–3). Cf. Rosenmeyer, *Ancient Greek Literary Letters*, 4–5; Wollenberg, *Closed Book*, 99; Reed, *Demons, Angels, and Writing*, 110.

Scholarship on Jewish Identity Formation

As the field of biblical studies developed into an academic discipline in the late nineteenth century, some Protestant biblical scholars treated the diaspora as a punishment exacted against an impious people whose sins earned them divine contempt.[2] Even Jewish scholars viewed the diaspora as disjunctive to the authentic traditions of early Judaism, which was thought to have taken shape in the land of Israel and, later, in eastern regions of the Roman Empire.[3]

Jewish studies scholars have only recently begun to vigorously engage with the question of how early Jews outside the land of Israel developed their identities under their host governments.[4] Among the first scholars to make the case that these Jews held a positive attitude toward diasporic Jewish identity was Thomas Kraabel, who argued that diasporic Jewish writers transformed an older and more negative notion of exilic living, which he called "Exile theology," into "Diaspora theology," a positive identity that affirmed God's covenantal promises to Israel.[5] One of the first collections of articles about the Jewish diaspora in the Hellenistic age was a 1992 volume that celebrated Kraabel's work.[6] It was soon followed by Shaye Cohen and Ernest Frerichs's 1993 edited volume *Diasporas in Antiquity*.[7] These studies marked the beginning of a new period in the scholarship of early Judaism. Outside of a few exceptions, scholars now take a positive approach toward the Jewish diaspora by rejecting the premise that it was characterized by abject longing for a return to the Jewish homeland.[8] Most agree that Jewish life outside Judea was characterized by successful integration into the Jews' host cultures.[9]

---

2. Martin Hengel was one of the first scholars to reject this negative approach. See Hengel, *Judentum und Hellenismus*. For a review of relevant scholarship, see Hicks-Keeton, "Putting Paul in His Place," 6–7.
3. See, for instance, Feldman, "Jews in Hellenistic Egypt," 215–37.
4. The present interest in Jewish diasporic identity is part of a general rise in interest in diaspora and displacement theory, which studies how identities are constructed amid tensions between loyalty to one's homeland and one's current location. See Tölölyan, "Rethinking Diaspora(s)," 3–36; Hall, "Cultural Identity and Diaspora"; Bhabha, *Location of Culture*.
5. Kraabel, "Unity and Diversity," 49–60.
6. Overman and McLennan, *Diaspora and Judaism*.
7. Cohen and Frerichs, *Diasporas in Antiquity*.
8. See, for instance, Barclay, *Jews in the Mediterranean Diaspora*; Barclay, *Negotiating Diaspora*; Gafni, *Land, Center, and Diaspora*; Scott, "Self-Understanding of Diaspora Jews," 173–220; Rutgers, *Hidden Heritage*; Gruen, "Diaspora and Homeland," 18–46; Gruen, *Diaspora*; Rajak, "Jewish Diaspora," 53–68; Rajak, "Synagogue and Community," 22–38.
9. Van Unnik's claim that diasporic Jews viewed their lives outside of Judea as fulfillments of a divine curse is an exception (*Das Selbstverständnis der jüdischen Diaspora*). Tuval's opposing position that Jews outside Judea were indifferent to Judean affairs is also an outlier. Present consensus is that Jews who lived outside Judea in the Hellenistic era expressed fealty to the Jerusalem Temple and, at the same time, embraced the cultural opportunities offered to them by their host empire. See Tuval, "Doing Without the Temple," 181–241; Tuval, *From Jerusalem Priest to Roman Jew*.

A positive approach toward diasporic Jewish life also pervades recent scholarship on identity formation in early Judaism. Among these works are John Collins's 2017 book *The Invention of Judaism*, which examines how Jewish law was interpreted and observed by Jews in the Second Temple period.[10] Ishay Rosen-Zvi and Adi Ophir's 2018 book *Goy: Israel's Multiple Others and the Birth of the Gentile* argues that fluid boundaries between Jews and non-Jews in the Second Temple period gave way to hardened boundaries in the rabbinic period.[11] Daniel Boyarin's 2018 work *Judaism: The Genealogy of a Modern Notion* demonstrates that the term "Judaism" did not enter common usage until Christians began to use the term as a marker of what they were not.[12] And Eyal Ben-Eliyahu's 2019 work *Identity and Territory: Jewish Perceptions of Space in Antiquity* describes the process by which Jews came to view the land of Israel not merely as a geographic space but as an idea that embodied God's covenantal promises.[13] Most recently, scholars have begun to speak of a Torah-centered theology that began to unite Jews in the second century BCE.[14]

These works, which consider how Jews in the Second Temple and rabbinic periods created normative theological ideas, presuppose that Jews who lived outside the land of Israel in the Hellenistic era viewed their lives in positive terms.[15] They also downplay or ignore evidence suggesting that most Judean Jews probably did not hold a positive attitude toward Jews who lived abroad.[16] These studies likewise do not explore the dialogic nature of diasporic identity construction. Instead, they ignore how Judean writers developed ideas about Judean exceptionalism and how writers outside Judea dissolved diasporic boundaries. My aim is to show that the diaspora was a construct that was enforced by some and negated by others. This construct produced a tension that lay at the core of the relationship between Jews who lived in Judea and Jews who lived in Egypt.

The Vocabulary of Early Judaism

One of the principal challenges facing historians today concerns the question of whether to describe a past time and place with words that did not exist at

---

10. Collins, *Invention of Judaism*.
11. Ophir and Rosen-Zvi, *Goy*.
12. Boyarin, *Judaism*.
13. Ben-Eliyahu, *Identity and Territory*.
14. Adler, *Origins of Judaism*; cf. Ben Zvi and Honigman, "*Tōrâ*-Centered Israel."
15. Trotter, *Jerusalem Temple in Diaspora*.
16. Many of these studies focus entirely on Judea. See, for example, Eckhardt, *Jewish Identity and Politics*, especially its cheekily titled introduction, "Introduction: Yet Another Book on Jewish Identity in Antiquity." The volume would have been less superfluous had it focused on Jewish life outside Judea.

that time and place. It is tempting, and sometimes useful, to describe early Jewish life with words that have no ancient equivalents. The terms *culture*, *holy land*, and *religion* were rarely used in correlating Greek and Latin forms. When they do appear in early Jewish and Hellenistic literature, these words evoke meanings that are different from their contemporary equivalents.[17] Still, it would be a mistake to avoid all words that were not used by Jews during the Second Temple period. Cultural concepts existed at this time that lacked corresponding terms that designated their meanings. One example concerns the notion of covenant. The word *covenant* barely appears in the writings of the late first-century historian Josephus, but the notion of a covenant with God's elect people drives Josephus's writings about early Israelite history.[18] The concept of martyrdom offers another example. The possibility that one could willingly sacrifice their life on behalf of their beliefs was an idea that circulated widely among Jews in the late Second Temple period.[19] And yet, the Greek word for martyr, *martus*, which means "witness" in most ancient sources, was not used to denote martyrdom until the second century CE.[20] And though it is only mentioned a few times in Second Temple literature, some form of the Greek word *Ioudaismos*, often translated as "Judaism," likewise existed in the late Second Temple period, though the question of what *Ioudaismos* actually meant is a matter of lively debate. The word appears in the second-century BCE work 2 Maccabees (2:21; 8:1; 14:38 [twice]), as well as in 4 Maccabees (4:26), a philosophical work dependent on 2 Maccabees. It also appears in the writings of Paul, who seems to have used it in reference to a transitive "Judaizing" (Gal 1:13–14).[21] The word *diaspora* was also rarely used by Jews in the Hellenistic era. Jews who had access to their Hebrew scriptures were aware that the Hebrew word *gôlâ* was used in these texts as a designation for the Babylonian

17. Reed, "Ancient Jewish Sciences," 195–253.
18. Halpern-Amaru, "Land Theology," 201–29.
19. Take, for example, 2 Maccabees, which was written by a Greek-speaking Jew in North Africa toward the end of the second century BCE. It preserves a story about a mother and her seven sons who are commanded by Antiochus IV Epiphanes to violate their ancestral law by eating pork on pain of death. The mother, who encourages her sons to die before giving up her own life, is lauded by the author as an exemplar of piety (2 Macc 7:1–42). On how martyrdom in antiquity played a role in identity formation, see Droge and Tabor, *Noble Death*; Moss, *Myth of Persecution*.
20. The first surviving text to use this word is a Christian text, the Martyrdom of Polycarp. See D. Schwartz, *Judeans and Jews*, 102–4, 164n38.
21. *Ioudaismos* resurfaces in the fourth century CE on two inscriptions found in Stobi (Macedonia) and Porto (Italy), which refer to the customs and practices linked to the people of Judea (Boyarin, *Judaism*, 50–51). Boyarin argues that the absence of the term *Judaism* (*Ioudaismos*) in early Jewish writings indicates the absence of the concept in early Jewish imagination. The reference to *Ioudaismos* in Galatians, therefore, must refer to the adoption of Judean practices and specifically to the practices of the Pharisees (Boyarin, *Judaism*, 50). A more well-known designation for Jews at this time was *Israel*, which by the end of the Second Temple period was used as a marker for both place and people. See Ben-Eliyahu, *Identity and Territory*, 17–30; Boyarin, *Judaism*, 15–17.

exile, but most Jews did not use the term *diaspora* as a Greek equivalent to *gōlâ*. Despite the rarity of the term *diaspora*, Jews in Judea and Egypt were probably aware of the concept of diaspora as a social category whose meaning was distinct from the *gōlâ*, and whose significance was contested.[22]

While writing this book, I had to make choices about when to use the term *Judeans* and when to use the term *Jews*. Both words are legitimate translations of the Hebrew word *yəhûdîm* and the Greek word *Ioudaioi*. Following Shaye Cohen's position that the shift from *Ioudaioi* as an ethnogeographic marker to an ethnoreligious designation took place sometime in the second century BCE, I use the term *Jews* in discussions regarding literature produced in the Hasmonean era (164–63 BCE) or later. As for *Judeans*, I use this term in two ways. In some contexts, I use it as a chronological designation that refers to descendants of Judahites who lived under Persian rule (539–334 BCE). Elsewhere, I use *Judeans* as a geographic term that refers to people who lived within the land of Israel. The multivalent nature of this term is endemic to its origins. Jews and Greeks alike who lived in the Hellenistic era were also perplexed about how to define *Ioudaioi*.

The opening chapters of this book consider how Judeans developed a concept of authoritative Torah, another multivalent term in the Second Temple period. In this book, I refer to *Torah* as an authoritative set of scriptural texts that early Judeans viewed to be a representation of an ancient tradition that preceded the Babylonian exile and, according to some, derived from Moses's revelation at Sinai.[23] I also occasionally use the lowercase term *torah* in reference to fluid teachings that were not thought to have been preserved in the written scriptures. In the early Second Temple period, the word *Torah* could convey either meaning. Since Hebrew does not use uppercase and lowercase type, I err on the side of referring to *Torah* rather than *torah*. Like the words *yəhûdîm* and *Ioudaioi*, the contemporary ambiguity of the word *Torah* is an outgrowth of the word's ancient multivalence.

Additionally, for the sake of clarity I use the term *Second Temple period* in this book, despite the fact that it presumes disproportionate focus on Jerusalem. I also use the term *rabbinic period*, despite the fact that Jews outside rabbinic communities lived throughout the Roman world during this time, though we know little about these Jews. I use the term *Septuagint*, despite the fact that the term implies that the entire Hebrew Bible was translated into

---

22. Dufoix, *Dispersion*, 32–34.
23. See Cohen, *Beginnings of Jewishness*. For the argument that Second Temple references to *Ioudaios* should be read as *Judeans*, see Mason, "Jews, Judaeans, Judaizing, Judaism;" Boyarin, *Judaism*, 52; cf. Lowe, "Who Were the ΙΟΥΔΑΙΟΙ?," 101–30; Lowe, "Ἰουδαῖοι of the Apocrypha," 56–90. A review of the debate regarding this term appears in Alexander and Berkowitz, *Religious Studies and Rabbinics*.

Greek all at once as an instantly cohesive and canonical collection. I occasionally use the term *religious*, although it is unlikely that people living in the ancient world thought with a conceptual category precisely analogous to what we refer to as "religious" today, with its individual and communal parameters. In this book, *religious* refers to the practices, rituals, materials, and texts that people in the Hellenistic era used to express their beliefs about the unseen divine forces that controlled the world.[24] Finally, with one exception that pertains to the author of Ben Sira's translation into Greek, I avoid using the term *Judaism*, and I use *diaspora* only in contexts where the term is not self-evident but a reflection of the conceptual category that Judean Jews were trying to build. These words were not widely used in the Second Temple period, and early Jewish writers did not view the meanings of their Greek and Hebrew corollaries as self-evident.

While scholars of the Second Temple period recognize the problems that arise from using terms such as *Judaism* or *religion*, most still treat the word *diaspora* as a self-evident category that bears uncontested meaning. Some scholars presume that Jews in the Hellenistic era were split into two populations: those who lived in Judea, and those who lived in the diaspora. Their treatment of these populations as fundamentally different has led to analyses that approach diasporic Judaism as a distinct and coherent whole. The historical reality, however, was more complex. Jewish communities outside Judea were decentralized and varied, and Jews who lived outside Judea were neither practitioners of Judean practices nor members of a cohesive group that opposed Judean Jewry. This study will examine the relationship between Jews who lived in Judea and Jews who lived in Egypt without assuming that either population represented a monolithic form of Judaism.

The Jews of Egypt

My reason for focusing on Jewish documents that address the relationship between Jews in Judea and Jews in Egypt is largely pragmatic. Many such texts survive, and their existence testifies to the fact that Jews living in these regions were interested in one another. Correspondences between Jews in Judea and Jews in Egypt, therefore, can be treated as a set of case studies that can

---

24. For differing perspectives on the term *religion* and *religious* in the Roman era, see Smith, "Religion, Religions, Religious," 269–84; Nongbri, *Before Religion*; MacRae, *Legible Religion*. On the question of whether a term that is analogous to the modern word *religion* existed among Greeks, see D. Schwartz, *Judeans and Jews*, 93–99, 103, 162, who argues that *thrēskeia* was a close analog. Boyarin dismisses this understanding as being overly reliant on dictionaries (*Judaism*, 20).

help modern readers better understand how Jews in antiquity negotiated the boundaries of diaspora.[25]

One of the central questions driving this study is whether correspondence between Judean and Egyptian writers can illuminate our understanding of how Jews negotiated the boundaries of diaspora in the broadest sense. Is the exceptionalism expressed in Judean letters to Jews in Egypt exclusive to the Judean-Egyptian relationship? And were Jews in Egypt the only Jews outside of Judea to produce literature that forged bonds between their communities and those in Judea?

My findings suggest that while the Judea-Egypt relationship was distinctive, at least some Judeans held negative attitudes toward all Jewish life outside their homeland. This antagonism is evident in Judean letters to Egyptian communities and in Judean documents intended for local Judean audiences. The question of whether Egyptian writings about Judea represent a broader "diasporic" attitude toward Judea is more elusive. Egyptian Jewish texts may well be representative of a unique outlook that negates diasporic boundaries by bonding Jews in Egypt to Judean Jewry. As far as we know, no other Jewish population outside Judea did more work to dismantle the association between Jewish life outside Judea and divine punishment than the Jews of Egypt. Given their efforts and the distinctive nature of the Judea-Egypt relationship, an exploration of this relationship's origins will be my starting point.

The Structure of This Book

The first section of this book, "Origins of Diaspora," explores early evidence of a tense dynamic between Judeans within and without the land of Israel and investigates rhetorical strategies that Judeans incorporated into their writings about life outside the land of Israel.

Chapter 1, "Sacred Writings and the Question of Exile," examines how biblical writers treated the notion of exile. After the Babylonian exile, Judeans struggled to reconcile the biblical idea that expulsion from the land of Israel was a mark of divine anger with the reality that pious Judeans chose to remain in exile rather than to return to their homeland. Judeans who did return to Judea began to highlight the authority of the Torah and the central role of the temple as points of connection that united Judeans. Paradoxically, the notion

---

25. On current approaches to a "split" Jewish diaspora in the Greco-Roman world, see Edrei and Mendels, "Split Jewish Diaspora," 91–137; Millar, "Rural Jewish Community," 351–74; Edrei and Mendels, "Split Jewish Diaspora Again," 305–11.

of an authoritative Torah played a key role in the failure of most Judeans to return to the land of Israel.

Chapter 2, "'A Letter They Did Not Send Us': An Early Case Study of Judea-Diaspora Relations," analyzes correspondences between Judeans living on the Egyptian island of Yeb, known today as Elephantine, and Judean leaders in Jerusalem in the late fifth century BCE. These correspondences indicate that in the early Second Temple period at least some Judeans in Jerusalem viewed themselves as arbiters of proper ancestral worship for all Judeans, even those who lived outside the land of Israel. They also clarify that even at this early stage, there existed a misalignment between how Judeans in the Persian province of Yehud and Judeans who lived elsewhere viewed their relationship.

Chapter 3, "The Judean Invention of the Diaspora," demonstrates that the writers of the Septuagint, the Greek translation of the Torah produced in the late third century BCE, played a major role in the development of a negative Judean attitude toward Jewish life abroad. These writers solidified the ancient association between exile and shame by inventing the word *diaspora* to translate passages of the Hebrew Bible that predict the Israelites' future expulsion from their land and exposure to the foreign nations. Some passages in the Septuagint that use the word *diaspora* link God's ancient curses to the future and thus to the Septuagint readers' present reality. The Septuagint, which may have been produced in Egypt but was influenced by Judean modes of thinking, can be read as a Judean missive intended for Egyptian Jewry. While the Septuagint's producers associated the ancient curse of exile with Judeans living outside the land of Israel in their own day, Judeans who lived outside the land of Israel made no such association.

Chapter 4, "The Hellenistic Strategies of Jewish Letter Writers," explores the rhetorical techniques that Egyptian and Judean letter writers used to strengthen their arguments about the theological meaning of Jewish life outside Judea. These writers used pseudepigraphy and ventriloquy to speak in the voices of Jews who represented their own communities or in the voices of Jews who lived across the diasporic line. They also employed mirroring techniques to convey an effect of continuous motion that stretched back into the earliest stages of Jewish history. Judean and Egyptian Jews used these strategies to conceptualize their identities through the prism of Jewish experiences across the diasporic line.

The second section of this book, "The Construction of Diaspora in Judean Letters," explores Judean texts produced in the second century BCE that treat Jewish life abroad as an embodiment of divine rejection. These texts reflect the disappointment that Judeans felt after the Hasmonean victory over the Seleucid Greeks. Judean Jews had anticipated that this victory would give way to a period of uncontested Judean power and an ingathering of all Jews to Judea, but they continued to experience conflicts with their neighbors, and no mass return to Judea took place. Judean texts produced during this period express anxiety that Jews living abroad were not sufficiently loyal to Judea. Letters dispatched from Jerusalem to Jews living in Egypt implore Egyptian Jews to observe holidays that affirm Judean exceptionalism and authority. Other novelistic texts written for Judean audiences speak in the voices of Jews who live outside the land, and who ask God to put an end to the exile. All figures in these texts portray Jerusalem as the authoritative epicenter of global Jewish life.

Chapter 5, "'Open Your Heart to His Law': Judean Letters to Egypt in 2 Maccabees 1:1–2:18," examines two Judean letters to Egyptian Jews produced in the late second century BCE that exhort Egyptian Jews to observe a newly established holiday commemorating the Hasmonean victory over the Seleucid Greeks. Both letters employ mirroring strategies that produce multiple layers of voices, and both letters cite older documents that affirm the authority of the Jerusalem Temple and its administrators. While the contents of these letters convey kinship and affection for Egyptian Jews, their rhetorical style enforces Judean exceptionalism and authority.

Chapter 6, "'For Those Living Abroad Who Wish to Gain Learning': The Transformations of Esther and Ben Sira into Judean Correspondence," explores how Judean authors of pietistic texts established boundaries between Judea and the land outside of it. This chapter compares a Greek version of the story of Esther with the wisdom text Ben Sira, which were both authored by Judean Jews in the late second century and early first century BCE. During this period, when Jews in Judea were reeling from Hasmonean infighting and Jews in Egypt were being pulled into partisan conflicts within the Ptolemaic dynasty, Judean writers refashioned popular Jewish works into texts aimed at an Egyptian Jewish audience. As missives to Egyptian Jews, these Judean documents reminded their readers that their religious and political identities should be shaped by their loyalty to Judea and the Jerusalem Temple. The prologue added by Ben Sira's translator and the additions produced by Esther's translator reflect a shared desire to convince Jews living in Egypt that Jewish authority derives from Judea. Both texts are also framed as dispatches from Judean Jews to Egyptian Jews that convey an intimate care for their Egyptian Jewish readers.

Chapter 7, "'There Is Open Shame upon Us': Fantasies of Exile in the Letter of Baruch," turns to a Judean document written for local Jews: the book of Baruch. Baruch's opening section is a fictional narrative that recalls how Jeremiah's scribe facilitated the dispatch of a letter from Judahites in the Babylonian exile to Judahite leaders in Jerusalem. Their letter expresses contrition for the people's sins and acknowledges that their exilic circumstances symbolize divine rejection. In attributing his work to Baruch, the author of this Judean text employed pseudepigraphy, which situated his story along a continuum of texts that argue for the centrality of Judea. By speaking in the voices of exiled Judahites, the author also used ventriloquy, which suggested that his position was unanimously supported by all Jews. These rhetorical devices, which were borrowed from real correspondences between Judeans and Egyptian Jews, assured Judean readers that the hardships of their kin who lived abroad reflected God's just punishment of a sinful people.

The third and last section of this book, "The Dissolution of Diaspora in Diasporic Letters," considers how Egyptian Jews shaped their identities in ways that bonded them to Judean Jews. These Jews did not affirm the Judeans' cosmological map, which divided the world into two parts. Instead, they embraced the dual identities that connected them to their host country and their ancestral homeland by dissolving the conceptual boundary between Judea and the diaspora. This dissolution is evident in Egyptian Jewish texts that present the God of Israel as universally present, powerful, and interested in all of humankind. These texts use the same rhetorical strategies present in Judean documents to buttress their claim that Egypt is a place where Jews can live and thrive.

Chapter 8, "'A Sign of Friendship and Love': Fantasies of Judea in the Letter of Aristeas," studies the Letter of Aristeas, an Egyptian Jewish text that recalls the circumstances in which the Hebrew Torah was translated into Greek and, in doing so, presents the relationship between Jews and Greeks as affectionate and enduring. The author takes pains to present Judean and Egyptian Jews as united in practice and belief to make the case that all Jews uphold traditions that are consonant with Hellenistic values. These Jews are devoted to Judea and the Jerusalem Temple but also believe that the Torah contains universal wisdom. Like Judean letters that employ strategies that create a ripple effect of continuous affirmation, Aristeas includes layered voices that portray Egyptian and Judean Jews as being in harmonious agreement about the Torah's value. Aristeas thereby legitimizes the Septuagint while assuring Judean Jews that Egyptian Jews are loyal to their ancestral homeland. The author of this novella may have been sensitive to the fact that Judean Jews of his time worried that political tensions in Egypt would cause Egyptian Jews to dissociate from Judea.

Chapter 9, "'Boundless and Immeasurable Earth': The Prayers of 3 Maccabees," analyzes the Egyptian Jewish novella 3 Maccabees. Because this novella is usually read as a critique of Jews who embraced Hellenistic culture, it is often contrasted with the Letter of Aristeas, which expresses a positive attitude toward Hellenism. Indeed, while Aristeas bonds Egyptian Jewry to Judean Jewry by presenting Jews in both regions as sharing values with Greeks, 3 Maccabees argues that Jews in both regions are subject to the same threats.

Nevertheless, Aristeas and 3 Maccabees share rhetorical features. They include letters written by Greeks and Judeans who embrace the Jewish community in Egypt, and they employ literary techniques such as ventriloquy, pseudepigraphy, mirroring, and *mise en abyme*. Like the author of Aristeas, the author of 3 Maccabees sought to assure his Judean kin that, despite his desire to maintain a safe environment for Jews living alongside their Greek neighbors, Egyptian Jewish loyalty to Judea remained steadfast.

This book's conclusion offers further reflections on the question of why Judean Jews developed the notion of diaspora while Jews living in Egypt dismantled it. Both populations produced works that aimed to convey the impression of unanimity, but both were responding to realities that were far from harmonious. In the late second century BCE, Jews in Egypt were under pressure to form uncertain political alliances, which they knew would impact their local communities and Jewish communities in Judea. These Egyptian Jews produced works that declared devotion to the Jerusalem Temple. But they also insisted that good relations with their Greek neighbors did not compromise their religious identities. The interest that Judean leaders showed in Egyptian Jews, meanwhile, was religious in content but political in nature. These Judeans wanted assurance that their Jewish kin in Egypt, many of whom were financially successful and politically powerful, would support and prioritize Judean interests.

This book argues that the diaspora, which was understood as a theologically meaningful category that encompasses all the space outside the land of Israel, was born out of a tenuous construct that required constant dialogic enforcement. It is not a comprehensive analysis of all early Jewish attitudes toward the category of diaspora that are expressed in literary and material evidence. There were certainly Jews living in the land of Israel during the Hellenistic era who were unconcerned with the religious welfare of their Jewish kin abroad. There were also Jews outside the land of Israel who embraced the idea that Judea and its Jewish inhabitants occupied an authoritative role in their religious lives. Rather than surveying all related evidence on this subject or focusing on the works of prolific intellectuals such as Philo and Josephus, this book conducts a limited textual study that focuses on letters and speeches. I have chosen to home in on such texts because I am not merely interested in what Judean and Egyptian Jews believed. I am interested in how these Jews presented themselves to one another, cared for one another, and cultivated connections with one another, even when they disagreed on important theological questions. The letters and speeches cited in this book bear a uniquely relational quality, and the commitment of their writers to an ongoing relationship with Jews who lived elsewhere, even during times of conflict, inspired me to write this book.

PART 1

Origins of Diaspora

CHAPTER 1

Sacred Writings and the Question of Exile

MANY JUDAHITES WHO LIVED during the First Temple period believed that Jerusalem was home to the sole legitimate temple dedicated to the God of Israel. These Judahites visited Jerusalem to pay homage to the god who had brought the world's most powerful empire to its knees, rescued their ancestors from slavery and anonymity, protectively escorted them through the wilderness, and communicated with them through Moses until the time came for them to enter the land of Canaan.[1] In the barren and uninhabited desert, the people's ancestors learned of their god's dominion, which spanned cultivated societies and vast stretches of uninhabited lands. These ancestors, the Israelites, settled in the land of Canaan, where they were destined to establish a society organized around one temple dedicated to the God of Israel.

Judahites believed that their capacity to live peacefully in the land of Israel was a barometer of their relationship with the God of Israel. Tranquil borders and fertile fields meant that God found the people's worship to be satisfactory. Threats from foreign nations, and the land's failure to produce food, meant that the people had not shown proper loyalty to God. During these dark times, the people turned to their scriptural traditions for assurance that God's covenantal promises were permanent. They remained hopeful that God would fulfill the promise to restore the people's independence in their land.

Prophetic traditions about God's loyalty to the people became especially resonant after the Babylonian invasions of Jerusalem that took place in 597–586 BCE, during which the Jerusalem Temple was destroyed and many Judahites were taken by force into exile. Judahite writers treated these catastrophes as marks of divine anger toward the people, who had failed to maintain exclusive devotion to God and their ancestral traditions. But the people's

---

1. I use the term *Judahites* in reference to people who lived in the land of Judah following the split of Solomon's kingdom shortly after his death. The Judahites' Israelite counterparts, who were exiled by the Assyrian Empire in 722 BCE, are thought to have been less devoted to Jerusalem and its temple.

fortunes changed in 539 BCE when the Persian king Cyrus conquered Babylon and permitted the exiled Judahites to return home. Cyrus's edict marked the beginning of a slow trickle of migration back to the land of Israel, now known as the Persian province of Yehud. Most Judahites, whom scholars refer to as Judeans in this new historical context, did not return. They elected to stay put or made their homes elsewhere along the Mediterranean coast. A schism began to develop between Judeans who believed that returning to Yehud was a divine imperative and a fulfillment of prophetic predictions of restoration, and Judeans who believed that their successful settlement abroad confirmed that the omnipresent God cared for and protected all Judeans equally, regardless of where they lived.

How did this split in attitude take place? And how did the Judean people manage to stay unified despite it? The observance of practices such as the Sabbath, dietary laws, and male circumcision may have contributed to the Judeans' cohesion. But the most significant uniting factor was probably their scriptural traditions, which they referred to as *tôrâ*, a Hebrew word that means *instruction*. In the Persian era, the word *tôrâ* referred to an amorphous collection of written and oral teachings that were thought to have derived from Moses, who received these teachings from God.[2] Judeans who returned to their land after the exile—and Judeans who remained outside of it—mined these teachings for meaningful material that would tell them how God wanted the people to live their lives. Judeans who heard and read *tôrâ* interpreted these words and produced new writings that cited them.

Jews in the later Hellenistic era also supported their ideas about the meaning of Jewish life outside the land of Israel by appealing to *Torah*. Using the genre of letter writing to establish a close connection with their audience, Jews in the land of Israel wrote letters to Egyptian Jews that cite Torah passages that highlight the land of Israel's central role in God's plan to safeguard the Jewish people. Egyptian Jews, likewise, cited Torah traditions in documents that point to how God protects the covenantal people who live outside Judea.[3] To clarify how sacred writings became central to these conversations, I will

---

2. Adler argues that Judeans only began to treat the Torah as an authoritative compendium of binding regulations in the Hasmonean period. References to *Torah* as authoritative written tradition, however, appear in Daniel, Ezra-Nehemiah, and other early Second Temple texts. Jews may not have practiced a uniform set of laws during this early period, but they were developing a system of ideas whose roots were thought to have been embedded in their scriptural traditions. See Adler, *Origins of Judaism*.

3. Exceptions to the rule existed on both sides of the diasporic line. Some Judean texts, like Jubilees and Ben Sira, show little interest in diasporic Jewry, while some texts produced outside of Judea, such as 2 Maccabees, show intense interest in the Jerusalem Temple. Yet the former texts do not encourage Jews outside of Judea to remain where they are, and 2 Maccabees does not wish for an ingathering of the exiles. See Simkovich, "Greek Influence," 293–310.

first address how Judahites and their Judean descendants developed opposing views about the meaning of exile, and will then consider how attitudes toward Torah brought these Judeans together.

Exile in the Hebrew Bible

Judahites living during the First Temple period heard their prophets speak about God's promise of a peaceful and bountiful life in the land of Israel. They also heard warnings that, should the people neglect the laws conveyed to them by the prophets, God would expel them from their land and throw them into exile. Living under foreign rule, the people would be unable to properly practice their ancestral laws, and assimilation would become nearly inevitable. Exile also came with a heavy emotional price. Ruled by people who did not recognize the power of their god, the people would experience public shame and degradation. One tradition preserved in Deuteronomy (28:15–30:4) cites Moses warning the people that, should they stray from God's instructions, "In the morning you shall say, 'If only it were evening!' and at evening you shall say, 'If only it were morning!'—because of the dread that your heart shall feel and the sights that your eyes shall see" (28:67). Images of battered bodies and crushed spirits terrified the Judahites.

To prevent this disastrous possibility, the people shared stories about their ancestors' enslavement in Egypt. They reminded one another that during this dark period, when their survival as a nation hung in the balance, God upended the natural world and transformed them from the lowly slaves of human rulers to the dignified servants of a powerful deity. In recognition of God's kindness, the people were expected to show God constant loyalty. Their return to Egypt, or even the expression of a desire to return to Egypt, was perceived as a rejection of the love that God had shown the people.[4] Such a rejection would result in exile and the reexperience of the suffering, enslavement, and near annihilation that their ancestors in Egypt had experienced. Yet this suffering would be followed by a restoration to the land that God had lovingly promised the Israelites following their redemption from Egypt.[5]

The Babylonian exile was perhaps the most transformative event in all of Jewish history. But it did not come as a shock. The seeds of exile were planted

---

4. On exile theology, see Kraabel, "Unity and Diversity," 49–60; Carroll, "Deportation and Diasporic Discourses," 63–88.

5. This land was viewed as home to God's presence but was not commonly described as sacred until the rabbinic period. Only a few Second Temple–era texts, 2 Maccabees, the Psalms of Solomon, the Testament of Job, the Sibylline Oracles, and the writings of Philo, describe Jerusalem as a holy city. See Ben-Eliyahu, *Identity and Territory*, 75, 85; Gruen, *Diaspora*, 239.

four centuries earlier, when David's monarchy split into two kingdoms following Solomon's reign. The kingdom of Judah, which included Jerusalem and its environs, occupied the southern half of David's kingdom, while the kingdom of Israel occupied the north. Prophetic writings preserved in the Hebrew Bible report that the Israelite kingdom faced distinct challenges. To maintain good relations with the kingdoms and city-states that neighbored it, some Israelite kings arranged political marriages between their children and the children of neighboring rulers. These arrangements weakened cultural borders and led to the Israelites' incorporation of foreign worship practices. Prophets who lived in the Northern Kingdom warned that disobedience to the God of Israel would lead to exile, but the Israelite people did not take heed. In 722 BCE, the Neo-Assyrian king Shalmaneser V invaded and exiled the Israelite Kingdom. Prophets in both Israel and Judah interpreted this disaster as an act orchestrated by the people's God, who had made good on the ancient promise to expel the people from their land as punishment for their disobedience. The exiled Israelites assimilated into their host culture, lost their cohesive identity, and never returned to their ancestral land.

Shortly after this catastrophe, in 701 BCE, the Neo-Assyrian king Sennacherib tried to conquer the kingdom of Judah, which at this time was ruled by the pious king Hezekiah. According to the biblical account, Hezekiah took counsel with the prophet Isaiah and prayed desperately for the people's salvation. That very night the Assyrian military suffered a plague that led to their last-minute retreat (2 Kgs 19:14–35). The Judahites took this as a sign: the same God who had thrown the sinful Israelites into oblivion had rewarded the Judahite king for his loyalty.

During the remaining years of the First Temple period, Judahites recalled these events as sobering reminders of what could happen if the people neglected to stay true to the God who took them out of Egypt. They continued to perceive exile as a terrifying sign of God's abandonment, though their prophets assured them that exile would be followed by reconciliation with their ever merciful God. The people's faith in this assurance was tested during the disastrous events leading up to the Jerusalem Temple's fall in 586 BCE. Biblical writers vividly described the starvation, disease, and devastation that the Judahites suffered as the Babylonian army invaded. Even worse than the physical suffering was the humiliation that the Judahites endured as foreign nations witnessed their subjugation. Later Judean writers imagined these nations gloating and gleeful as they watched the Judahites, whose ancestors had proclaimed that their God controlled all nations, being led into exile. This exile came to be known as the *gōlâ*.[6]

---

6. 2 Kgs 24:14–16; Jer 28:6 (35:6 LXX); 29:1 (36:1 LXX); 29:4 (36:4 LXX); 29:16, 20, 31 (36:31 LXX); 46:19 (26:19 LXX); 48:7 (31:7 LXX), 11 (31:33 LXX); 49:3 (30:19 LXX); Ezek 1:1; 3:11, 15;

The question of how Judahites managed to preserve their identity in exile continues to befuddle scholars. Yet literature produced after the people were permitted to return to their homeland suggests that they emerged from this ordeal as a transformed people. Unlike their Israelite predecessors, Judahites responded to the trauma of displacement by generating strategies that ensured their cohesion and prevented their assimilation. These strategies included the sharing of ancestral memories conveyed in oral and written formats and the development of a new approach toward the concept of written torah. Before the Jerusalem Temple's destruction, many Judahites understood *tôrâ* as a term that denoted teachings derived from earlier prophets and Moses, who received these teachings from God. In exile, however, the meaning of *tôrâ* took on a more central and expansive quality. As a result, prophets, scribes, and teachers familiar with oral and written traditions took on prominent leadership positions in Judahite society.

Cyrus's edict permitting Judahites to return to Yehud produced an unprecedented demographic split that divided the people. Judahite leaders exhorted the people to return to their homeland, rebuild the temple in Jerusalem, and restore their old way of life that had been lost in exile.[7] Their pleas were only moderately successful. Most of the people chose to stay put or relocated to western regions of the empire outside of Yehud. According to the book of Ezra, the initial wave of returnees included just 42,360 people in addition to 7,337 servants and two hundred singers (2:64–65).[8]

The spread of the people referred to by scholars as Judeans throughout the Persian Empire presented new challenges. The biblical prophets had promised that the exile would end with the restoration of the people to their homeland and the rebuilding of Jerusalem, but these promises had only been partly fulfilled. The temple was rebuilt, and the Persians had granted Judeans in Yehud some independence to govern their local affairs. But these Judeans lacked the independence that their predecessors had enjoyed during the First Temple period. Even more problematically, other Judeans now lived all over the Persian Empire, and the promised ingathering of Judeans had not taken place. Judeans living in Yehud were left to debate complex questions: Had the exile come to an end with Cyrus's decree, or was it ongoing? And if the exile

---

11:24–25; 12:3–4, 7, 11; 25:3; Amos 1:15; Zech 6:10; 14:2; Ezra 1:11; 2:1; 4:1; 6:19–21; 8:35; 9:4; 10:6–8, 16; Neh 7:6. The Hebrew word *gôlâ* also appears in six Qumran fragments (1QM I, 2–3 [twice]; 4Q169 3–4 IV, 1; 4Q385a 17a–e II, 7; 4Q391 77 2; 6Q9 1 2).

7. Some Judahites continued to live in the region after 586 BCE, but little is known about them. Lipschits, "Persian-Period Judah," 187–211; Gadot, "Valley of the King," 3–26; Faust, *Judah in the Neo-Babylonian Period*.

8. Another wave of return is recorded in Ezra 8:1–32, but these returnees likely represented a small percentage of the exiled population in Babylonia. See Becking, "We Are All Returned," 1–18; Grabbe, *Yehud*; Lipschits, "Demographic Changes in Judah," 323–76.

was over, was the presence of Judeans outside of Yehud perpetuating God's disfavor?

Judean writers in Yehud struggled to reconcile their conviction that exile marked divine rejection with the reality that pious Judeans had chosen to remain in exile. These Judeans, such as the authors of Ezra-Nehemiah, did not explicitly claim that all space outside of the land of Israel conveyed monolithic negative meaning.[9] Instead, they maintained that the *gōlâ* was a temporary location where the sinful people resided until their term of punishment was complete. They also insisted that God wanted all Judeans to live in the land of Israel, and they appealed to scriptural teachings about the centrality of Jerusalem and its temple to make their case. The authors of Ezra-Nehemiah drew upon scriptural traditions to support their proscription of cultural mixing with outside communities. They condemned Judean men who returned to Yehud with foreign wives and insisted that they separate from their families on the basis that intermarriage threatened the survival of Judean identity (Ezra 10:1–44; Neh 23:31).[10] Ezra and Nehemiah are credited in these works with protecting the fragile communal structures that were at risk of foreign infiltration and consequent destruction.

Some Judeans outside of Yehud, however, tolerated intermarriage. They even suggested that limited integration with outsiders was desirable, if it served the interests of the Judean people. Collaboration with powerful subjugators, moreover, was often perceived as necessary. Judeans who were sympathetic to these views sometimes grounded their arguments in scriptural stories, such as the legend of Joseph's time in the Egyptian court, to claim that Judeans could live harmoniously under foreign rule.[11] The image of a Judean serving in the court of a foreign king became a powerful trope in Judean literature produced in the early Second Temple period. The story of Esther, for example, recalls how the Persian king Ahaseurus selects a beautiful Judean woman named Esther to be his queen. When Ahaseurus empowers his wicked advisor Haman to devise a scheme to annihilate all Judeans who live in his kingdom, Esther collaborates with her cousin Mordecai to expose Haman as

---

9. For the position that Ezra and Nehemiah were written by the same hand, see Boda and Reddit, *Unity and Disunity*. For a refutation, see Amzallag, "Authorship of Ezra and Nehemiah," 271–97.

10. While intolerance of non-Judean wives can be interpreted by modern readers as xenophobic, this is not quite accurate; see Southwood, *Mixed Marriage Crisis*, 75–122; Japhet, "Expulsion of the Foreign Women," 100, 151–61; contra Lester Grabbe's characterization of Ezra in *Introduction to Second Temple Judaism*, 130.

11. Second Temple era legends about Judean courtiers such as Esther and Daniel drew from the biblical account of Joseph's career in the house of Potiphar and the court of Pharaoh. See Kugel, *In Potiphar's House*; Wills, *Jewish Novel*.

an enemy of her people and of the state. By the end of the story, Esther is a beloved Persian queen, and Mordecai is a celebrated Persian courtier.

Rabbinic interpreters read the story of Esther as a cautionary tale about what can happen to Judeans in exile.[12] According to these rabbis, the Judeans of Esther's story were responsible for their own exposure to the threat of annihilation. They should have chosen to reside in the land of Israel at the moment that Cyrus permitted them to return. Since these Judeans chose to stay in the place of their exile, God punished them for their disobedience. There is no evidence, however, that Jews who lived outside their homeland in the late Second Temple period similarly interpreted the story of Esther as a warning against the dangers of living in exile. At some points during this era, Jews in Judea faced a barrage of existential threats, and Jews outside Judea were in no more danger than their Judean counterparts. Jews in both regions probably celebrated Esther and Mordecai as heroes who saved the Jewish people, even though these heroes express no interest in the question of whether their exiled kin would ever return to the land of Israel.[13]

The first half of the book of Daniel also centers on the adventures of a Judean affiliated with a foreign court. Daniel 1–6 comprises a collection of stories about Daniel's experiences as a royal courtier during the Babylonian exile and the years following the Persian defeat of Babylon. Daniel is presented in these tales as the ideal Judean. He is so devoted to Jerusalem that he prays three times a day facing the city (6:10). But Daniel is also invested in the welfare of his host kingdom. In return for his loyalty, Babylonian and Persian kings show respect for him and for the god he worships. They admire Daniel for his piety and wit and welcome his participation in their court.[14]

Esther and Daniel were admired by Judeans for navigating the complexities of exilic life without assimilating into their host culture. Their stories and others like them that were produced and circulated outside the land of Israel reflect a shift in attitude among Judeans who lived outside the land of Israel. For these Judeans, the notion that God continuously scorns Judeans who lived outside the land was untenable. Instead, they claimed that the existence of a global Judean population enhanced the relationship between God and Israel. They advanced the following ideas:

12. See b. Megillah 15b; Esth. Rab. 1:15; 2:1, 11.

13. The story of Esther, which shows no interest in the land of Israel, functions not to rebuke Jews into returning to the land but to convey a lack of faith in the Persian regime. As Jon Levenson notes, "This is a stratum that has come to terms with diaspora, and, indeed, the book of Esther can be read as the story of the transformation of the *exile* into the *Diaspora*" (*Esther*, 15; cf. Levenson, "Scroll of Esther," 440–51).

14. On how Daniel "narrativizes" material in Jeremiah that engages the theme of exile, see Segal, *Dreams, Riddles, and Visions*; cf. Collins, *Daniel*.

- God maintains universal control over the entire world and over unseen aspects of the universe.[15]
- In exile, Judeans fully repented of their sins, and God's punishment of Judeans came to its full completion.
- The foreign nations' role in Judean suffering was potentially—but not necessarily—a sign of divine wrath.

Whether they embraced or lambasted the exile, Judeans appealed to their authoritative traditions to make their arguments about the exile more compelling. As torah turned into *the* Torah, that is, a set of stable and authoritative writings, Judeans began to cite these texts to signal that their writings were part of a chain of unbroken tradition. To understand how the concept of Torah became central to debates about the exile, we must turn once again to the early Israelites. This time, we will explore the growing tension between the content and the modality of written Torah. The Torah's content underscored the centrality of the land of Israel. But its modality of transmission accommodated the absence of a temple and the land that was its home. Paradoxically, it was the adherence to Torah teachings that enabled Judeans to live outside of their homeland and remain connected to their ancestral traditions. The developing concept of Torah would play a central role in the failure of many Judeans to return to the land of Israel.

Sacred Writing and the Survival of Judean-ism

In the early Second Temple period, Judeans did not work with the notion of a closed canon that contained authoritative scriptures.[16] They did, however, believe that Moses received authoritative teachings from God.[17] The word for this concept, *tôrâ*, often conveyed oral teachings rather than a particular written document.[18] Indeed, Moses's instruction that the Israelites record "all the

---

15. This idea has its basis in the exodus story and variations of the story's key phrase, "for all the land is mine" (Exod 19:4; cf. 5:2; 6:2–9; 9:4, 24; 10:2; 11:7; 14:1, 18.). The land in question was understood by early Jews as a reference not to Egypt, but to the earth and even the cosmos. See Psalm 114, which may have inspired the tradition in Mekilta de Rabbi Ishmael 14:21 that all the earth's waters split at the moment of the splitting of the Reed Sea.

16. On the relationship between the formalization of scribal practices during this period and the increasing fixity of Torah, see Ska, "History Writing to Library Building," 145–69; Leith, "New Perspectives on the Return," 148; Niditch, *Oral World and Written Word*; Schniedewind, *How the Bible Became a Book*; Carr, *Writing on the Tablet*.

17. Zahn, "Talking about Rewritten Texts," 93–119; Mroczek, *Literary Imagination in Jewish Antiquity*.

18. For an examination of how the notion of *tôrâ* came into development in the postexilic Persian period, see Collins, *Invention of Judaism*; Knoppers and Levinson, *Pentateuch as Torah*.

words of this law [*tôrâ*]" (Deut 27:3) suggests that *tôrâ* was not exclusively associated with written texts. Biblical writers, therefore, often modified the word when they referred to written records of these teachings. The phrase "the scroll of the *tôrâ*" (*sēper hatôrâ*) in Deuteronomy (29:20; 30:10; inter alia), for instance, suggests that a modifier, *sēper*, was needed because *tôrâ* referred primarily to oral teachings. Some biblical authors referred to the "*tôrâ* of Moses," while others referred to the "*tôrâ* of God."[19] The postexilic authors of Nehemiah 8–9 refer to the same scroll by both names.[20]

Biblical writers treated written scriptures as potent and authoritative because the human act of writing scriptures was considered to be imitative of divine writing. In Exodus and Deuteronomy, God writes on both sets of tablets presented to Moses.[21] Later prophets received visions from God, recorded them, and read them aloud to public audiences. Scrolls that contained writings attributed to a divine source were viewed as powerful conduits that linked God with the people.[22]

By the middle of the seventh century BCE, prophets critiqued administrators of the Jerusalem Temple for being negligent of these traditions. Local prophets declared that exile would become inevitable if they did not repent.[23] In the years leading up to the Babylonian exile, written Torah began to take on a more stable quality that distinguished it from oral traditions. Qualifiers that had once transformed the term *tôrâ* into a written object were slowly dropped, and the term *Torah* came to be understood as a sacred object. When the exile ended, Judeans began to consult what "was written in the Torah" (*kātûb batôrâ*) and mined it for clues regarding how to properly practice their ancestral traditions (Neh 8:14–15). Torah soon took on a central role in representing

---

19. References to the "scroll of the teaching of Moses" (*sēper tôrat Mōšeh*) also appear in Josh 8:31; 23:6; 2 Kgs 14:6. In Josh 24:26, Joshua adds to a book referred to as the "scroll of the teaching of God" (*sēper tôrat 'ĕlōhîm*). For references to the "scroll of the teaching of the Lord" (*sēper tôrat* YHWH), see 2 Chr 17:9 and 34:14.

20. Neh 8:1 (*sēper tôrat Mōšeh*), 18 (*sēper tôrat 'ĕlōhîm*); 9:3 (*sēper tôrat* YHWH).

21. Exod 31:16–18; 32:15–16; 34:1–2; Deut 9:9–11.

22. On God as the writer of the Decalogue and progenitor of the scriptural writings that follow it, see Graham, *Beyond the Written World*, 52; Childs, *Introduction to the Old Testament*, 84–108.

23. Scholars who present the temple's priestly leadership as lying in ethical tension with prophetic teachings presume a false binary that undermines the fact that some Judahite and Israelite kings collaborated with both priests and prophets who worked in their courts. This false binary is often inspired by New Testament passages that are interpreted as rejecting priestly rituals in favor of the prophets' ethical teachings. See Brueggemann, *Prophetic Imagination*; Hansen, *Dawn of Apocalyptic*; Bousset, "Die Bedeutung der Person Jesu," 14–17; Bultmann, *Primitive Christianity*, 74–75; Jeremias, *Jesus and the Message*, 10, 19; Harnack, *New Testament Studies*, 14. Jeremias's point that "the attitude of late Judaism toward non-Jews was uncompromisingly severe" and that Jesus rectified this narrowness by universalizing God's covenant is representative of this thought (*Jesus' Promise to the Nations*, 40).

the prophetic message that rebuked Jerusalem's leaders and the people who supported them.

An example of this changing dynamic appears in a story set during the reign of King Josiah (r. 640–609 BCE) (2 Kgs 22:1–20). Unlike his father, Amon, and grandfather, Manasseh, Josiah was praised by Judean writers for his piety and in particular for his reform of the temple administration and his eradication of private altars in the kingdom. Josiah instituted this reform after instructing his officials to restore the Jerusalem Temple, which had fallen into disrepair. During this process the high priest, Hilkiah, alerted Josiah to the discovery of an ancient scroll. The king may have known that the scroll included passages that warned of the consequences of abandoning the people's ancestral traditions. The scroll's very existence, moreover, also likely reminded him of the ancient association between the people's loyalty to God and God's promise that they would live in the land. Either way, the discovery of the scroll led Josiah to restore the people's ancestral practices. Josiah and the Judahites who supported him believed that the written Torah embodied God's authoritative will, and that the Jerusalem Temple was the central locus of God's presence on earth. Over time, however, perceptions of the relationship between the temple and the Torah loosened and shifted.

The book of Jeremiah preserves a story about the emerging separation between Torah and temple that took place just one generation after Josiah's reform. This story centers on a conflict between King Jehoiakim, the son of Josiah, and the prophet Jeremiah. Both parties believed that they possessed symbolic objects that signified their authority and power. Jehoiakim and his loyalists were in control of the Jerusalem Temple and were confident that they could retain the Judahites' loyalty and fend off a Babylonian invasion. Jeremiah and his scribe, Baruch, on the other hand, were expelled from the royal court, but they had access to prophetic messages that they recorded on scrolls that were meant to be read aloud to the king and the people. The Judahite populace soon became split between those who heeded the words written in these scrolls, and those who dismissed their warnings as immaterial.

After Jeremiah's expulsion from Jehoiakim's court, God tells Jeremiah to dictate a prophecy to Baruch, who is to write it on a scroll that will be read to the Judahites (36:1–4). Because Jeremiah is at risk of being assassinated, he asks Baruch to bring the scroll to the royal courtyard and read it before the king and his courtiers (36:5–8). Baruch arrives at the temple and reads from the scroll in the chamber of Gemariah son of Shaphan, where the king's scribe, Micaiah son of Gemariah, hears his words and alerts the king's officials (36:9–13). Micaiah was likely startled by the scroll's prediction that an unprecedented disaster would soon befall the Judahites. But he may have also been startled by the mode of its transmission. Given that Jeremiah had been expelled from the court, Baruch's entry into the royal courtyard and his reading from a scroll is a sign that God had rejected the king's own prophets and scribes and is now working with others outside the court. As the grandson of Shaphan, the scribe who worked for King Josiah when the discovery of a Torah scroll in the temple generated a period of reform, Micaiah comprehends the symbolic import of a prophet or scribe reading from a scroll produced outside of the monarchy's inner circles. The other court officials understand this too and summon Baruch to read the scroll to them (36:14–19).

After hearing Baruch's recitation, Jehoiakim's officials ask him for information about how the scroll was produced. When Baruch informs them of Jeremiah's dictation, they instruct Baruch to find Jeremiah and stay in hiding. They avoid mentioning Jeremiah's name, which suggests that they fear being overheard and betrayed by courtiers who would not have looked kindly upon their protection of Jeremiah's scribe (36:17). The officials then convey the scroll's message to the king, who instructs a courtier to retrieve the scroll and read it before him (36:20–26). As the courtier reads, the king rips columns off the scroll and tosses them into a fire. He then demands that Baruch and Jeremiah be located and arrested (36:27–32). Jeremiah, meanwhile, receives a prophetic message to produce a replica of the scroll that the king has destroyed. Perhaps a duplicate was necessary because the scroll was meant to be carried into exile as a resource for Judahites who would no longer have access to the temple or to prophecy. If so, this scroll was to become the primary means by which the people could access God's message outside the land of Israel. Its words would remind the Judahites that they were responsible for their exilic circumstances and assure them that a restoration would soon come. The second scroll that Baruch produces also includes supplementary material that the first scroll did not contain. This augmentation suggests that Jeremiah's power—and by extension, God's power—has not diminished in the wake of the king's insults. The act of writing both scrolls is a claim to power that the scribe, and the prophet he works for, continues to wield over the king and his court.

We do not know how Jeremiah's scroll and other scrolls containing scriptural and authoritative teachings were used by Judahites living in exile. We do know, however, that by the time they entered exile, at least some Judahites conceived of written Torah as a medium by which the people could transmit God's teachings in the absence of the temple. As the divine message traveled from God to the prophet, from the prophet to the written page, and from the page to the people, Torah scrolls were transformed into binding agents between the Judahite people and God's divine realm. By the time the period of exile came to a close, Judeans had already begun the process of developing a new approach to written scriptures that included study and interpretation. Interpretation helped to establish the stable nature of the people's scriptures, and the notion of stable and interpretable scriptures enabled Judean life outside the land of Israel to survive.[24] Over time, however, a conflict emerged between Judeans in the land of Israel, who appealed to passages in the written Torah that stated that worship of God was to take place in the land, and Judeans outside the land of Israel, who appealed to the modality of the written Torah as evidence that God had sanctioned their settlement outside Judea by providing them with the tools to stay connected with their ancestral traditions.

The Return from Exile

Torah interpretation became a central project for Judeans in the early years of the restoration. The book of Ezra alludes to this focus in its description of the eponymous Judean leader as a scribe, priest, and creative reader of the written Torah:

> [9]On the first day of the first month the journey up from Babylon was begun, and on the first day of the fifth month he came to Jerusalem, for the gracious hand of his God was upon him. [10]For Ezra had set his heart to study [*lidrōš*] the law of the Lord, and to do it, and to teach the statutes and ordinances in Israel. (Ezra 7:9–10)

While earlier biblical writers used the verb *dāraš* in reference to prophetic inquiry (Lev 10:16; 1 Kgs 22:8), the author of this passage used *dāraš* in reference to interpretation of the written Torah. This new meaning points to a change in Judean attitudes toward their scriptural texts. Judeans at this time began to imbue themselves with the agency to produce biblical interpretations that reframe older scriptural traditions to justify their attitudes toward Judean life outside the land of Israel.

During this transitional period, Judeans consulted priestly leaders and authoritative written texts for guidance regarding how to structure religious leadership and restore the role of priestly families. This process is referenced in the book of Nehemiah, which recalls a crisis concerning unverified claims of priestly lineage. Some Judeans who had returned from exile claimed to come from priestly families, but their names did not appear on the official registration lists available to Nehemiah. The status of these Judeans, therefore, was unclear:

> [64]These sought their registration among those enrolled in the genealogies, but it was not found there, so they were excluded from the

---

24. Mandel, *Origins of Midrash*, 21–86.

priesthood as unclean; ⁶⁵the governor told them that they were not to partake of the most holy food, until a priest with Urim and Thummim should come. (Neh 7:64–65)

Nehemiah takes a moderate approach to this crisis by instructing Judeans who claim to come from priestly families to abstain from eating food that has been designated for priests until a senior priest arrives and consults the Urim and Thummim for a divine message that will clarify the Judeans' status. In contrast to the written Torah, the registration records in this story are viewed as fallible, and the matter of whether they have omitted Judean names can only be answered with prophetic consultation.[25]

The temple's reconstruction amplified the question of how written and cultic modes of interpreting divine messages were meant to interact. Did the Second Temple mitigate the elevated status of the written scriptures? Some Judeans must have worried that the new approach to scriptural texts would destabilize the temple's central authority. After all, the written Torah was a collection of portable documents that provided a mechanism by which Judeans could survive—and stay—in exile. Other Judeans, however, insisted that there was no tension between gathering at the temple to offer sacrifices and gathering elsewhere to study the written scriptures. These scriptures affirmed the central role of the temple and contained prophetic promises that a divine restoration would one day bring the people back to their homeland.

The role of scriptural interpretation as a legitimate method of worship lies at the fore of a story preserved in Nehemiah 8, in which Judeans gather to hear Ezra read from a scroll following the completion of Jerusalem's walls. The scene is resonant of the scriptural injunction in Deuteronomy that Israelite kings must write a scroll of Torah and read it to the people at a public gathering (17:18–20). Ezra is not a king, of course, but this story refers to him as a priest and also a scribe, which implies that he has written the scroll from which he reads.[26] Ezra therefore functions as the monarch described in Deuteronomy, and his reading symbolizes the same affirmation of loyalty to God that the monarchic reading was meant to represent. The identification of Ezra as both priest and scribe in this passage is intentional. Ezra's priestly lineage links him to the leadership that once administered in the temple and authorizes him to oversee the restoration. His scribal training, moreover, gives him access to the people's scriptural traditions and developing interpretations. Judeans at this

---

25. Fishbane, *Garments of Torah*, 66.
26. The NRSV renders *sēper tôrat Mōšeh* as "the book of the law of Moses." "Scroll" is a more precise rendering of *sēper*, and "teaching" is a better word for *tôrâ* than "law," since the scroll was probably not merely a legal code. The preferred rendering of this phrase, therefore, is the "scroll of the teaching of Moses."

time needed both forms of authority. Properly interpreted, the written Torah would enforce the centrality of the temple.

The Judeans who hear Ezra recite from the Torah do not comprehend his words. Perhaps the people, most of whom were born in exile, spoke a Persian dialect of Aramaic and did not understand the Hebrew scriptures. It is also possible that the Judeans understood the meaning of Ezra's words but struggled to comprehend their deeper import. Both possibilities are likely correct. Many Judeans probably did not speak Hebrew fluently but might have understood passages that had been transmitted to them orally or that they had studied with their teachers. While they may not have understood Ezra's words, the Judeans did comprehend the call to obey the terms of the covenantal relationship:[27]

> [6]Then Ezra blessed the Lord, the great God, and all the people answered, "Amen, Amen," lifting up their hands. Then they bowed their heads and worshiped the Lord with their faces to the ground. [7]Also Jeshua, Bani, Sherebiah, Jamin, Akkub, Shabbethai, Hodiah, Maaseiah, Kelita, Azariah, Jozabad, Hanan, Pelaiah, the Levites, helped the people to understand the law, while the people remained in their places. [8]So they read from the book, from the law of God, with interpretation. They gave the sense, so that the people understood the reading. (Neh 8:6–8)

As Ezra reads from the scroll, Levite teachers help the Judeans understand the written Torah by providing clarification and interpretation.[28] By depicting Levites as teachers of Ezra's Torah, the authors of this story implied that even Judean leaders whose ancestors administered in the Jerusalem Temple endorsed Ezra's reading of the Torah as a powerful act of communal worship.

The precise status of Ezra's Torah is not clear. The scroll is first referred to as the "scroll of the teaching of Moses" (*sēper tôrat Mōšeh*), which suggests that it derives from Moses but is divinely authorized (Neh 8:1; cf. 8:14). Later in the story (8:18), the scroll is referred to as the "scroll of the teaching of God" (*sēper tôrat hā'ĕlōhîm*). This change might represent a shift that the people undergo over the course of Ezra's two-day reading. While they initially associate Ezra's scroll with teachings that Moses passed on to the people, they come to view the written Torah as an embodiment of God's actual words.

---

27. The people respond to Ezra's reading by proclaiming "Amen, Amen," a phrase that is at times used to publicly affirm communal trust in God's curses; see Deut 27:15–26 and Num 5:22. In the Psalms, *'āmen* affirms collective blessing (Pss 41:13; 72:19; 89:52; inter alia).

28. The Levites are also associated with the kind of wisdom that provides the people with *śēkel* in 2 Chr 30:22.

The different descriptors of the written Torah in this story might also reflect the writers' ambivalence concerning its status. Were these written scriptures divine and equal to the oral traditions conveyed by the prophets, or were they inferior, human-made records that sought to mimic oral messages transmitted from God to the prophets? One thing is certain: the elevated status of the written scriptures generated a new stage of interpretive activity. When Ezra reads about the Feast of Tabernacles on the second day of his recitation and the people realize that this holiday is fast approaching, they are not content to merely listen to Ezra. Instead, they consult the Torah and interpret its words:

> [13]On the second day the heads of ancestral houses of all the people, with the priests and the Levites, came together to the scribe Ezra in order to study the words of the law. [14]And they found it written in the law, which the Lord had commanded by Moses, that the people of Israel should live in booths during the festival of the seventh month, [15]and that they should publish and proclaim in all their towns and in Jerusalem as follows, "Go out to the hills and bring branches of olive, wild olive, myrtle, palm, and other leafy trees to make booths, as it is written." [16]So the people went out and brought them, and made booths for themselves, each on the roofs of their houses, and in their courts and in the courts of the house of God, and in the square at the Water Gate and in the square at the Gate of Ephraim. (Neh 8:13–16)

The Torah verse that the Judeans read instructs the people to "go out to the hills and bring branches of olive, wild olive, myrtle, palm, and other leafy trees to make booths" (Neh 8:15). No version of this biblical verse, which seems to be a quotation of Lev 23:40–42, contains this precise language.[29] The Judeans may have been reading a different version of these verses or a different text altogether. Alternatively, the authors may have been paraphrasing Leviticus 23 rather than citing it. The mandate in Leviticus 23 to gather plants does not clarify what the Israelites are to do with the plants that they select. The Judeans in Nehemiah 8, however, come up with a solution. They use the plants that they have gathered to build their booths. If they were indeed reading Leviticus 23, they probably noticed the juxtaposition between the mandates to gather plants and build booths and interpreted this juxtaposition by using the plants to build the booths. If so, this story suggests that the Judeans' first public

---

29. Lev 23:40–42 reads, "On the first day you shall take the fruit of majestic trees, branches of palm trees, boughs of leafy trees, and willows of the brook; and you shall rejoice before the Lord your God for seven days. You shall keep it as a festival to the Lord seven days in the year; you shall keep it in the seventh month as a statute forever throughout your generations. You shall live in booths for seven days; all that are citizens in Israel shall live in booths."

reading of their written scriptures following the exile was also the first time that they interpreted them. The written Torah's public transmission marks the beginning of its development into a stable body of texts that were subject to interpretation. The writers of Nehemiah 8 believed that, with the correct interpretation, the written Torah could guide the people toward the proper worship of their God in the land of Israel. According to these writers, Judeans who chose to remain in exile while expressing loyalty to the Torah were missing the essence of its message.

Not all Judean writers, however, cited the Torah toward these same ends. The authors of the book of Daniel adopted a more optimistic approach toward life outside the land of Israel, and treated the Torah as a legitimate mode of worship that enabled Judeans to discern God's desires far from the temple. In Daniel 9, the eponymous hero begs God to put an end to the exile by appealing to scriptures that promise that God will always protect the people:

> ⁸Open shame, O Lord, falls on us, our kings, our officials, and our ancestors, because we have sinned against you. ⁹To the Lord our God belong mercy and forgiveness, for we have rebelled against him, ¹⁰and have not obeyed the voice of the Lord our God by following his laws [*lāleket bətôrōtāyw*], which he set before us by his servants the prophets. ¹¹All Israel has transgressed your law [*tôrātekā*] and turned aside, refusing to obey your voice. So the curse and the oath written in the law of Moses [*kətûbâ bətôrat Mōšeh*], the servant of God, have been poured out upon us, because we have sinned against you. ¹²He has confirmed his words, which he spoke against us and against our rulers, by bringing upon us a calamity so great that what has been done against Jerusalem has never before been done under the whole heaven. ¹³Just as it is written in the law of Moses [*kātûb bətôrat Mōšeh*], all this calamity has come upon us. (Dan 9:8–13a)

In this prayer, *tôrâ* denotes a collection of teachings that Moses received from God and transmitted to the people. The story's references to "written" words of Torah suggest that Daniel perceives Torah to be a set of blueprints that Judeans in exile can consult to ascertain how to repent of their sins.[30] Torah here transcends the provincial function of bringing Judeans home and embodies God's entry into the human realm.

---

30. Other hints that the author viewed writings as potent and authoritative appear in Dan 5:5–9, when King Belshazzar observes a disembodied hand writing on a wall of the royal palace. The king's terrified reaction contrasts with King Jehoiakim's behavior in Jeremiah 36.

The Emerging Split Between the Judeans of Yehud and Egypt

During the early Persian period, Judeans produced texts that were later read as authoritative, even though their human derivation was uncontested. The book of Esther, for example, was considered by Jews in the Hellenistic era to be authoritative and scriptural, even though it specifies that Mordecai wrote Esther's story and Esther issued a letter authorizing Mordecai's account (Esth 9:20–32). Jews interpreted the book of Esther in the same way that they interpreted older scriptural texts, and they looked to it for insight regarding the meaning of exile.

Other Judean documents, such as personal letters, novellas, and wisdom texts, were never read as scriptural and authoritative. Yet some of these texts are remarkably similar to books that were ultimately included in the Hebrew Bible. Like the book of Esther, they were read as documents that address questions about life outside the land of Israel and that participate in a fundamental disagreement. Texts produced in the land of Israel appeal to scriptural traditions to affirm the centrality of the temple and the land of Israel. Texts produced in Egypt, however, tend to invoke the authority of the written Torah to argue that all Judeans are deserving beneficiaries of God's infinite love. In the coming chapters, I will trace the development of this disagreement, beginning with an early set of correspondence between Judeans in Yehud and Judeans living on an island in the Nile River that they called Yeb.

CHAPTER 2

"A Letter They Did Not Send Us": An Early Case Study of Judea-Diaspora Relations

JUDEANS LIVING UNDER PERSIAN RULE used the word *tôrâ* to denote a collection of teachings that represented the sayings of prophets who received messages from God and recorded them onto scrolls. These scrolls possessed an audial quality. They preserved oral communications from God that were meant to be read to the people in public spaces. At this early stage, the separation between written traditions and oral traditions was not complete. But as teachings from the written Torah were transmitted, they took on a fixed quality that distinguished them from oral traditions, and they became subject to interpretation. The increasingly important role of written Torah is connected to two developments in the Persian period that impacted how people communicated with one another.

The first development concerns how the Persian royal court produced authoritative writing. Officials in this court wrote declarations, edicts, and other documents that cite earlier traditions. These texts, which establish political authority by invoking ancient writings, represent a new era of antiquarian culture that placed a high value on ancient precedent.[1] The second change took place beyond the halls of the Persian court on newly built roads that snaked throughout the massive empire. These interconnecting highways were constructed to facilitate the swift transmission of royal dispatches, and they generated new opportunities for dispersed families to maintain ties with one another.

Judeans within and without the land of Israel took advantage of both of these developments by writing letters that adopted strategies found in official Persian documents.[2] Their letters, as well as other documents that they produced, are rife with allusions, citations, and interpretations of earlier authoritative texts that respond to questions about how Judeans were to practice their traditions outside of Yehud. By citing earlier traditions, these texts participate in broader conversations about God's attitude toward the global Judean population.

1. Ska, "History Writing to Library Building," 145–69.
2. Leith, "New Perspectives on the Return," 147–69.

An early example of such correspondence comes from a Judean community that settled on Elephantine, a small island on the Nile River in Upper Egypt.

The Judean Letters at Elephantine

Excavations on Elephantine in 1907 and 1908 revealed a significant cache of ancient papyri that included a collection of Aramaic documents produced by Judeans who lived on the island, which was known at the time as Yeb. The Judeans (*Yəhûdāyeʾ* in Aramaic) may have come from the region of Yehud sometime earlier, but the circumstances in which these Judeans came to settle in the Nile River are not known.[3] Perhaps they first came to the region in the middle of the seventh century BCE, during the reign of King Manasseh, as members of a Judahite military garrison sent to help Psammetichus I fight Nubia and the Assyrian Empire.[4] Alternatively, they may have fled to the island as refugees when the Babylonian Empire began to exile Judahites in 597 BCE (Jer 43:5–7).[5] Or perhaps they came in 594–589 BCE as soldiers dispatched by Psammetichus II to fight the Ethiopians.[6] They may have also arrived later as mercenaries for the Achaemenid Empire in the postexilic period.[7] It has even been recently suggested that the authors of these papyri descended not from Judahites at all but from people who migrated from Samaria in the seventh century BCE.[8] It seems most likely, however, that waves of Judahites arrived on the island during some or all of these periods.[9]

---

3. Becking, "Yehudite Identity in Elephantine," 404.
4. Ahlström, *History of Ancient Palestine*, 751–60.
5. Kraeling, "Elephantine Colony," 142.
6. Tcherikover, *Hellenistic Civilization*, 270. This community of Judean soldiers may be the same alluded to in Let. Aris. 13: "Now even before this time large numbers of Jews had come into Egypt with the Persian [king], and in an earlier period still others had been sent to Egypt to fight as allies of Psammetichus in his campaign against the king of the Ethiopians. But these were nothing like so numerous as the captives whom Ptolemy the son of Lagus carried off." All translations of The Letter of Aristeas in this study are from White and Keddie, *Jewish Fictional Letters*, 55–172.
7. Becking, "Yehudite Identity in Elephantine," 405.
8. Van der Toorn, *Becoming Diaspora Jews*. Van der Toorn argues that this community comprised Arameans who came from Samaria. As Judeans migrated to Egypt and became a "majority minority," these Arameans refashioned themselves as Judeans to receive advantages that came with the Judeans' semiautonomous status. This theory depends on a liturgical document, P. Amherst 63, which comprises thirty-five Aramaic hymns and blessings written in demotic script and references numerous gods, including the god Yaho. Building on the document's references to Samarian soldiers fleeing to a city with a "fortress of palms," van der Toorn suggests that some Samarians settled in Palmyra, where they began to self-identify as Arameans before migrating to Elephantine. For other theories regarding how Judeans at Elephantine fused Israelite practices with local Egyptian cultic practices, see Vincent, *La religion des judéo-araméens* and Grelot, *Documents araméens d'Égypte*, 94. For a rebuttal of van der Toorn, see Silverman, "Religion of the Elephantine Jews," 377–88.
9. On the cultural diversity of Yeb's inhabitants; see van der Toorn, "Anat-Yahu," 80–101; Grabbe, "Israel's Reality After the Exile," 25.

The archive of documents discovered on Elephantine includes day-to-day contractual records, such as property sales, loans, and betrothals, and reveals key information about how Judeans conducted their social activities and ritual practices. One letter found in this cache addresses the role of a Judean temple that was built on the island.[10] The letter, which survives in two drafts, is addressed to a "Lord Bagavahya governor of Judah," and signed by "Jedaniah and his colleagues the priests."[11] Dated to November 25, 407 BCE (i.e., "the 20th of Marcheshvan, year 17 of Darius the king"), the letter petitions Bagavahya, the governor of Yehud, to permit the Judeans to rebuild their temple after it was vandalized by Egyptian priests of Khnum about three years earlier. A reconstruction of the original version reads:

RECTO ¹To our Lord Bagavahya governor of Judah, your servants Jedaniah and his colleagues the priests who are in Elephantine the fortress.

The welfare ²of our lord may the God of Heaven seek after abundantly at all times, and favor may He grant you before Darius the king ³and the princes more than now a thousand times, and long life may He give you, and happy and strong may you be at all times.

⁴Now, your servant Jedaniah and his colleagues thus say:

In the month of Tammuz, year 14 of Darius the king, when Arsames ⁵had departed and gone to the king, the priests of Khnub the god who are in Elephantine the fortress, in agreement with Vidranga who was ⁶Governor here, (said), saying:

---

10. Porten, *Elephantine Papyri*, 139.

11. Porten, *Elephantine Papyri*, 141–46 (B19), TAD A4.7 Cowley 30 (Sachau Plates 1–2). The first draft of this letter was written by two scribes. The first scribe wrote lines 1 through the middle of line 12, and the second scribe, who completed lines 12 through 30, also wrote the second draft. Scholars believe that the second version, which is torn down the middle and missing the end of each line, is the revised one since it contains fewer mistakes. The second draft makes about fifty adjustments to the original version. Differences between these versions are listed in Cowley, *Aramaic Papyri*, 121–22. Most of these changes are minor, but a few serve to strengthen the letter's message.

Bagavahya (*bgwhy*), referred to as Bagoas by Cowley and Bagohi by Becking, was probably a Judean official with ties to temple administrators. See Porten, *Elephantine Papyri*, 79, 141; S. Schwartz, "Law in Jewish Society," 58. Ezra 2:2 and Neh 7:7 mention a Bigvai (*bigway*) who seems to have been a Judean that returned to Jerusalem from exile and entered the employ of Persian authorities. Cowley identifies him as *strategos* of Artaxerxes II who, according to Josephus, imposed a seven-year fine on the temple cult after the high priest Johanan murdered his brother Jeshua (*Aramaic Papyri*, 108).

References in the first letter (A4.7) to the writer's colleagues as priests may suggest that Jedaniah was a layperson, but line 1 of the second version (A4.8) identifies Jedaniah as a priest. This clarification may reflect a desire to draw parallels between the Elephantine Judean community and the Judean community of Jerusalem by imbuing Jedaniah with priestly authority. See Hays, "Yedaniah's Identity," 521–41.

"The Temple of YHW the God which is in Elephantine the fortress let them remove from there."

Afterwards, that Vidranga, [7]the wicked, a letter sent to Naphaina his son, who was Troop Commander in Syene the fortress, saying:

"The Temple which is in Elephantine [8]the fortress let them demolish."

Afterwards, Naphaina led the Egyptians with the other troops. They came to the fortress of Elephantine with their implements, [9]broke into that Temple, demolished it to the ground, and the pillars of stone which were there—they smashed [them]. Moreover, it happened (that the) [10]5 gateways of stone, built of hewn stone, which were in that Temple, they demolished. And their standing doors, and the pivots [11]of those doors, (of) bronze, and the roof of wood of cedar—all (of these) which, with the rest of the fittings and other (things), which [12]were there—all (of these) with fire they burned. But the basins of gold and silver and the (other) things which were in that Temple—all (of these) [they] took [13]and made their own.

And from the days of the king(s) of Egypt our fathers had built that Temple in Elephantine the fortress and when Cambyses entered Eg[ypt] [14]—that Temple, built he found it. And the temples of the gods of Egypt, all (of them), they overthrew, but anything in that Temple one did not damage.

[15]And when this had been done (to us), we with our wives and our children sackcloth were wearing and fasting and praying to YHW the Lord of Heaven [16]who let us gloat over that Vidranga, that cur. They removed the fetter from his feet and all goods which he had acquired were lost. And all persons [17]who sought evil for that Temple, all (of them), were killed and we gazed upon them. Moreover, before this, at the time that this ev[il] VERSO [18]was done to us, a letter we sent (to) our lord, and to Jehohanan the High Priest and his colleagues the priests who are in Jerusalem, and to Ostanes [the] brother [19]of Anani and the nobles of the Jews. A letter they did not send us.

Moreover, from the month of Tammuz, year 14 of Darius the king [20]and un[til] this day, we, sackcloth are wearing and are fasting; the wives of ours as widow(s) are made; (with) oil (we) do not anoint (ourselves), [21]and wine do not drink.

Moreover, from that (time) and until (this) day, year 17 Darius the king, meal-offering and ince[n]se and burnt-offering [22]they did not make in that Temple.

Now, your servants Jedaniah and his colleagues and the Jews, all (of them) citizens of Elephantine, thus sa[y]:

[23]If to our lord it is good, take thought of that Temple to (re)build (it) since they do not let us (re)build it. Regard [24]your obligees and your

friends ^(who are) here in Egypt. May a letter from you be sent to them about the Temple of YHW the God ²⁵to (re)build it in Elephantine the fortress just as it had been built formerly.

And the meal-offering and the incense and the burnt-offering they will offer on the ²⁶altar of YHW the God in your name and we shall pray for you at all times—we and our wives and our children and the Jews, ²⁷all (of them) who are here. If thus they do until that Temple be (re)built, a merit you will have before YHW the God of ²⁸Heaven more than a person who will offer him burnt-offering and sacrifices (whose) worth is as the worth of silver, 1 thousand talents and about gold.[12]

About this ²⁹we have sent (and) informed (you).

Moreover, all the(se) things in a letter we sent ^(in our name) to Delaiah and Shelemiah sons of Sanballat gov^(er)nor of Samaria.

³⁰Moreover, about this which was done to us ^(all of it) Arsames did not know.

On the 20th of Marcheshvan, year 17 of Darius the king.[13]

This letter's formal conventions and expressions of warm familiarity suggest that it was composed by a skilled scribe trained in Aramaic letter writing practices.[14] It opens with a conventional fourfold greeting that wishes its recipients good welfare, divine favor, long life, and happiness and strength.[15] The letter's body comprises a report and a petition. The report describes how Egyptian priests of Khnum conspired with the local Persian governor, Vidranga, and his son, Naphaina, against the Judean community (ll. 4–13). It then cites earlier Egyptian and Persian authorization of the temple and recounts the temple's vandalization.

The origins of the conflict between Judean leaders and the priests of Khnum are unclear. Perhaps it began when Khnum priests started to extend their temple toward the Judean temple and constricted the road that separated them. The Judeans' sacrificing of animals such as rams, which were viewed as sacred, might have also irritated these priests. Alternatively, the conflict may have been due to a precious stone that was stolen from Egyptians and

---

12. Sprengling's rendering is smoother than Porten's more literal but awkward reading. Sprengling's version reads "to the value of 1 thousand talents. And as for (the) gold, concerning this we have sent information" ("Aramaic Papyri of Elephantine," 440).
13. Porten, *Elephantine Papyri*, 141–44.
14. Porten, *Elephantine Papyri*, 139; Cf. Lindenberger, *Ancient Aramaic*.
15. Fourfold blessings appear in Egyptian letters as well, but the letter's reference to being blessed a thousand times over may have borrowed from biblical scriptures. See P. Valençay 1.2–6; Deut 1:11.

discovered in the possession of Judean traders, an incident referenced in other Elephantine letters.[16] The conflict, whatever its source, was likely percolating over a long period of time, given the extensive destruction that was meant to antagonize local Judeans. The letter moves on to describe the aftermath of the incident, highlighting the Judeans' mourning and the silence of authorities in Jerusalem following this crisis (ll. 13–14).[17] The second half of the letter's main body is a petition that asks Bagavahya and his colleagues to respond. The letter concludes with a blessing, references to earlier letters sent by the community to other authorities, and, finally, the letter's date.

Jedaniah and his colleagues crafted their case by affirming the legitimacy of their temple as well as the authority of the Jerusalem Temple and its administrators. Since temple destruction could have been interpreted as signifying the defeat of the community's god, or taken as a sign that the god said to reside in this temple did not approve of it, Jedaniah and his colleagues wanted to clarify that the destruction of their temple did not signify the defeat of their god or their god's displeasure.

To legitimize the temple, Jedaniah and his fellow colleagues underscored the Judeans' attention to ancestral practice. They presented their piety in scriptural terms, particularly in descriptions about their mourning practices of wearing sackcloth and fasting as well as abstaining from wine and from anointing with oil (ll. 20–21).[18] The writers' devotion to their temple, moreover, was not a deviation that distracted them from the Jerusalem Temple. Instead, it was an act of homage. The authors were careful to note that their temple faced Jerusalem and that its dimensions were similar to those of the Temple of Solomon.[19] While the temple at Yeb was an imitation of the Jerusalem Temple, as evident in its replicative dimensions of the latter, it was by no means a symbolic replacement of this temple, as evident in its orientation toward the Jerusalem Temple.[20] The writers of this letter also referred to their temple's priests as *kahănîn*, the same Aramaic word used for the priests of Jerusalem, but referred to the Egyptian priests

---

16. Van der Toorn, "Previously, at Elephantine," 255–70; von Pilgrim, "Tempel des Jahu," 303–17.

17. If Porten's reconstruction is correct, another papyrus also refers to the vandalization of the Judean temple. This letter's top three lines and bottom are missing, but it was likely addressed to Persian authorities. Like the letter to Bagavahya, it may also highlight the corruption of the priests of Khnum. See Porten, *Elephantine Papyri*, 136–39 (B17), TAD A4.5 Cowley 27 (Strasbourg P. Aram. 2 = Sachau Plate 75).

18. Cf. Joel 1:8–13, which links mourning to refraining from temple practice.

19. Archaeological research suggests that the temple may have been modeled after the tabernacle rather than the Jerusalem Temple, but Jedaniah presents the temple only as an imitation of the latter. See Porten, "Structure and Orientation," 38–39; Rosenberg, "Jewish Temple at Elephantine," 12; cf. 1 Kgs 6:2.

20. Silverman, "Religion of the Elephantine Jews," 377–88.

of Khnum as *kûmārîn*, a word used in 2 Kings to refer to idolatrous priests.[21] By identifying themselves with their kin in Jerusalem, the authors implied that their temple was endorsed by Judeans in Yehud and by the god they worshipped.

The authors also legitimized their temple by invoking political precedent. They claimed that Cambyses (probably Cambyses II, the son of Cyrus the Great) sanctioned and protected it, though he destroyed all temples devoted to Egyptian gods. This detail suggests that, prior to the Persian conquest of Egypt in 525 BCE, native Egyptian Saite rulers also permitted the Judean temple to stand.[22] The authors of this letter likely did not know with certainty whether this was true. For our purposes, the value of their claim lies not in whether Cambyses truly did destroy every sanctuary in Egypt aside from the Judean temple, but in the fact that Jedaniah and his colleagues felt the need to fortify their argument with political precedent to argue for their temple's legitimacy in an address to Judean leadership.

While Jedaniah and his colleagues sought to legitimize Judean cultic practices at Yeb, they were also careful to express loyalty to authorities in Yehud. In their opening salutation, they pray that "the God of Heaven" will provide Bagavahya with longevity, happiness, and strength (l. 3). Their closing blessing, which identifies the Judean (*Yəhûdāye'*) community of Yeb as one that prays on behalf of its Judean kin in Yehud, similarly highlights the community's devotion to the Jerusalem community (l. 26). A cursory reading of this letter suggests that it recognizes the authority of officials in Yehud as extending into Egypt. Scribal changes in the letter's second version, however, indicate that the writers sometimes used performative obsequiousness to flatter their audience and prime them for their requests. In the letter's first version, Jedaniah and his colleagues note that the community sent messages to the *nobles of the Judeans* (*ḥarê Yəhûdāye'*), which implies a reciprocal and connective kinship between the two communities based on shared Judean identity (l. 19). The revised version adjusts this phrase to the *nobles of Yehud* (*ḥarê Yəhûd*). This change can be taken as an attempt to limit the administrative realm of Jerusalem-based officials and as an indication that Judeans in Yeb live outside the realm of Jerusalem-based leadership.

Both versions of this letter defer to the authority of Judean leaders in Yehud by asking for permission to rebuild the Judean temple at Yeb. Jedaniah and his colleagues probably did not need formal permission to move forward with the project to restore their temple. Their request was a performative assurance

---

21. Reference to *kəmārîm* appears in 2 Kings, when the Judean king Josiah commands temple priests to remove idolatrous objects from the temple and deposes idolatrous priests as part of his reform (2 Kgs 23:5).

22. Porten, *Elephantine Papyri*, 144. Becking views this reference as historically unreliable ("Yehudite Identity in Elephantine," 405).

that the reestablishment of the Yeb temple was an act of loyalty rather than an act of separatism. The writers' obsequious homage to authorities in Yehud, moreover, coupled with their personal view that the Judean temple of Yeb was legitimate, produced a dissonance in this letter. Jedaniah and his colleagues likely knew that their readers would not see eye to eye with them regarding the legitimacy of their temple. They allude to this concern in the complaint that when the Judeans of Yeb first appealed to Yehud authorities for help in the wake of conflict with their Egyptian neighbors, they received no response. The authorities' silence, which may have reflected tacit disapproval of the temple and a desire to avoid formally endorsing it, forced Jedaniah and his colleagues to contact Bagavahya. While they viewed their local temple as a legitimate affirmation of loyalty to Jerusalem, Jedaniah and his colleagues did not want to move forward with their project to restore their temple without the support of authorities in Yehud.

Memorandum of a Response

A surviving record of the authorities' response to the leaders of Yeb confirms what these leaders suspected. Authorities in Yehud did not want Judeans in Yeb to worship in a local temple in a manner that suggested any equivalence to the Jerusalem Temple. The same scribe who wrote the second draft of Jedaniah's petition recorded their response as follows:

> ¹Memorandum. What Bagavahya and Delaiah said ²to me. Memorandum. Saying, "Let it be for you in Egypt to say ³before Arsames about the Altar-house of the God of ⁴Heaven which in Elephantine the fortress built ⁵was formerly before Cambyses (and) ⁶which Vidranga, that wicked (man) demolished ⁷in year 14 of Darius the king: ⁸to (re)build it on its site as it was formerly ⁹and the meal-offering and the incense they may offer upon ¹⁰that altar just as formerly ¹¹was done."[23]

Judean leaders in Yehud granted permission to the Judeans of Yeb to rebuild their temple. But whereas Jedaniah and his colleagues asked to reinstate "the meal-offering and the incense and the burnt-offering," Judean leaders in Yehud permitted only "the meal-offering and the incense." The omission of burnt offerings in the leaders' response suggests that animal sacrifice at the Yeb temple would render it unacceptably similar to the Jerusalem Temple.[24] Because the Jerusalem Temple was the locus of worship for all Judeans, the

---

23. Porten, *Elephantine Papyri*, 150–51 (B21), TAD A4.9 Cowley 32 (Sachau Plate 4).
24. Porten, *Elephantine Papyri*, 150.

Judean priests of Yeb were to abstain from bringing animal sacrifices as a performative recognition of the Jerusalem Temple's centrality.

The memorandum also contains hints about the identities of the people who issued this ruling. Jedaniah's letter addresses only Bagavahya, but this response comes from Bagavahya as well as Delaiah, who is identified in Jedaniah's petition as a son of Sanballat, governor of Samaria. Delaiah's name indicates that he worshiped the Judeans' ancestral God, though his father Sanballat may have been the same Sanballat who was known to be a Samaritan enemy of Nehemiah.[25] The attribution of this response to both Bagavahya and Delaiah also reflects a degree of collaboration among Judean political offices. Since the matter of animal sacrifice at Yeb would not have been of great concern to Persian authorities, Bagavahya must have had contact with temple authorities in Jerusalem who conveyed the caveat that the Judeans of Yeb were not to bring animal sacrifices.

This memorandum makes no mention of the Judeans' Egyptian neighbors or of local Egyptian authorities. Its writers represented Judean and Persian interests in Yehud, and they had little reason to help the Judeans of Yeb improve their relations with Egyptians. The focus of these writers was on providing readers with historical precedent that buttressed their decision to permit the temple's construction with limitations in place.[26]

Jedaniah's Acceptance of the Terms

It appears that the Judeans of Yeb accepted the memorandum's terms of permission. Another papyrus discovered in Jedaniah's archive has been reconstructed as follows:

> ¹Your servants—
> Jedaniah son of Gem[ariah] by name, 1
> ²Mauzi son of Nathan by name, [1]
> ³Shemaiah son of Haggai by name, 1
> ⁴Hosea son of Jathorn by name, 1
> ⁵Hosea son of Nattum by name, 1:
> all (told) 5 persons, ⁶Syenians who in Elephantine the fortress are heredi[tary-
> property-hold]ers—⁷thus say:
> If you lord [...] ⁸and the Temple-of-YHW-the-God of ours be (re)built ⁹in Elephantine the fortress as former[ly] it was [bu]ilt—¹⁰and sheep, ox, and goat (as) burnt-offering are [n]ot made there ¹¹but (only)

---

25. Porten, *Elephantine Papyri*, 146.
26. Porten, *Elephantine Papyri*, 148.

incense (and) meal-offering [*they offer there*]—²and should our lord a statement mak[e *about this afterwards*] ¹³we shall give to the house of our lord si[lver ... and] ¹⁴barley, a thousa[nd] ardabs.²⁷

The intended recipient of this letter is not known. Some scholars suggest that it was sent to Bagavahya or another official in Yehud.²⁸ There are a number of reasons, however, why it is unlikely that this letter was sent to Yehud. First, the letter implies that Jedaniah and his colleagues had already been granted by the Judeans permission to rebuild their temple under restrictive limitations. The conditional nature of this permission would have been unlikely to prompt a desire to send gifts, as the writers of this letter promise to do. Second, the letter's writers identify themselves as coming from Syene, an Egyptian city in Upper Egypt. This affiliation would have reminded Judeans of scriptural traditions that condemned the people of Syene and other inhabitants of Egypt, and thus it is unlikely that Judeans in Yeb would have made this connection in a letter to Judean kin in Yehud.²⁹ It is more likely that this letter was intended for local Persian officials in Egypt.³⁰ Perhaps it was directed to Arsames, an Achaemenid satrap who was sympathetic to the local Judean population. Arsames is mentioned in Jedaniah's petition and in other documents found in Jedaniah's archive. By identifying as Syenians, the Judean writers would have made themselves more recognizable to local officials in Egypt.

If Jedaniah and his colleagues were writing to local officials, however, why did they mention the plan to refrain from bringing animal sacrifices at their reconstructed temple? What significance would such a specific detail have had for these officials? One possibility is that the letter writers added this detail to assure Egyptian leaders that Judeans of Yeb were mindful of the Egyptians' worship of Khnum, whose head was depicted as a ram. The Khnum priests were likely antagonistic toward the Judean practice of sacrificing goats, and Jedaniah and his colleagues may have sought to put their new policy to diplomatic use by repackaging it as a gesture of goodwill that would mend their relationship with local Egyptians.³¹

The absence of a lengthy opening greeting and farewell blessing in this letter also points to an Egyptian audience. Such greetings and farewells would have

---

27. Porten, *Elephantine Papyri*, 152–53 (B22), TAD A4.10 Cowley 33 (Sachau Plate 4); Cowley, *Aramaic Papyri*, 124–25. Crossed-out text represents erasures in the original manuscript.

28. Cowley, *Aramaic Papyri*, 124.

29. Ezek 29:10; 30:15–16; cf. Isa 49:12. Babylon is depicted as Egypt's conqueror in Ezek 29:18–20; 30:10–11, 24–25. See Siljanen, "Judeans of Egypt in the Persian Period," 50–51.

30. Porten, *Elephantine Papyri*, 153n10.

31. Perhaps this god was the four-headed, ram-faced god Banebdjedet. See Mélèze Modrzejewski, *Jews of Egypt*, 39.

been unnecessary in a letter that did not seek to affirm mutual kinship. While the writers emphasize their capacity to make a substantial payment (ll. 5–7), their letter is neither exhortatory nor polemical. Unlike Jedaniah's petition, its formal structure supports rather than undermines its rhetorical content.

The fact that the Judeans of Yeb felt compelled to bribe local officials to guarantee the reconstruction of their temple raises the likelihood that these Judeans did not require permission from authorities in Yehud to rebuild their temple. Their letter to authorities in Yehud was primarily a gesture meant to show loyalty to Judeans in Jerusalem. The Yeb community's letter to officials in Egypt shows another strain of loyalty directed toward its host government. The authors of both letters skillfully presented the Yeb community's identity with their intended audience in mind. Their goal was not to achieve sly manipulation but to maintain good relations with their Judean kin and their local government. These efforts were effective: documents from the island dated to 402 BCE mention the temple of Yeb, which suggests that it was rebuilt by that year.[32]

From Yehud-Yeb Tension to Judea-Diaspora Schism

The correspondence between Judean authorities who lived in Yehud and Judeans who lived on Yeb suggests that Judean leaders in Yehud wanted Judeans in Egypt to recognize their wide-ranging authority. These leaders may have been especially interested in Egyptian Judeans because their scriptural traditions presented Egyptian worship practices as both alluring and reprehensible. To prevent Judeans in Egypt from succumbing to these temptations, they sought to establish normative Judean practices that affirmed their own authority. The Judeans of Yeb seem to have accommodated this desire, and they even agreed to modify their temple practices to demonstrate their loyalty to the Jerusalem Temple and its administrators.

The difference between Judeans who lived within and without the land of Israel became starker after Alexander the Great defeated the Persian Empire and Hellenistic ideas began to rapidly spread throughout the Mediterranean world. By the end of the third century BCE, Judeans had produced a Greek version of their Hebrew scriptures that enforced the association between exile and divine punishment. This translation rendered Deuteronomy's description of exile—"You shall become an object of horror to all the kingdoms of the earth"—by replacing the Hebrew word for horror, *za'ăwâ*, with a Greek word,

---

32. Rosenberg, "Jewish Temple at Elephantine," 9.

diaspora (Deut 28:25; cf. Neh 1:9). Over time, *diaspora* came to denote the population of Jews who lived outside the land of Israel.

The hundreds of thousands of "diasporic" Jews who were viewed by Judean Jews as embodiments of divine punishment were mostly unconcerned with the fact that their scriptures were read by some as condemnations of diasporic life. These Jews practiced their ancestral laws such as the Sabbath, circumcision, and dietary laws. They also wrote novellas, stories, prayers, poems, and wisdom texts that presented the God of Israel as benevolent toward all Jews, regardless of where they lived.[33] Some of these Jews produced texts that carefully dissociate scriptural passages about the curse of exile from their own lives.[34] These texts deny a qualitative difference between Judean Jews and Jews who live elsewhere, underscore common elements of human experience, and highlight the universality of the covenantal God.[35] To understand how the category of diaspora was produced, I will next examine literature produced by Judean Jews who created and enforced this category. I will begin with an overview of how Jewish life outside the land of Israel posed a theological problem for Judean Jews and how they used the Torah to try to solve it.

---

33. An exception to this rule is 2 Maccabees, a late second-century BCE novella that was produced in Cyrene. Its surviving version is an abridged work that centers on events taking place in Judea and thus quite naturally shows little interest in events outside the homeland. The novella's acceptance of Judean exceptionalism makes it an outlier among Jewish texts produced outside Judea during this time. See 2 Macc 2:19, 22; 3:2, 4, 12, 30; 4:15, 34, 42; 5:15, 21; 6:2, 4; 8:2; 9:16; 10:1–5; 11:3, 25; 13:15, 23; 14:4, 31–33; 15:17–18, 33; Simkovich, "Composition of 2 Maccabees," 293–310.

34. Kraabel, "Unity and Diversity," 49; Scott, "Self-Understanding of Diaspora Jews," 182; Carroll, "Exile! What Exile?," 62–79. Van Unnik holds that Jews who lived outside the land of Israel viewed their lives as actualizations of the biblical curse of exile, noting that *diaspora* appears in contemporary Greek sources disparagingly (Diogenes Laertius, *Lives of the Eminent Philosophers* 10.65; Plutarch, *Moralia* 1105a; 1109f; 1110f–1111a; Herodotus, *Hist.* 3.68; Plato, *Leg.* 3.699d). See van Unnik, *Das Selbstverständnis der jüdischen Diaspora*. A study of these texts, however, suggests that these passages are far less disparaging than Van Unnik claims.

35. *Let. Aris.* 190, 195, 197, 207, 210; *Joseph and Aseneth* 15:6–8; Philo, *Decalogue* 41, 64, 99, 178; *Spec. Laws* 1.97, 169, 304–5, 327; *Rewards* 9; *Cherubim* 109; *Flaccus* 94; *Hypothetica* 7.1–9; *Alleg. Interp.* 161, 306; *Virtues*, 109–24, 141, 147, inter alia.

CHAPTER 3

The Judean Invention of the Diaspora

IN THE FIRST CENTURY CE, Judea was home to hundreds of thousands of Jews as well as to Greeks, Romans, Egyptians, and other people, many of whom had been hired by the Herodian government to do manual labor and had settled nearby after their contracts were completed. Judea was also a destination spot for Jewish visitors and pilgrims who would make the trip to Jerusalem to worship at the temple on their holidays. As all of these people interacted with one another and exchanged ideas, Judea became an epicenter of cultural encounter that brought together people from different regions of the Roman Empire.[1] Inscriptional evidence and Jewish documents produced at this time indicate that Jewish life in Judea and abroad was more cohesive than disparate. Jews in Judea, and elsewhere in the Roman Empire, observed their ancestral dietary laws, kept the Sabbath and holidays, and practiced male circumcision.[2] They also regularly gathered to read and interpret their scriptures in Hebrew, Aramaic, and Greek, depending upon where they lived. What divided Jews in Judea from Jews who lived elsewhere was miniscule compared to what bound them together, and the cultural borders separating Judea from the space outside of it were far from self-evident.

Why, then, did a category of diaspora come into existence at all? Who enforced this concept and toward what ends?

The concept of diaspora has its origins in the Greek translation of the Torah known as the Septuagint. The Judeans who produced the Septuagint in the late third century BCE associated Judean life outside the land of Israel with divine anger. They believed that the exile denoted a particular place to which Judahites had been sent during the Babylonian exile as a punishment for their sins. This catastrophe, as well as the Assyrian expulsion of Israelites from the

---

1. See Acts 2:5–11, which describes Jerusalem as a cultural meeting ground and recalls a miracle in which the ethnically diverse Jews, gathered together for the Pentecost, are "filled with the Holy Spirit" and speak in foreign languages.
2. Sanders, *Jewish Law*, 260–72.

Northern Kingdom in 722 BCE, was a fulfillment of God's promise of retribution against sinful Israelites that was preserved in Deuteronomy (4:26–28; 28:63–65) and prophetic literature.[3] Yet the question of whether Judean life outside the land of Israel was a continuation of the biblical exile in the translators' own time remained unresolved.

The translators of the Septuagint, who came from Judea or had cultural ties to Judea, believed that contemporary Jewish life outside Judea was an extension of biblical exile. They enforced this idea by inventing a new Greek word, *diaspora*, and by using two other Greek words for captivity and displacement, *aichmalōsia* and *apoikia*.[4] With these words, the dual themes of subjugation and exile threaded their way through the Greek version of the Jewish scriptures and pulled them all together. The word *diaspora* came to mean something more expansive and long-lasting than exile. It came to signify a monolithic space and implied that the people's divine punishment of exile had spilled into the present. To understand how the diaspora developed as a concept, we must first trace its development as a word.[5]

The successful establishment of Judean communities throughout the Hellenistic world prompted Judeans to wonder why their ancestral prophets perceived exile to be a catastrophic event. How could it be that life outside the land of Israel signified God's wrath, when life there was so good?[6] The problem of how to distinguish between Jews who lived within and without the land of Israel was amplified by the fact that during the Hellenistic period, there was just one term in Greek to designate Judeans: *Ioudaioi*. This ambiguous ethnonym was freely applied as an ethnogeographic designation and then, over time, as an ethnoreligious designation. The transition of *Ioudaioi*'s meaning had not fully taken place by the late Second Temple period, and thus *Ioudaioi* was a word that had ethnic, national, and religious valances. As the meaning of *Ioudaioi* became less ethnogeographic, Judeans in the land of Israel worried that their *Ioudaioi* kin who lived abroad were not properly oriented toward their homeland.[7]

---

3. A thorough list of biblical passages that blame foreign invasion on the people's sins are too numerous to cite here, but see Isa 3:13–17 and Jer 17:1–10.

4. Simkovich, "Diaspora as a Word," 153–70.

5. Khachig Tölölyan argues that contemporary diasporas are discursive constructions ("Rethinking Diaspora(s)," 3–36). Jill Hicks-Keeton nuances this position by demonstrating that early Jewish texts such as 3 Maccabees, Joseph and Aseneth, and Tobit engage in discursive debate concerning the notion of diaspora as well ("Putting Paul in His Place," 20). Hicks-Keeton does not differentiate between texts produced within and without Judea. Of the pre-Pauline documents she studies, only Tobit enforces a separation between Judea and the lands outside it, and only Tobit has Judean provenance.

6. Rajak, "Jewish Diaspora," 146–62. On the Judeans' challenges under Persian rule, see Koller, *Esther*, 8–10.

7. Cohen, *Beginnings of Jewishness*, 69–104. The full debate on the meaning of *Ioudaios/Ioudaiois* is too extensive to fully cite here, but see our discussion above on p. 8, n. 23.

Judeans living outside the land of Israel could have invalidated the notion that they remained under the authority of their kin in the land of Israel, and that they lived in a state of divine disfavor, in two ways. They could have dissolved the concept by moving to Judea en masse, thereby reducing or eliminating Jewish life outside of Judea. Alternatively, they could have dissolved the idea by reinterpreting their scriptures to minimize the potency of exile as an expression of divine rejection. As far as we know, Jews outside of Judea did neither. Although they showed loyalty to the Jerusalem Temple by making pilgrimages to Jerusalem and donating the *didrachmon* (an annual half-shekel tax), there is no evidence of a mass migration to Judea in the Hellenistic era.[8] And while many Jewish writers radically interpreted difficult passages in their scriptures, there is no evidence that Jews allegorized passages in Deuteronomy that treat exile as the tragic result of sinful behavior.

Beginning in the second century BCE, Jews in Egypt began to approach the fact that they were being treated as symbols of divine rejection in another way. They redefined the space outside Judea as space sanctioned by God, and as space where God resides. In doing so, they rejected an essentialist distinction between the land of Israel and the lands outside of it. These Jews did not even use the word *diaspora*, perhaps because they knew that it was used in the Septuagint in connection with exile and divine punishment.[9] There is little evidence that suggests that Jews in Egypt viewed their lives as fulfillments of biblical predictions concerning the Israelites' displacement.[10] There is also little evidence that they perceived loyalty to their homeland and to their host empire as operating in tension with one another. These Jews saw themselves as members of a cohesive Jewish population, not one that was split into two halves. Indeed, there was probably little practical difference between a Jew living in Antioch and a Jew living in Jerusalem. Jewish practice and biblical interpretation may have varied from region to region, but not in a way that drew a boundary line around Judea.

---

8. Elephantine Papyrus (B19–B20) TAD A4.7–8 Cowley 30–31; Philo, *Heir* 75; *Drunkenness*, 85; Josephus, *Ant.* 18.312; Matt 17:24; 2 Macc 2:22; 3:12; Let. Aris. 84; Sib. Or. 3.274–302.

9. Schmidt argues that Jews in the Hellenistic era began to use the term *diaspora* rather than the Septuagint's words for captivity and displacement (*aichmalōsia* and *apoikia*) because they wanted to avoid giving the impression that their diasporic lives were actualizations of biblical curses. Given the rarity of the word *diaspora* at this time, Schmidt's argument is peculiar. See Schmidt, "διασπορά," 98–104.

10. Gruen rightly notes that Jews in the Hellenistic era were content to be loyal to both their homeland and host country, but he does not address the fact that Judean texts such as Ben Sira, Tobit, and Judith express a negative attitude toward Jews outside the homeland. Gruen classifies texts that extol the centrality of the homeland as Hellenistic texts, and he adds that for Philo and Josephus, "no breach existed, no discernible difference even, between the practices of Palestinian Jews and of those abroad." This assessment misses the point that Philo and Josephus wrote outside Judea. Though reared in Judea, Josephus was attuned to the expectations of his Roman audience. See Gruen, *Diaspora*, 249; cf. Cohen, *Josephus in Galilee and Rome*.

Still, some Jews drew this line themselves. The appearance of the word *diaspora* in the Septuagint marks the beginning of a process by which Judean Jews established a protective boundary that separated the land of Israel from the rest of the world. Jews in Judea would soon begin to write letters, historical archives, novellas, and wisdom texts that enforced this boundary and depicted the Jerusalem Temple as the global center of Jewish worship. Because the boundary around the land of Israel required constant reinforcement, Judean Jews asked Jews living in Egypt to affirm the notion of Judean exceptionalism. For these Judean Jews, the insurmountable separation between Jews within and without the land of Israel would only be resolved in the end-time, when a Jewish ingathering to the land would eliminate Jewish life abroad.

Many scholars believe that Jews at this time mostly dissociated Jewish life outside Judea from the biblical exile and instead adopted a broadly positive approach toward life outside Judea.[11] A few suggest that the majority of Jews held a negative view toward life outside the land. Scholars on both sides of this debate tend to miss the fact that the word *diaspora* entered the Jewish lexicon with a trickle rather than a bang. Jews who wrote about land and exile in the Hellenistic era may not have even known that the word existed. Nevertheless, the scarcity of the word *diaspora* does not suggest an absence of the concept.[12] Jews within and without Judea seemed to be aware of the diaspora as an idea,

---

11. Kraabel notes that there is little evidence that suggests that Jews who lived outside Judea viewed their lives as fulfillments of the biblical *gālût*. Still, his claim that "diaspora was not Exile; in some sense it became a Holy Land, too," goes too far. Van Unnik's position that these Jews viewed their lives as embodied fulfillments of scriptural promises to punish Israel with exile is also too extreme. See Kraabel, "Roman Diaspora," 452; van Unnik, *Das Selbstverständnis der jüdischen Diaspora*, 95–101. For a moderate approach, see Scott, "Self-Understanding of Diaspora Jews," 182.

12. The near absence of the Greek word for *Judaism* raises the question of whether Jews perceived their ancestral practice to be a system that was external to Hellenistic practice. This question centers on how language and thought serve to shape one another. While Boyarin argues that the absence of the word *Judaism* indicates that a conceptual notion of Judaism could not have existed at this stage, most scholars of language development agree that thought and language are interdependent processes that inform and shape one another. Present consensus is that children acquire language, either innately or with training, in response to and in interaction with emergent language. A child cannot call a spoon a "spoon" until she develops a perception *of* the spoon. Nor can a toddler say "I love you" to her mother until she becomes conscious of the bond that connects them. In the earliest stages of human development, thought precedes language. Once language is established and users come to an understanding of a word's basic contours, they can adjust and subvert its conceptual meanings. Vygotsky, *Thought and Language*; Piaget, *Le Langage*; Skinner, *Verbal Behavior*; Chomsky, *New Horizons*; Pinker, *Language Instinct*. D. Schwartz applies this approach to early Judaism, noting that "we may legitimately speak, today, about ancient Jewish 'culture,' 'ethics,' 'sovereignty,' 'nationalism' or the like, although ancient Jewish languages had no words for such concepts. Indeed, frequently terms for phenomena come into vogue only after the phenomena have been around long enough for the language to recognize them" (*Jews and Judeans*, 104; cf. Lowe, "Concepts and Words").

and Jews outside Judea subverted the idea of diaspora without using the word itself.

The Invention of the Word *Diaspora*

The Septuagint is not the work of a single author. According to early Jewish tradition, this Greek translation of the Torah was produced by seventy-two Judean scholars who traveled to Egypt during the reign of King Ptolemy II Philadelphus (284–246 BCE) and who worked on the project on the island of Pharos off the coast of Alexandria. Greek translations of other Hebrew books were produced over the next few centuries and were later included in this collection. By the second century, the Septuagint comprised a diverse collection of books that were produced within multiple cultural contexts. Many of these books were translated by scholars who were somehow connected to Judea, even if they had been living in Egypt for some time. This connection is evidenced in the presence of Aramaic loan words in the Septuagint, which suggests that its translators may have been Aramaic speakers who had come from Judea, or whose parents and grandparents had come from Judea, where they spoke Aramaic fluently.[13] The Septuagint is often studied as a cultural bridge between Judean and Egyptian communities. But it can also be read as a Judean missive produced for Egyptian Jews that is comparable to epistolary works that were produced by Judean Jews and intended for Egyptian Jews.

The Greek noun *diaspora* is a neologism in the Septuagint, which means that it does not appear in earlier extant sources.[14] To readers coming across it for the first time, *diaspora* would have conveyed an image of seeds being scattered upon foreign lands.[15] Its prefix *dia-* indicates a motion of moving

---

13. Aitken reviews recent scholarship on the Septuagint's provenance in "Ptolemaic Setting," 398–414.

14. Oddly, most scholars interested in how Jews viewed the diaspora in the Hellenistic era do not study how Jews used the word *diaspora*. One of the more thorough analyses of *diaspora* comes from van Unnik, who argues for a negative diasporic self-understanding on the basis that the word's usage in Greek and Roman sources is negative and appears within the context of colonization. He concludes that Septuagint translators adopted *diaspora* from these sources and reframed the term as a referent to God's punishment of Israel. He also claims that because *diaspora* is used negatively in the Septuagint, diasporic Jews must have perceived their lives negatively. Van Unnik's research, however, contains errors. He notes that *diaspora* appears in the writings of Thucydides (*Peloponnesian War* 2.27), but the word there is the verb *speirō*. And whereas the verb *diaspeirō* appears as early as the fifth century BCE, the noun only first appears in the Septuagint. See van Unnik, *Das Selbstverständnis der jüdischen Diaspora*, 95–101. See also Dufoix's thorough refutation of van Unnik in *Dispersion*, 30–37; cf. Scott, "Self-Understanding of Diaspora Jews," 183–84.

15. The verb *diaspeirō* appears sixty-six times in the Septuagint and is most often used to translate nāpaṣ, which means "to shatter."

through or over a particular space and refers to separation or division. Its main root, the verb *speirō*, means "to sow." *Diaspora* appears just fifteen times in the thousands of pages of literature that Jews produced in the late Second Temple era.[16] Besides its ten appearances in the Septuagint, *diaspora* appears twice in the writings of Philo of Alexandria: once in a citation of the Septuagint (*Confusion* 197), and once in a metaphorical comment about how vice leads to dispersion of the soul (*Rewards* 115). Philo does not betray any awareness that *diaspora* was a word used to identify Jewish populations outside of Judea. *Diaspora* also appears twice in the Psalms of Solomon, a collection of poems that were likely composed in the years following the Roman invasion of Jerusalem in 63 BCE. Both references to *diaspora* in the Psalms of Solomon appear within descriptions of a temporary punishment that will be resolved on account of God's mercy (Pss. Sol. 8:28; 9:2).[17] *Diaspora* also appears once in the Testaments of the Twelve Patriarchs, a collection of texts that was probably edited and assembled during the first century CE, perhaps in Syria. The word appears in a section called the Testament of Asher, when the eponymous patriarch envisions Israel's future captivity and dispersion (T. Ash. 7:2).[18] This reference may have been written by an early follower of Jesus, since the phrase that follows it predicts that a figure will come to "save Israel and all the nations, God speaking like a man" (7:3).[19] Finally, *diaspora* appears three times in the New Testament. Two references appear in the opening verses of 1 Peter and James, when the respective writers identify their addressees, and one appears in the Gospel of John, when Jews ask one another whether Jesus intends to go to the *diaspora* to teach the Greeks (7:35). These scanty references indicate

---

16. In the Septuagint, *diaspora* appears in Deut 28:25; 30:4; Isa 49:6; Jer 15:7; 41:17; Dan 12:2; 2 Esd 1:9; Jdt 5:19; 2 Macc 1:27; and Ps 146:2.

17. Pss. Sol. 8:28; 9:2: "Bring together the dispersed [*tēn diasporan*] of Israel with mercy and goodness ... The dispersion of Israel [*hē diaspora tou israel*] (was) among every nation, according to the saying of God; that your righteousness might be proven right, O God, in our lawless actions. For you are a righteous judge over all the peoples of the earth." I treat the Psalms of Solomon as outside of the Septuagint collective since they only appear in the fifth-century CE Codex Alexandrinus manuscript of the Septuagint and not in the early fourth-century CE Codex Vaticanus or Codex Sinaiticus. See Goswell, "Order of the Books," 466; Eckhardt, "Psalms of Solomon," 7–30.

18. T. Ash. 7:2: "For I know that you will sin and be delivered into the hands of your enemies; your land shall be made desolate and your sanctuary wholly polluted. You will be scattered to the four corners of the earth; in the dispersion [*en diaspora*] you shall be regarded as worthless, like useless water, until such time as the Most High visits the earth." Translation from Kee, "Testaments of the Twelve Patriarchs," 1:818.

19. At least part of this passage represents a later Christian interpolation; see Kee, "Testaments of the Twelve Patriarchs," 1:818. The Testament of Asher's reference to *diaspora* and its emphasis on exile as divine punishment for Israel's sins may reflect the work of a Jewish follower of Jesus who viewed the dispersion as a signifier of God's rejection that was predicted in the early biblical period. As we will see, however, some Jews who lived well before Jesus's time espoused the notion that dispersion signifies divine punishment.

that Jews barely used the word, let alone collectively agreed that it was a referent to God's retributive punishment.

The authors of the Septuagint rarely used *diaspora* to translate the Hebrew words for banishment and exile (*gālût* and *gōlâ*). Of the three words used in the Septuagint to denote the stages of exile—captivity (*aichmalōsia*), displacement (*apoikia*), and dispersion (*diaspora*)—*aichmalōsia* is the most common, appearing 124 times in the Septuagint.[20] *Apoikia* appears just twenty-eight times in the Septuagint, all in references to the recent or contemporary exile.[21] *Diaspora* is by far the rarest, appearing just ten times in the Septuagint. Most of the references to *diaspora* in the Septuagint appear in the context of a catastrophic exile that will occur as an expression of God's wrath and rejection.[22] Captivity and displacement are conceptual precursors to the diaspora, but the Septuagint translators sometimes used *diaspora* as an umbrella term that included the experiences of captivity and displacement.[23]

The authors of the Septuagint did not use *diaspora* to translate any particular word of the Hebrew Bible. In three instances (Deut 30:4; Neh 1:9;

20. Josephus uses *aichmalōsia* twenty-nine times but Philo uses it just once in a citation of the Septuagint's rendering of Num 31:25–26, which concerns the laws of taking spoils in war (*Alleg. Interp.* 2.35). *Aichmalōsia* appears twenty-two times in other early Jewish texts. Most uses of *aichmalōsia* allude to the Israelites' slavery in Egypt and potentially to later exiles as well (T. Benj. 7:2; T. Dan 5:7–8, 11; T. Naph. 4:2; 5:8; T. Levi 13:6–7). In some passages, the word refers to spoils (T. Jud. 4:3; 5:6; 6:3; 7:8; 23:5) or captivity (T. Jos. 1:5; Pss. Sol. 2:6; 3 Baruch prol. 2–3; 4 Baruch 6:19; 2 Esdras 5:16–18; Demetrius 6.1, preserved in Clement of Alexandria, *Miscellanies* 1.14). The fifteen references to *aichmalōsia* in the Testaments of the Twelve Patriarchs may represent the work of an early Christian editor. See de Jonge, *Testaments*, 128; Bickerman, "Date of the Testaments," 260. The Septuagint also occasionally renders *gōlâ* as *aichmalōsia* (2 Kgs 24:14; Ezek 1:1; 3:11, 15; 11:24–25; 12:3–4, 7, 11; 25:3; Amos 1:15; Zech 6:10; 14:2; 1 Esd 2:1; 8:35; 2 Esd 7:6).

21. In the LXX, see 1 Esd 1:11; 2:1; 4:1; 9:4; 10:6, 16; 2 Esd 7:6; Jer 13:9; 30:19; 31:7; 35:4; 35:6; 36:1, 4; 36:22, 31; 37:3; 39:44; 40:7, 11; 47:11; Bar 3:7–8; 3 Macc 6:10; Wis 12:7. Some appearances of *apoikia* are translations of the Hebrew *gōlâ*; see 2 Kgs 24:14–16; Jer 28:6 (35:6 LXX); 29:1 (36:1 LXX); 29:4 (36:4 LXX); 29:16, 20, 31 (36:31 LXX); 46:19 (26:19 LXX); 48:7 (31:7 LXX), 11 (31:33 LXX); 49:3 (30:19 LXX); Ezra 1:11; 4:1; 6:19–21; 9:4; 10:6–8, 16; Neh 7:6. *Apoikia* appears forty-four times in the writings of Philo, who uses it in reference to the two-phase experience of departing one's ancestral homeland and colonizing another land, mostly in passages regarding the biblical patriarchs. Philo views displacement and colonization positively, perhaps because he was influenced by the Egyptian tradition that communities throughout the world derived from Egypt. Philo, *Creation* 135; *Migration* 176; *Heir* 98; *Prelim. Studies* 84; *Flight* 36, 95; *Abraham*, 66, 68, 72, 77, 85; *Moses* 1.71, 103, 163, 170, 195, 222, 233, 236, 239, 254–255, 232, 246, 288; *Spec. Laws* 2.25, 146, 150, 158; 3.111; 4.178; *Virtues* 77, 102, 219; *Rewards* 16, 80; *Contempl. Life* 22; *Embassy* 281; *QG* 1.27; esp. *Confusion* 77–78; *Flaccus* 46–47. Cf. Diodorus Siculus, *Library of History* 1.28.1–3; Scott, "Self-Understanding of Diaspora Jews," 183; Scott, "Philo and the Restoration of Israel," 553–755; Gruen, *Diaspora*, 242. Josephus likewise uses *apoikia* to refer to colonization, and uses the word eight times (*Ant.* 1.110–112, 120, 216, 255; 10.223; *Ag. Ap.* 2.38).

22. The sole exception is the book of Judith, which uses the word in reference to a past event. Dufoix, *Dispersion*, 47; cf. Dufoix, "Diaspora," 13–21.

23. Schmidt, "διασπορά," 98–104.

Ps 147:2), *diaspora* is used to describe those who, in the Hebrew account, are portrayed as *niddăḥ*, "scattered." In these verses, *diaspora* designates a population rather than (or in addition to) a designated space. More often, however, the Septuagint authors used *diaspora* to translate or editorially expand upon a word connected to the theme of divine punishment. *Diaspora* first appears in the Septuagint in Deut 28:25 within a passage that lists a series of curses that God will exact upon the Israelites should they violate the covenantal laws. The Hebrew version of this passage first refers to the Israelites being subject to foreign colonization in verse 36, which declares that "the Lord will bring you, and the king whom you set over you, to a nation that neither you nor your ancestors have known." The Septuagint transfers this punishment to the passage's opening pericope by rendering "you shall become an object of horror [*ləzaʿăwâ*] to all the kingdoms of the earth," as "you shall be in dispersion [*en diaspora*] in all the kingdoms of the earth" (Deut 28:25 LXX). In defining *zaʿăwâ* as *diaspora*, the Septuagint clarifies that Israel's source of shame will come in the form of dispersion and the consequent exposure of its broken covenant with God to the nations. The nations, in turn, will delight in Israel's fate and be reminded of God's fearsome power.

While the Septuagint's first reference to *diaspora* links Israel's expulsion with public shame, its second reference to *diaspora* appears shortly afterward in the context of reconciliation. Deuteronomy 30:4–5 reads, "Even if you are exiled [*niddaḥăkā*] to the ends of the world, from there the Lord your God will gather you, and from there he will bring you back. The Lord your God will bring you into the land that your ancestors possessed, and you will possess it; he will make you more prosperous and numerous than your ancestors." By rendering *niddaḥăkā* as *diaspora*, the Septuagint authors implied that the shameful dispersion envisioned in the earlier pericope is temporary. The juxtaposition of both usages of *diaspora*, moreover, points to the word's dual aspect: the diaspora will exacerbate the deteriorating relationship between God and Israel, but it will also be a harbinger of their future reconciliation.

The Septuagint also renders *zaʿăwâ* as *diaspora* in Jeremiah 34, which warns that God will not release the people from punishment, just as the people did not grant financial releases to their neighbors. Instead, they will become a source of horror to other nations. A translation of the Hebrew verse reads:

> Therefore, thus says the Lord: You have not obeyed me by granting a release [*dərôr*] to your neighbors and friends; I am going to grant a release [*dərôr*] to you, says the Lord—a release to the sword, to pestilence, and to famine. I will make you a horror [*ləzaʿăwâ*] to all the kingdoms of the earth. (Jer 34:17)

The Septuagint version of this verse clarifies that the horror that God promises will be experienced as a diaspora:

> Therefore, thus did the Lord say: You have not obeyed me by calling for a release each pertaining to his fellow. Behold, I am calling for a release for you to the dagger and to death and to the famine, and I will give you as a dispersion [*eis diasporan*] to all the kingdoms of the earth. (Jer 41:17 LXX)[24]

The Septuagint builds on the Hebrew version's reference to *dərôr*, a term that appears elsewhere in the Hebrew Bible in reference to the nullification of land contracts in the Jubilee year, to clarify the *quid pro quo* nature of the people's punishment (Lev 25:10).[25] Because they refused to grant such releases, the people will lose their own land. Clarifying God's punishment as dispersion resolves a difficulty with the Hebrew verse: how can the people be a horror to all kingdoms when they reside in Judea? The answer is that they will not reside in Judea at all. They will be dispersed throughout the world, and this dispersion will constitute the source of their humiliation.[26]

Besides Deut 30:4, the Septuagint translates the participle *niddāḥ* as *diaspora* in two other passages: Neh 1:9 and Ps 147:2. In Nehemiah, *niddaḥăkem* appears in a prayer that asks God to remember the promise to gather the outcasts of Israel from exile.[27] The Septuagint's translation of *niddaḥăkem* as *hē diaspora humōn* follows the Septuagint's translation of *niddaḥăkā* as *diaspora* in Deut 30:4.[28] Perhaps the translator of Nehemiah noted thematic links between

---

24. This verse corresponds to Jer 34:17 in the Masoretic Text.
25. *Dərôr* also appears in conjunction with the release of captives (Isa 61:1; Jer 34:8, 15; Ezek 46:17) and occasionally means *sparrow* (Ps 84:4; Prov 26:2).
26. The fact that the Septuagint authors did not always render *za'ăwâ* as *diaspora* in verses that mention exile suggests an absence of a systematic approach toward the connection between shame and exile. Besides Deut 28:25, *za'ăwâ* appears in Jer 15:4; 24:9; 29:18; 34:17; Ezek 23:46; and 2 Chr 29:8. All of these verses outside of Ezek 23:46 refer to the Israelites' forced displacement as an act of divine rejection. *Za'ăwâ* is not translated as *diaspora* in the Septuagint in these verses (Jer 29:18 may be an exception, but no Septuagint translation of this passage survives). In some of these verses, translating *za'ăwâ* as *diaspora* would make some sense in context, such as in Jer 15:4: "I will make them a horror [*ləza'ăwâ*] to all the kingdoms of the earth because of what King Manasseh son of Hezekiah of Judah did in Jerusalem."
27. Neh 1:8–9 paraphrases the curses of Deut 30:4, but changes *niddaḥăkā* to *niddaḥăkem*: "Remember the word that you commanded your servant Moses, 'If you are unfaithful, I will scatter you among the peoples; but if you return to me and keep my commandments and do them, though your outcasts [*niddaḥăkem*] are under the farthest skies, I will gather them from there and bring them to the place at which I have chosen to establish my name.'"
28. "Remember now the word that you commanded your servant Moyses, saying, 'You, if you are faithless, I will scatter you among my peoples, and if you return to me and keep my commandments and do them, if your dispersion [*hē diaspora humōn*] is to the farthest skies, from there I will

the two passages and identified the returnees to Yehud with the exiled Israelites alluded to in Deuteronomy 30. The Septuagint also renders *nidḥê Yiśrā'el*, "the scattered ones of Israel," in Ps 146:2 as *tas diasporas*.[29] Perhaps the translators of Psalm 147 took note of how the Hebrew Bible associates *niddāḥ* with exile and reconciliation and followed suit by translating *nidḥê* as *diaspora* in a psalm that imagines how God will compassionately gather the outcasts of Israel back to Jerusalem.

The Septuagint authors also employed *diaspora* to clarify difficult Hebrew phrases. Its rendering of Isa 49:6, for example, uses *diaspora* as a way to resolve ambiguities in the verse. Isaiah 49:6 cites God as declaring that "it is too light a thing [*nāqel*] that you should be my servant to raise up the tribes of Jacob and to restore the survivors of Israel [*nəṣûrê Yiśrā'el*]; I will give you as a light to the nations, that my salvation may reach to the end of the earth." The phrase "it is too light a thing that you should be my servant" implies that the prophet's burden should be even more difficult than it currently is. The identity of the "survivors of Israel," whom the prophet is meant to restore, is also obscure, and the reference to the tribes of Jacob and the survivors of Israel seems repetitive. The Septuagint resolves all of these difficulties with the following translation:

> And he said to me, "It is a great thing for you to be called my servant so that you may set up the tribes of Iakob and turn back the dispersion [*ten diasporan*] of Israel. See, I have made you a light of nations, that you may be for salvation to the end of the earth." (Isa 49:6 LXX)

The rendering of the Hebrew phrase "it is too light a thing" as "it is a great thing" clarifies that the stewardship of Israel is a crucial role. The rendering of "survivors" (*nəṣûrê*) as *diaspora*, moreover, resolves the problem of repetition and clarifies the survivors' identities. The servant's task, according to this rendering, is to gather the Israelites who are scattered abroad and initiate the process of divine restoration.

The Septuagint also uses *diaspora* as a clarifying word in Jer 15:7, which cites God as declaring, "I have winnowed them with a winnowing fork [*'ēzrem bəmizrēh*] in the gates of the land. I have bereaved them, I have destroyed my people; they did not turn from their ways." The Septuagint interprets the verse's winnowing imagery as a scattering of Israel: "And I will disperse them in a dispersion [*kai diaspeirō autous en diaspora*] in the gates of my people.

---

gather them and lead them to the place where I have chosen my name to encamp there'" (2 Esd 11:8–9 LXX). 2 Esdras 11 LXX corresponds to Nehemiah 1 MT.

29. Compare the Hebrew's "The Lord builds up Jerusalem; he gathers the outcasts of Israel [*nidḥê Yiśrā'el*]" with the Septuagint's "The Lord builds up Jerusalem; he gathers the outcasts [*tas diasporas*] of Israel" (Ps 146:2 [147:2 MT]).

I was made childless; I destroyed my people because of their evils" (Jer 15:7 LXX). The Septuagint replaces *mizrēh*, "winnowing fork," with *diaspora*, which denotes the dispersion of seeds. The two words share an obvious agricultural connection. But the preceding pericope, which predicts that the people will be taken captive and exiled to a foreign land, also offers insight as to why the Septuagint renders *winnowing fork* as *diaspora*:

> ¹And the Lord said to me: If Moyses and Samouel stood before me, my soul would not be toward them. Send this people away, and let them go! ²And it shall be, if they say to you, "Where shall we go?" you shall also say to them: This is what the Lord says: Those destined for death, to death, and those destined for a dagger, to a dagger; and those destined for famine, to famine, and those destined for captivity, to captivity.... ⁴And I will hand them over for anguish to all the kingdoms of the earth on account of the King Manasse son of Hezekias of Iouda concerning all he did in Ierousalem. (Jer 15:1–2, 4 LXX)

The Septuagint preserves the agricultural imagery of Jer 15:7 while developing the prediction of expulsion outlined in Jer 15:2 by clarifying that the winnowing image in Jer 15:7 refers to the scattering of Israel. This translation modifies the meaning of the Hebrew version. Whereas the Hebrew has God winnowing the people as a punishment that takes place within the land, the Septuagint predicts that God will scatter the people outside the land. This difference correlates with the Septuagint's rendering of the Hebrew "gates of the land" as "gates of my people." By transforming the image of gated cities into an image of scattered communities, the Septuagint transforms this verse into a forecast of dispersion.[30]

Other references to *diaspora* in the Septuagint build on its first appearance in Deuteronomy 28 by enforcing the connection between dispersion and shame. One such example occurs in the Septuagint's rendering of Dan 12:2. The Hebrew reads, "Many of those who sleep in the dust of the earth shall awake, some to everlasting life, and some to shame and everlasting contempt." This verse appears in a passage that fuses eschatological themes about divine judgment with the notion that the dead will be revived in the end-time. In this scenario, the dead will awaken to wonderful reward or terrible punishment.[31] The Septuagint situates this punishment within the experience of the diaspora: "And many of those who sleep in the flat of the earth will arise, some to everlasting

---

30. Cf. Isa 41:16 LXX, which renders the Hebrew's image of winnowing (*tizrēm warûaḥ tiśśā'ēm ûsə'ārâ tāpîṣ 'ōtām*) into one of scattering with the term *diaspeirō* (*kataigis disperei autous*).

31. Cf. Ezekiel's vision of the valley of the dry bones in Ezek 37:1–14.

life but others to shame and others to dispersion [*hoi de eis diasporan*] and contempt everlasting" (Dan 12:2 LXX). The repetitive *laḥărāpôt lǝdir'ôn 'ôlām* is rectified by interpreting *lǝdir'ôn* as *eis diasporan*, thereby envisioning two distinct but related punishments. According to this version, only some people will be doomed to dispersion. Perhaps the translators viewed dispersion as an extreme form of punishment meant to shame only the worst sinners.[32]

Nearly every reference to *diaspora* in the Septuagint imagines a future scattering that will take place following Israel's abandonment of the covenantal laws. The sole exception appears in the book of Judith, which treats the diaspora as a space occupied by Israel in the past. An Ammonite named Achior informs the Assyrian general Holofernes that the Israelites can only be defeated when they are disobedient to their God. In the past, Achior explains, God punished Israel for their disobedience with dispersion, but in recent times the Israelites have "come back from the places where they were scattered" (*ek tēs diasporas ou diesparēsan ekei*; Jdt 5:19). This verse is unusual because it references a past diaspora, and because it refers to *diaspora* as a plural noun.[33] Perhaps the author of Judith, who lived in Judea under Hasmonean rule, was optimistic that the Hasmonean Kingdom had already experienced a full restoration. Jews who lived outside Judea, therefore, could no longer be living in a state of punishment.

The Septuagint's association of *diaspora* with experiences of punishment, horror, and shame complicates the prevalent view that Jews in the Hellenistic period generally viewed the diaspora as a source of pride.[34] Given this association, the absence of the word *diaspora* in Jewish literature produced outside Judea is not surprising. Jews in these lands wrote documents that depict their communities as places where Jews could thrive while practicing their ancestral laws. Over time, the negative meaning of the word *diaspora* became dissonant with the lived reality of most Jews who resided outside their homeland.

The Judean Interest in the Jews of Egypt

The first five books of the Septuagint were produced for Greek-speaking Jews living in Egypt by people who had an affiliation with Judea. The production of

---

32. The second-century CE Jewish translator Theodotion removed this reference to the dispersion in his Greek rendering of Daniel and translated the verse as, "And many of those who sleep in a mound of earth will be awakened, these to everlasting life and those to shame and everlasting contempt" (Dan 12:2). This omission may suggest discomfort with the association between divine judgment and diaspora.

33. The only other appearance of a plural form of *diaspora* is in Ps 146:2 (LXX).

34. For the view that most Jews in the Hellenistic era embraced the diaspora, see Kraabel, "Unity and Diversity," 49–60; Kraabel, "Roman Diaspora," 445–64.

this collection, and of other Judean documents produced for Egyptian Jewish readers, suggests that Judean Jews took a special interest in the Jews of Egypt. Many of these documents ask Egyptian Jews to adopt an approach toward Jewish life outside Judea that matched the approach found in the Septuagint. Before we examine these texts, we must consider why Judean Jews were especially interested in the affairs of Jews in Egypt.

Judean attention to Egypt goes back to at least the early sixth century BCE, when Jeremiah cautioned Judeans who had settled there to refrain from worshiping false gods (Jer 44:1–30). Egypt, Jeremiah insisted, is a place that lures Judeans into sin and even self-destruction. "I will take the remnant of Judah who are determined to come to the land of Egypt to settle," Jeremiah was cited as predicting, "and they shall perish, everyone; in the land of Egypt they shall fall" (44:12).[35] The damning words of Jeremiah may have rung in the ears of Judean Jews four centuries later, following reports that Jews in Egypt were in peril. Hearing these reports from afar, Judean leaders may have felt a duty to reiterate Jeremiah's message that Judeans could avoid destruction by demonstrating loyalty to the Jerusalem Temple. Judean Jews who remembered Jeremiah's message, however, did not simply communicate doom and gloom to their kin in Egypt. They also shared words of comfort and guidance while gently inviting Egyptian Jews to accept Judean Jewish authority.[36] Above all, they took care not to sever the fragile ties that kept these communities in relationship.

By the late Second Temple period, Egypt was special for another reason as well: it was home to Jews who came from elite Judean families that had escaped Jerusalem for fear of losing their lives. One such figure was a high priest named Onias, who fled Jerusalem for Egypt after falling out with a Hellenized Jew named Alcimus. Onias formed an alliance with Ptolemy VI Philometor (r. 186–145 BCE) and received permission from Ptolemy to build a Jewish temple in a region of Egypt called Leontopolis. According to Josephus, Onias informed Ptolemy that the temple would be modeled after the Jerusalem Temple and would serve to unite disparate Jewish communities in Egypt. Onias and his supporters, it seems, did not dare to make the bold suggestion that the Leontopolis temple would be considered equal to the Jerusalem Temple.[37] Knowing that such a claim would have been viewed by Judean

---

35. The verse continues: "by the sword and by famine they shall perish; from the least to the greatest, they shall die by the sword and by famine; and they shall become an object of execration and horror, of cursing and ridicule."

36. Evidence of contact between these communities appears in 1 Macc 10:46–56, which notes that Jews allied with Alexander Epiphanes, who claimed to be the son of Antiochus IV Epiphanes, after he defeated Demetrius I in late 153 or early 152 BCE. Alexander Epiphanes allied with Ptolemy VI Philometor, making the Jews of Judea and the Jews of Egypt allies by extension.

37. Honigman, "Birth of a Diaspora," 108.

Jews as untenable, they instead presented their temple as a symbol of homage to the great Jerusalem Temple. Such expressions of loyalty were not merely cynical gestures. The fact that Egyptian Jews began to give their children traditional Hebrew names at this time suggests that events in Judea, along with the rising perception in Egypt that Jews belonged to a separate class, generated nationalistic sentiment among the Jews of Egypt.[38]

While Onias may have truly intended to redirect Egyptian Jewish loyalties to Jerusalem, Judean leaders in Jerusalem may have felt ambivalent about how Judean transplants were successfully shepherding Jewish communities in Egypt. On the one hand, Onias and his supporters came from Judean families and represented Judean power. And yet, for most Judean leaders in Jerusalem, any support of the temple in Leontopolis undermined the Jerusalem Temple and its administrators, especially in light of scriptural depictions of Egypt as the antithesis of the land of Israel.[39]

The two communities also shared organizational similarities. Like Jews in Judea, Jews in Egypt worshiped their ancestral God in both temple and synagogue, and they adopted similar, though not identical, systems of local governance, including the establishment of the position of ethnarch.[40] For Judeans, the shared practices and overlapping connections between Jews in Egypt and Jews in Judea required clarification that these regions were not equal in significance.[41] Judean leaders, therefore, drew a sharp distinction between Judea and Egypt and, ultimately, between Judea and the rest of the world. This distinction helped to discursively create the Jewish diaspora.

Judean writers believed that Jewish life outside the land of Israel was both a sin and a punishment. They also believed that as Jews continued to make the incorrect choice to settle outside the land of Israel, God continued to punish them by withholding a restoration. Jews with Judean ties produced a Greek version of the Hebrew scriptures that reminded Greek-speaking Jews that they did not belong in the lands outside Judea, and that they should remain loyal

---

38. Honigman, "Birth of a Diaspora," 124; Stern, "Relations Between the Hasmonean Kingdom," 81–196; Smallwood, *Jews Under Roman Rule*, 34–37, 224; cf. Josephus, *Ag. Ap.* 2.49–55.

39. Deut 28:68 warns the Israelites that, should they abandon the covenantal relationship with God, "the Lord will bring you back in ships to Egypt, by a route that I promised you would never see again; and there you shall offer yourselves for sale to your enemies as male and female slaves, but there will be no buyer." Cf. Ezek 29:10; 30:15–16.

40. Josephus, *Ant.* 14.73, 184, 194, 208–210; *J.W.* 1.153, 194; Sharon, "Title Ethnarch," 472–93. Judea and Egypt also shared the category of *gerousia*; see Josephus, *Ant.* 4.186, 218, 220, 222, 255–256, 324–325; 5.15, 23, 55, 57, 80, 103, 115, 135, 151, 170, 332, 335, 353; 7.294. Cf. Philo, *Flaccus* 74–80; Philo, *Embassy* 229; 3 Macc 1:8.

41. On Judean interest in Jewish affairs in Egypt, see Mélèze Modrzejewski, *Jews of Egypt*, 122–24; Kasher, "Political and National Connections," 24.

to the Jerusalem Temple and its authorities. And yet, these very scriptures enabled Jews to remain connected to their traditions without returning to their homeland.

The tension between the mode and content of the Septuagint parallels tensions between the mode and content of the Hebrew Torah. Judeans who did not live in proximity to the Jerusalem Temple were aware that their scriptures associated Judean settlement outside the land of Israel with shame and divine rejection.[42] But they also viewed the Torah as the central medium around which they could gather to serve their ancestral God.

A similar tension appears in letters that Judean Jews wrote to Jews living in Egypt. These letters encourage the observance of Judean holidays with the apparent intention of ensuring Jewish uniformity. And yet, the very *act* of exhortatory letter writing to Egyptian Jewish communities reinforced imagined boundaries around Judea by fortifying Judean authority. While Judean letters to the Jews of Egypt express friendship and mutuality with Egyptian Jews, they also express a desire to bring Egyptian Jews under the protective wing of Judean leadership and indicate that Egyptian Jews are members of a distinct population that cannot fully assimilate with its Judean kin. Before turning to these letters, I will examine the rhetorical strategies that helped Judean writers to make their case.

---

42. Diaspora is associated with shame in Dan 9:11 and Bar 1:15–22, which we will discuss in chapter 7. It also appears in Ezra 9:7: "From the days of our ancestors to this day we have been deep in guilt, and for our iniquities we, our kings, and our priests have been handed over to the kings of the lands, to the sword, to captivity, to plundering, and to utter shame, as is now the case;" cf. 1 Esd 8:74–77.

CHAPTER 4

The Hellenistic Strategies of Jewish Letter Writers

BEGINNING IN THE SECOND CENTURY BCE, Judean Jews wrote letters to their kin in Egypt and produced other documents that were framed as letters, which highlight the centrality of the Jerusalem Temple. Some Jews living outside the land of Israel rebutted the ideas expressed in these documents by citing scriptural texts that support the establishment of Judean life outside the land of Israel. Other Jews appealed to the notion that the Torah's mode of transmission enabled all Jews, regardless of where they lived, to cultivate a sense of connection with Jews who were reading and interpreting the same texts.[1]

As I noted in chapter 1, the Hebrew Bible presents the God of Israel as the paradigmatic writer who dictates messages to prophets, who in turn instruct their scribes to record these messages onto scrolls. In the case of the two sets of tablets that were given to Moses on Mount Sinai, God even writes the written scriptures directly.[2] Biblical writers depicted official writings produced by the Israelite king, meanwhile, as mere imitations of the divine word that signify the king's obedience to God. Moses tells the Israelites that once they enter the land and establish a monarchy, the king of Israel must produce a copy of written Torah and read from it aloud at a public assembly each year.[3] While kings in the ancient Near East used inscriptive writing to proclaim their divinely imbued power, the Israelite king was to write a copy of God's scriptures and publicly read from it as an act of mimicry and obeisance. The production of God's words, in these traditions, signified sacred transmission but not empowering independence.

---

1. Scholars of earlier generations tend to treat epistles as artificial and historical letters as more genuine, but contemporary scholars reject this distinction. Compare Deissman, "Prolegomena to the Biblical Letters," 1–59 with White and Keddie, *Jewish Fictional Letters*; Doering, *Ancient Jewish Letters*, 20.
2. Exod 3:1–2; 9:9–11; 31:16–18; 32:15–16; Mal 3:13–4:6 (3:13–24 MT).
3. Deut 17:14–20; cf. 2 Kgs 22:1–20; Jer 36:1–32.

Judeans believed that the written Torah bore a sacred quality even before they developed ideas about a fixed canon that held their sacred writings.[4] The process of transmitting these written scriptures was not considered to be distinct from the process of transmitting oral traditions. Numerous texts preserved in the Hebrew Bible testify to how prophetic documents were read aloud in public spaces. People who heard the recitation of these documents were expected to share them with others long after the prophet or scribe had ceased to speak. These documents contained meanings that were transmitted orally and that outlasted the text's initial reading. The written word was just one part of an ongoing cycle of hearing, recording, reading, sharing, and copying, which, taken together, comprised a continuous process of transmission.[5]

Writing also bore a stabilizing quality. Jewish communities throughout the Hellenistic world were different from one another and internally diverse. The comparative stability of scriptural documents as they changed hands from town to town and village to village enabled Jews to treat their past as a stable history in which they shared equal stake. As an embodiment of this history, the written scriptures were a unifying force for Jews scattered throughout the Hellenistic world. Jewish writers at this time treated the scriptures as authoritative and authentic but simultaneously viewed them as malleable resources that could be developed.[6] Interpretations of a text's meaning often shifted from place to place and from generation to generation, but the message in question was always framed as a dispatch that came directly from God.

During this period, letter writing became increasingly admired as a skill that served the needs of individuals as well as broad populations.[7] Anyone who knew how to write could produce correspondence on their own, but letter writing was especially prominent in wealthier communities, where literacy rates were relatively high and someone could dictate a letter through a scribe

---

4. Carr, *Formation of the Hebrew Bible*; Carr, *Writing on the Tablet*; Person, "Text Criticism"; Person, "Literary Unity"; Knoppers and Levinson, *Pentateuch as Torah*.

5. On the interplay between oral and written scriptural transmission, see Graham, *Beyond the Written Word*, 45–48. On written text as a significant mode of authoritative transmission to which Jewish writers appealed, see Jaffee, *Torah in the Mouth*; Newman, *Praying by the Book*; Zahn, "Talking About Rewritten Texts," 93–119; Mroczek, *Literary Imagination in Jewish Antiquity*. Wollenberg highlights the anxieties about written scriptures in the Hellenistic era that the rabbis inherited in *Closed Book*.

6. A full examination of early Jewish reading and writing practices cannot be conducted here. For a review of how early Jewish reading practices were impacted by broader reading cultures, see Wollenberg, *Closed Book*, 7–11.

7. On how letter writing occupied a central role in Greek society and particularly in Greek pedagogical circles, see Cribiore, *Gymnastics of the Mind*; Exler, "Ancient Greek Letter." On writing practices in the Roman era, see Morgan, *Literate Education*, 224; Peirano, *Rhetoric of the Roman Fake*, 14.

or a person in their employ. Many Hellenistic letters produced in the second century BCE were written in an exhortatory style that seeks to persuade a community or individual to conform to a certain kind of behavior. In its most sophisticated form, this style reflects specialized skills and extensive training in rhetorical strategy. Greek and Roman handbooks on the art of writing expound on exhortatory style but define it in varying and overlapping terms.[8]

Jews living in the Hellenistic world were naturally impacted by this literary environment, even if they did not receive formal Greek educations. These Jews were aware that a key feature of Hellenistic exhortatory letters was that they cite earlier correspondence and older authoritative texts. Jews therefore began to perceive letter writing as an opportunity to address questions about Jewish identity and practice by drawing from their own scriptural traditions.[9] Whereas Judean Jewish authors drew from scriptural passages that portray Jerusalem as the epicenter of Jewish life and treat Judeans as conservators of scriptural tradition, Egyptian Jewish authors drew from traditions that legitimize life outside the land of Israel.

Jewish writers who were exposed to Hellenistic ideas soon began to incorporate new rhetorical techniques into their letters. Ironically, some writers used these techniques to express resistance against the cultural changes that were taking place around them. They wrote texts that depict a harmonious bond shared by all Jews that was chronologically stable in its transcendence and geographically stable in its universality. Written texts and personal correspondences in particular became a stabilizing force for Jews who wanted to establish a firm grip on an unstable reality.[10]

Among these correspondences are Judean letters to Egyptian Jews that try to enforce Jewish cohesion by exhorting Egyptian Jews to observe holidays that had been recently established in Judea.[11] Two such letters ask Egyptian

---

8. Such works include the pseudonymous Demetrius of Phalerum's *On Style*, written in the first century BCE, as well as *Epistolary Styles*, which was composed at around the same time and later attributed to Libanius. The former classifies letter writing into twenty-one distinct styles, while the latter has forty-one styles. See Stowers, *Letter Writing*, 34.

9. Stowers, *Letter Writing*, 95; Ong, *Orality and Literacy*, 45–46.

10. Written texts take on an increasingly central role as a social stabilizer in turbulent times. As Davis and Womack have put it, "In a climate of cataclysmic upheaval, the role and meaning of a given text altered radically, taking on the increasingly important but harrowingly illusive role of stabilizer. The stability or security of a given text—most often a poem for the formalists—was found within itself... [T]he chaotic world beyond the borders of the text need not intrude; within the boundaries of the text all might be saved" (*Formalist Criticism*, 15–16).

11. The pool of exhortatory Judean letters to diasporic communities expands if one includes the writings of Paul. On Paul as a diasporic writer, see Barclay, "Paul Among Diaspora Jews," 89–120; Hicks-Keeton, "Putting Paul in His Place," 1–21. For references to other letters written by Judean Jesus followers to diasporic communities; see Acts 15:23–29. One rare example of a Judean

Jews to observe the holiday of Purification, which later became known as Hanukkah. These documents can be read as festal letters, a form of exhortatory letter writing that asks readers to modify their calendrical observance.[12] Some exhortatory festal letters are paraenetic: they offer advice by referring to early wisdom traditions that provide guidance concerning how to achieve consistency between one's behavior and one's ideals.[13] Other letters are protreptic: they explicitly ask their readers to adopt a radically new way of life. Both kinds of letters appeal to historical figures who made similar changes. Both kinds of letters also take care to affirm the personal friendship between writer and recipient, though this friendship is not always one of equals. Some letters speak to their audience as peers, whereas others speak to them as superiors.[14]

Scholars tend to analyze these letters as festal documents that prove that holiday observance was integral to producing a cohesive network of normative Jewish practice.[15] Judean letters to Egyptian Jews do indeed use strategies that appear in other exhortatory festal writing. Nevertheless, scholars are incorrect to read these letters as texts that are singularly focused on the observance of Jewish holidays. For Judean writers, such observance was merely a means to an end. They wanted to encourage cohesion among Jews in Judea and Egypt and also wanted to enforce Judean authority over a region where Jews were so numerous that they were beginning to develop independent social and religious systems. Observance of holidays, especially ones that affirmed the importance of the land of Israel, could strategically ensure Jewish unity and the position of Judea as the locus of global Jewish life. According to this view, Egyptian Jews who observed these holidays implicitly affirmed that Judean

---

document purportedly written to diasporic Jews outside of Egypt is 2 Baruch 78–86, though this text was composed in the late first century CE at the earliest. See Whitters, *Epistle of Second Baruch*. On later correspondences between Judean and diasporic Jews, see Alon, *Jews in Their Land*.

12. Whitters, "Some New Observations," 274.

13. Stowers has not found paraenetic letters in papyri (*Letter Writing*, 96). The papyri letters between Judean leaders in Yeb and Judea, however, though not strictly paraenetic, can be read as precursors to later correspondence between Jews who were influenced by Hellenistic epistolary writing. Cf. Aune, *New Testament*, 174–80; Fitzmyer, *Wandering Aramean*, Lindenberger, *Ancient Aramaic*.

14. Stowers, *Letter Writing*, 92–95.

15. Torrey, "Letters Prefixed to Second Maccabees," 139; Wacholder, "Letter from Judah Maccabee," 132n101; Doran, *Temple Propaganda*, 113; Goldstein, *II Maccabees*, 138–39. For a broader reading see Bergren, "Nehemiah in 2 Maccabees," 251; Bickerman, "Colophon," 339–62; Fox, *Character and Ideology*. Similar festal letters are preserved in 2 Chr 30:1–9; cf. t. Sanh. 2:5–6; b. Sanh. 11a–b. All of these letters participate in multiple genres simultaneously and bore different functions and meanings depending on who was reading them. On genre theory and early Jewish writing, see Newsom, "Spying Out the Land"; Collins, "Epilogue," 418–30. Wright, "Joining the Club," 294n14; Najman, "Idea of Biblical Genre," 307–23; Najman, *Destruction, Mourning and Renewal*.

leaders were conservators of a tradition whose authentic modes of practice emanated from Judea.[16]

The letters that Judean Jews wrote to Egyptian Jews, and the fictional letters that Egyptian Jews wrote and attributed to Judeans, are complex and multilayered. They reference earlier correspondence either through allusion or through direct quotation. They embed the voices and actions of people who do not represent their community into their texts, drawing upon the pasts of others to make claims about the present. They also allude to scriptural texts, indicating that they are participants in a chain of oral and written transmission. Both Judean and Egyptian Jews employed these strategies to produce a "surround-sound" effect that amplified their positions so that they seemed to represent a diverse chorus of voices from across space and time. Today, these strategies are known as pseudepigraphy, ventriloquy, mirroring, and a layered form of mirroring called *mise en abyme*.

Pseudepigraphy

One widespread strategy that Jewish writers used in the Hellenistic period is the attribution of their work to another person. This practice, known as pseudepigraphy, was not unique to these writers. It was common for Romans to attribute their writings to older sources while neglecting to cite or engage with literature produced by their contemporaries.[17] Writers who used pseudepigraphy did not merely intend to conceal their identities by using a generic pseudonym. Nor did they seek to lie or trick their audience. They attributed their works to well-known ancestral heroes whose legacies were related to their message in order to situate their works within an ancient tradition. Such attributions signaled to readers that the text before them was authorized to support, nuance, and sometimes subvert the legacy of the attributed author.[18] Even pseudepigraphic works that altered the legacies of ancestral heroes legitimized these figures by scaffolding new work onto older stories.[19] The

---

16. Whitters, "Some New Observations," 272–88.

17. On pseudepigraphic practices among Roman Latin writers, see Peirano, *Rhetoric of the Roman Fake*, 1–14. Peirano's insight that falsely attributed writings are not "inferior counterfeit objects, but ... creative readings and interpretations" (6) apply to Jewish texts as well.

18. As Peirano has noted, "fakes are part of a continuum of pervasive cultural phenomena that treat canonical texts as amenable to expansion, continuation, and creative refashioning" (*Rhetoric of the Roman Fake*, 13–14).

19. Pseudepigraphy involves the attempt to restore the authority of the person to whom the text is attributed and works to construct "a discourse tied to a founder: a practice ascribing texts to an ideal figure, in order not only to authorize the texts in question but also to restore the figure's authentic teaching." See Najman, Manoff, and Mroczek, "Pseudonymous Attribution," 326.

authors of such texts also elevated the status of their own writings by engaging with scriptural themes and by imaginatively taking these themes into new directions.[20]

Ventriloquy

Greek and Roman writers showed off their skills by producing works that address ancient questions whose answers were thought to be self-evident.[21] They often utilized older literary traditions and embedded citations of ancient texts into their writings to strengthen arguments that were perceived as obvious or weak. Jewish writers, too, embedded citations into their texts that they attributed to figures who lived outside their communities and that parroted their own positions. They employed this practice, which I refer to as ventriloquy, to convey the impression that outside parties agreed with their perspectives. Judean Jewish writers produced letters that cite older texts and correspondences that present the land of Israel as the locus of Jewish life and the leaders of this land as the sole conservators of Jewish practice. Their writings often speak in the voices of exiled Judahites who associate their exilic circumstances with their collective sins. In these Judean texts, Judahites in exile beg God to forgive them of their sins and restore them to the land of Israel. Egyptian Jewish writers, meanwhile, expressed no such desire. Instead, they produced texts that cite figures who legitimize the presence of Judeans outside the land of Israel. Some Egyptian Jewish writers acknowledged that the presence of Jews outside Judea derived from God's justified anger toward the people. But even these writers tempered this admission by featuring heroes in their stories who praise the piety of Egyptian Jewry and celebrate God's universal love for humanity. Their stories cite Judean Jews who declare their admiration for Egyptian Jewry, and cite Greeks and Romans who express high regard for the sophistication of all Jewish people.

Ventriloquy became an indispensable tool for Egyptian Jewish writers who sought to transform their identities so that they would no longer be viewed as marginalized by both their Judean kin and their Hellenist neighbors. Rather than being doubly marginalized, Egyptian Jews used ventriloquy to argue that they were doubly embraced, first by their Judean kin, who esteemed them as worthy of divine love, and by their neighbors, who admired them as wise philosophers. Whereas pseudepigraphy was unlikely to truly deceive readers into thinking that an attributed author wrote a given work, ventriloquy

---

20. Najman, "Torah of Moses," 202–16.
21. Aristotle, *Rhetoric* 1402a24; Cicero, *Brutus* 30.

operated internally within a text and, at times, may have truly convinced readers that the author's position was corroborated by outsiders.

Mirroring and *Mise en Abyme*

Mise en abyme is the effect produced when an author or artist miniaturizes an event or image within a text, play, drawing, or video. This miniaturization represents a larger medium and contains self-representation. The effect is akin to placing a mirror in front of another mirror: it produces continuous self-perpetuation.[22] In literature, *mise en abyme* produces a complex structure that frames and embeds storytelling, and invites the reader to encounter the text as identical to the text that it describes. A classic example of such mirroring in modern English literature is Mary Shelley's 1818 *Frankenstein*, which uses letter writing to speak to the reader from three first-person perspectives. In art, this form of imaging reflects the artist's desire for observers to encounter their work in relationship to its context. Diego Velázquez's 1656 painting, *Las Meninas*, for instance, uses *mise en abyme* in a way that encourages viewers to engage with the painting from multiple perspectives. In popular culture, *mise en abyme* is used on consumer items such as cereal boxes, which contain an image of a person holding that same box of cereal, which itself contains a tiny image of a person holding a box of cereal.

In the Hellenistic era, the practice of *mise en abyme* seems to have been known to Jewish writers who were interested in the relationship between Jews who lived within and without the land of Israel. These writers used *mise en abyme* to build on the idea that a text attains authority by presenting itself as part of an intellectual continuum that stretches into ancient times. Citing authoritative texts that cite yet older texts, which in turn cite even older texts, these writers collapsed the interval of time that separated them from their ancient traditions.

Many Jewish letter writers at this time wrote about collected writings. In one such letter, Judean writers ask Jews in Egypt to observe the holiday of Purification. They inform these Jews that they possess an ancient library of books that contains information about this holiday. The letter's reference to this library transforms this text into a conversation partner with older authoritative texts that, in turn, build on scriptural tradition. The newer letter thus becomes an embodied culmination of an ongoing transmission process that

---

22. On *mise en abyme* in contemporary art and literature, see Dickmann, *Little Crystalline Seed*; Dällenbach, *Mirror in the Text*; D. Cohn, "Metalepsis and Mise en Abyme," 105; Genette, *Narrative Discourse*.

expands Jewish tradition without disrupting its stable nature. By producing texts that required continual copying, reading, transmitting, and circulating in order to preserve their lasting message, Jewish writers imitated older acts of scriptural transmission. Building on the work of their ancestors, these writers affirmed the authority of older texts and tapped into their power. Their letters were not quite Torah, but moved within the world of Torah.

Jewish authors produced documents that used images of letter writing and speech making to produce the impression of a surround-sound chorus whose voices represented different communities that united to express a single argument. Instead of producing texts that claim to represent a single voice or a monolithic minority group, these writers employed pseudepigraphy, ventriloquy, and *mise en abyme* to broadcast their arguments about Jewish life outside Judea from multiple points of view. Judean letter writers who implemented these techniques needed the authority of older texts to produce a discursive boundary around the land of Israel that centripetally pulled all Jews toward Jerusalem. These writers viewed themselves as sharing a common past and an ongoing relationship with Jews in Egypt. The similarities between Judean Jews and Egyptian Jews, however, and the fluidity in movement between the two communities, threatened to undermine the scriptural binary between Judea and Egypt. Such similarities also destabilized the idea that God rejected the Judahites and their descendants in exile and bestowed favor only upon those who returned to Judea.

Judean writers addressed these similarities by writing letters that clarify that Judea was, and had always been, the center of Jewish life. Their exhortations that Egyptian Jews observe the Purification holiday were not motivated merely by their interest in the successful establishment of the festival. These writers viewed the observance of the Purification holiday as an act that recognized Judean exceptionalism and authority. Using Hellenistic strategies, Judeans wrote letters that indicate that the land of Israel takes center stage in Jewish life, and that Jewish life outside Judea is a source of communal shame. In the next two chapters, I will explore how Judean authorities borrowed from earlier writers to develop this idea, which would later become known as *diaspora*.

PART 2

The Construction of Diaspora in Judean Letters

CHAPTER 5

"Open Your Heart to His Law": Judean Letters to Egypt in 2 Maccabees 1:1–2:18

IN THE HELLENISTIC PERIOD, authorities in Jerusalem sent letters to Jewish leaders in Egypt asking them to observe a newly established holiday that celebrated the central role of Jerusalem and its temple. These letters refer to the close relationship between Judean Jews and Egyptian Jews, and to the widespread reverence that all Jews have for the Jerusalem Temple, as self-evident facts. Such letters were not mirroring reality as much as they were pushing against it. Consensus about the role that Jerusalem and its temple played in the lives of Jews who lived far from the city did not exist. Jews who established communities outside the land of Israel, moreover, invested in infrastructure that testified to an optimistic outlook for their long-term future. These Jews, particularly those who lived in Egypt, were growing increasingly independent from Judea and its authorities.

Judean leaders wanted Jewish communities in Egypt to function as colonies of Judea that remained ever loyal to its interests. They had good historical basis for clinging to this expectation. Many of Egypt's Jewish residents had cultural and ethnic connections to their homeland. Beginning in the late seventh or early sixth century BCE, Egyptian rulers hired Judean mercenaries to aid them in their military campaigns, which generated a series of Judean migrations to Egypt.[1] More Judeans arrived in the late sixth century or early fifth century BCE, when Persian leaders employed Judean mercenaries and stationed them in Egypt. As I noted in chapter 2, some of these Judeans might have settled on the island of Yeb and built a temple there to their god. In the Hellenistic era, Judean Jewish authorities were probably most interested in Judean Jews who relocated to the Egyptian city of Leontopolis with Onias IV in the second

---

1. Psammetichus I (r. 664–610 BCE) and his son Necho II (r. 610–595 BCE), members of the twenty-sixth pharaonic dynasty, oversaw significant migration to Egypt on the basis of mercenary needs. Verse 13 of the Letter of Aristeas refers to Judean mercenaries in the armies of Psammetichus and Ptolemy I Soter (r. 305/304–282 BCE), identified as the "son of Lagus"), but it is unclear whether Aristeas is referencing Psammetichus I or Psammetichus II (r. 595–589 BCE). See Kahn, "Judean Auxiliaries," 507–16.

century BCE. According to Josephus, Onias fled to Egypt and established a Judean temple there shortly after the Syrian Greeks installed Onias's pro-Seleucid opponent Alcimus as high priest in 162 BCE.[2] Since their scriptures prohibited Israelites from settling in Egypt (Deut 17:16; Jer 44), Judean authorities might have felt that Onias's relocation to Egypt was a public embarrassment.

The problem was not simply that a Jewish temple had been erected in Egypt. Numerous other Judean temples may have existed in Egypt at this time as well (Josephus, *Ant.* 13.65–67). The problem was Onias himself. As an heir to the high priesthood whose family boasted prestigious Zadokite lineage, Onias had likely been educated by an elite circle of Judean leaders. In Egypt, however, Onias forged ties with Ptolemy VI Philomotor (r. 186–145 BCE) and his sister-wife Cleopatra. He may have even been active in Ptolemy VI's campaign to regain control of Judea in the Sixth Syrian War (170–168 BCE) in the hopes of being reinstated as high priest of the Jerusalem Temple.[3] Onias's initiative to build the temple at Leontopolis probably occurred after Ptolemy failed to win this war.[4] The temple's construction in a region later known as "Onias's Land" may have suggested to Judean Jews that this new temple was not a physical homage to the temple in Jerusalem but instead a symbol of Egyptian Jewish independence from Judea.

Surviving sources from the late Second Temple period are not consistent on the matter of Onias's intentions. In a letter to Ptolemy cited by Josephus, Onias insists on his loyalty to Judean leadership and predicts that his temple will buttress Judean authority over Jewish communities in Egypt. He explains that he seeks to unify Egypt's disparate Jewish communities, many of which had their own temples that competed with one another for worshipers. Onias also claims that by seeking to establish harmony among these communities,

---

2. Josephus's reports on the establishment of this temple are contradictory. In *Antiquities*, Josephus identifies Onias as Onias IV (12.43, 157). In *Jewish War*, however, Josephus notes that Onias fled to Egypt after a conflict with Judean supporters of Antiochus IV Epiphanes (1.31–33). This places the establishment of Onias's temple in 167–164 BCE. In *J.W.* 7.421–436, moreover, Josephus refers to Onias as the "son of Simon," which identifies him as Onias III, who held the high priesthood until 175 BCE. This association is corroborated in rabbinic texts (t. Soṭah 13:6–8; y. Yoma 6:3; b. Yoma 39a; b. Menaḥot 109b). Most scholars believe that the Onias who established the temple at Leontopolis was Onias IV. Besides Josephus's detailed account in *Antiquities*, 2 Maccabees reports that Onias III died in Daphne and makes no reference to him resettling in Egypt (4:4–34). See also Tcherikover, *Hellenistic Civilization*, 276–78; Gruen, "Origins and Objectives," 47–70; Delcor, "Le temple d'Onias," 188–205; Frey, "Temple and Rival Temple," 171–205. For the argument that Onias III built the temple, see Parente, "Le témoignage de Théodore de Mopsueste," 429–36. For analysis of Josephus's conflicting accounts, see Taylor, "Second Temple in Egypt," 297–321; Noy, "Jewish Communities of Leontopolis," 162–82.

3. On Onias IV's role in aiding Cleopatra in her conflict against Ptolemy VIII, see Tcherikover, *Hellenistic Civilization*, 280–81. For a challenge to this view, see Gruen, "Origins and Objectives," 59–66.

4. Kasher, "Political and National Connections," 30.

he was fulfilling the prophet Isaiah's prediction that a single Judean temple would one day be built in Egypt.[5] This letter casts doubt on the theory that Onias was a dissident of Judea, though the question of whether the letter is trustworthy is open to debate. Perhaps Onias really was a loyalist who hoped to unite the Jews of Egypt by encouraging them to find common ground in their devotion to Judea (Josephus, *Ant.* 13.65–67; *J.W.* 7.423–424).[6]

Judean letters to the Jews of Egypt do not mention Onias's temple. But they do express a sense of conservatorship similar to the sentiment that Onias expresses to Ptolemy in his letter cited by Josephus.[7] These letters were not aimed at Egyptian Jews who had fully assimilated into Hellenistic life. They were aimed at Jews whose similarities to Judean Jews served as potential evidence that one could express equal loyalty to Judea and to a foreign host government. Judean leaders considered these dual loyalties to be risky and intolerable.

Judean letter writers were also sensitive to political events that threatened to diminish their standing with other Jews. Judeans gained political autonomy from the Seleucid Greeks in 164 BCE, but Hasmonean rulers of the new monarchy were soon imperiled by internal debates regarding how to position Judeans amid a broader conflict between the Seleucid and the Ptolemaic Kingdoms. The relationship between the Jews of Judea and the Seleucid Kingdom, moreover, remained stormy even after the Jews' successful rebellion (Josephus, *Ant.* 13.240–245; *J.W.* 1.61). Conflict between the two kingdoms came to a head after Ptolemy the son of Abubus, who was appointed governor of Jericho by the Seleucid ruler Antiochus VII Sidetes (r. 138–129 BCE), entered

---

5. "On that day there will be five cities in the land of Egypt that speak the language of Canaan.... [O]ne of these will be called the City of the Sun. On that day there will be an altar to the LORD in the center of the land of Egypt, and a pillar to the LORD at its border" (Isa 19:18–19). Onias likely selected Heliopolis as a choice city that would be included in the "land of Onias" to fulfill Isaiah's prediction about the City of the Sun. Josephus adds that Isaiah's prophecy was interpreted as referring to a Judean who would construct this temple (*Ant.* 13.64).

6. Tcherikover suggests that if Onias was truly motivated to bring glory to Egyptian Jews (*Ant.* 13.62–63) and to encourage Judeans to resettle in Egypt (*J.W.* 7.431), he would have settled in Alexandria, where a large concentration of Jews already lived. Onias was more likely a military figure who controlled a Jewish force in the region of Leontopolis and built a military colony around 145 BCE (*Hellenistic Civilization*, 177–79). Other scholars suggest that a possible site for the temple is Tell el-Yehoudieh, the "Mound of Judea," about eight miles northeast of Heliopolis. The site, whose ancient name suggests that it was viewed as a "little Judaea of some kind," sits between two valleys like the Jerusalem Temple. See Petrie, *Hyksos and Israelites Cities*, 19–27; Kasher, *Jews in Hellenistic and Roman Egypt*, 123–30. Other scholars take a more skeptical view; see Bohak, *Joseph and Aseneth*, 28–30; Taylor, "Second Temple in Egypt," 316–19.

7. The absence of references to Leontopolis in these letters is not enough to suggest, as Kasher does, that Judeans perceived Egyptian Jews to be their close brethren, but only that this particular temple was not as unique as one might sense from reading Josephus. See Tcherikover, *Hellenistic Civilization*, 278, Kasher, *Jews in Hellenistic and Roman Egypt*, 132–35.

a political marriage with the daughter of the Hasmonean leader Simon (r. 142–135 BCE), one of Mattathias's five sons. Ptolemy held a banquet for his father-in-law Simon, during which he murdered Simon as well as two of Simon's sons, Mattathias and Judah. A surviving son, John Hyrcanus, took the throne.

The early years of Hyrcanus's monarchy were beset by conflicts with the Seleucids. In 132 BCE, Antiochus VII Sidetes laid siege to Jerusalem (Josephus, *Ant.* 13.240). The siege lasted a year and only came to an end when Hyrcanus accepted humiliating terms of surrender. Hyrcanus was compelled to pay Sidetes three thousand talents of silver and dispatch his own soldiers to support the Seleucids' military campaign against the Parthians. According to Josephus, Hyrcanus had to raid the tomb of David to come up with the money. The Hasmonean monarchy and the Seleucid kingdom lived alongside one another in a tense truce until Sidetes died, at which point Hyrcanus embarked on a successful campaign that led to a period of independence and expansion for the tiny Judean state (*Ant.* 13.249). By the time his reign ended in 104 BCE, Judea had achieved a level of power that Judeans had not enjoyed since the First Temple period. Hyrcanus was briefly succeeded by his son, Aristobulus, until he died due to poor health, and another son, Alexander Jannaeus (r. 103–76 BCE), took over. The Seleucid Kingdom was significantly weakened during these years, and Judeans now had to contend with an increasingly powerful player in the geopolitical sphere: the Ptolemies.

The Ptolemies were embroiled at this time in a civil war between Cleopatra III and her son Ptolemy IX Soter, also known as Lathyrus (r. 116–107, 88–81 BCE), and the Judean king Alexander was under pressure to choose a side to support. While he initially indicated that his plan was to ally with Soter, Alexander ultimately made an alliance with Cleopatra. This decision may have been informed by the fact that Cleopatra had shown herself to be malleable to Jewish influence. According to Josephus, Cleopatra's army was controlled by two Jews, Ananias and Chelkias, the sons of Onias IV. After Cleopatra pursued Soter to Judea with the intention of quelling his insurrection and annexing Judea, Cleopatra's Jewish generals convinced her to withdraw from Judea on the basis that doing so would lead to the loss of her Jewish support base in Egypt. Cleopatra agreed to withdraw and entered into negotiations with Alexander in the Judean city of Scythopolis.

Judean Jews who resisted Ptolemaic control likely worried that their kin in Egypt would pity them for being vanquished by one enemy neighbor only to be rendered powerless by another. Any comparison between Egyptian Jewish experiences and Judean Jewish experiences with their respective host governments would have led to the conclusion that Egyptian Jews were more politically successful than Judean Jews. The contrast between their roles in the military campaigns of their host governments was especially stark. Whereas

Cleopatra's army was run by Jews whose father held a prominent position in the Ptolemaic army, the Seleucid army had forced Judean leaders to accompany its king on military campaigns as terms of their surrender. The Egyptian Jews' participation in Egyptian affairs was a sign of their high status. The Judean Jews' involvement in Seleucid military excursions was a sign of their humiliation.

Jews in Judea wanted their Egyptian kin to perceive them as widely respected religious authorities. In the face of political powerlessness vis-à-vis the Seleucid enemy, they also wanted to show Egyptian Jews, whose ancestors had migrated from Judea, that they were far from powerless. Despite their political failures, Judean Jews had achieved remarkable territorial expansion. More importantly, they still perceived themselves as conservators of Jewish tradition, even amid political turmoil. These Judeans believed that Jews in Egypt should neither pity nor condescend to them. Instead, they wanted Egyptian Jews to admire Judeans as authorities and to recognize their disadvantages as Jews who lived outside of Judea. Judean Jews also wanted Egyptian Jews to acknowledge the ancient association between life outside the land of Israel and God's rejection and wanted Egyptian Jews to yearn to come home. Judean Jews asked their Egyptian kin to observe the Purification holiday, which commemorated the Hasmonean reclamation of the Jerusalem Temple, as a sign of these emotions, even though peace between Judea and its neighbors was elusive.

Judean Letters to Egyptian Jewry

Judean letters that implore Egyptian Jewish communities to observe the Purification holiday reflect a broader effort to enforce good relations between Judean and Egyptian Jews.[8] Rhetorical flourishes in these letters, however, reveal tensions between Judean and Egyptian Jewish administrators and between the institutions that they represented. Two letters appended to the book of 2 Maccabees indicate that by the first century BCE, Judean scribes were repackaging older Judean literature into letters that were dispatched to Egyptian Jews. These letters ask their recipients to express fealty to Judea and cite biblical heroes who express a negative attitude toward exile that matches the writers' perspective. Their use of ventriloquy conveys the impression that Judean Jews are conservators of an unbroken message that associates life outside the land of Israel with divine rejection.

---

8. Mélèze Modrzejewski, *Jews of Egypt*, 122; Kasher, "Political and National Connections," 31; cf. Gruen, *Heritage and Hellenism*, 233n192; Collins, *Between Athens and Jerusalem*, 129n88.

The Judean letters preserved in 2 Macc 1:1–9 and 1:10–2:18 probably circulated independently from the rest of 2 Maccabees until around 78 BCE, when they were added to the book and dispatched to Egyptian Jewish communities.[9] Both letters include Greek phrases that suggest a Hebrew or Aramaic original or indicate that the scribe who recorded them was a native Hebrew or Aramaic speaker.[10] The first letter (1:1–9) closes with a note that dates its composition to the month of Kislev in the year 188 and cites an earlier message from Judean Jews to Jews in Egypt during "the reign of Demetrius, in the year 169." Since Judeans adopted the practice of dating the beginning of the Seleucid era to the spring of 311 BCE, these years correspond to 124/123 BCE and 143/142 BCE, and the Demetrius here is likely the Seleucid king Demetrius II. The second letter (1:10–2:18) is dated to the period following Antiochus IV's death in 164/163 BCE, but this setting is problematic. Judean Jews could not have received the news of Antiochus IV's death this early. Nor would they have been able to swiftly dispatch this news, given the hostilities at this time between Egypt and the Seleucid Empire. The letter may have been misdated and written slightly later. Alternatively, it may be a forgery that was written in the late second century BCE.[11]

As texts that were copied alongside 2 Maccabees, these letters should not be read independently of the longer work. All three documents express concern over honoring the Jerusalem Temple, which they deem to be the locus of God's presence.[12] They also present God as the sole savior of the Jewish people and tend to eclipse the role of the Hasmonean family in the story of the Jews' rebellion and their restoration of the Jerusalem Temple. In training their focus

---

9. The letters were likely added by a later editor who noted thematic commonalities between all three documents. See Wacholder, "Letter from Judah Maccabee," 132n101; Doran, *Temple Propaganda*, 113; Bergren, "Nehemiah in 2 Maccabees," 251. Torrey suggests that the letters were appended as an introduction to the main text (the *epitomē*) of 2 Maccabees by the same writer who condensed Jason of Cyrene's now lost five-volume work ("Letters Prefixed to Second Maccabees," 139). Mélèze Modrzejewski suggests that the second letter was composed to support the contents of the first letter, a theory that implies that the forger had involvement in the letters' attachment to one another and to 2 Maccabees (*Jews of Egypt*, 123).

10. Goldstein believes that the second letter was written in Greek, while Bickerman argues it was written in Hebrew. See Goldstein, *II Maccabees*, 164; Bickerman, *Studies*, 2:136–37.

11. Wacholder suggests that the letter is misdated and was written in the spring or summer of 163 BCE ("Letter from Judah Maccabee," 131–32).

12. The emphasis on the Jerusalem Temple in 2 Maccabees, which was produced in Cyrene, does not undermine my thesis that Jews in Egypt sought to dissolve diasporic boundaries that separated them from Judea. Egyptian Jews, and Jews living elsewhere outside Judea, regularly expressed devotion to the temple. Like other early Jewish authors working outside Judea, the author of 2 Maccabees does not express a wish for Jewish life outside Judea to come to an end. Nor does his work express the wish for an ingathering to Jerusalem or embrace the global authority of Judean leadership. On the temple as 2 Maccabees's central theme, see Simkovich, "Greek Influence," 293–310.

on the temple, these documents construct a notion of Jewish authenticity that establishes leaders in Jerusalem as the arbiters of Jewish worship.

Efforts to discern links between 2 Maccabees and its appended letters concentrate on the letters' exhortation to observe a holiday commemorating the temple's rededication on the twenty-fifth of Kislev.[13] The first letter refers to this holiday as "the Days of Tabernacles in the month of Kislev," and the second refers to it as the "Purification" (1:18; 2:16). The regulation of time-bound practices rather than space-bound practices helped to establish the notion of a cohesive global Jewish network and simultaneously affirmed Judean authority over Egyptian Jews.[14] As we will see, the Egyptian Jewish writers of 3 Maccabees and the Letter of Aristeas responded to these efforts by recounting the observance of holidays that commemorate events that took place in Egypt (3 Macc 7:17–20; Let. Aris. 310–311).[15]

A close study of the letters appended to 2 Maccabees indicates that the observance of the Purification holiday is not their primary interest. Neither letter mentions the Hasmonean victory over Antiochus IV Epiphanes. Nor do they reference members of the Hasmonean family, though perhaps the second letter's initial greeting has them in mind. The observance of the dedication holiday is only significant insofar as it serves the writers' true goal, which was to convince Egyptian Jews to show loyalty to their Judean kin. To make their point, both letters employ rhetorical strategies that serve contradictory purposes. The first is to establish a bond with Egyptian Jewry based on its shared history with Judean Jewry. The second is to distinguish Judean Jewry from Egyptian Jewry on the basis of Judean exceptionalism.

These interests are evident in the letters' indication that Egyptian Jews must repent, though they do not clarify what, precisely, Egyptian Jews have done that requires repentance (2 Macc 1:2–6; 2:17–18). They also affirm the sole authority of the Jerusalem Temple and implicitly discredit Onias's temple at Leontopolis.[16] Like other Hellenistic exhortatory letters, the letters seek to persuade their audience to adopt a particular behavior and desist from an alternative behavior. They want Egyptian Jews to express uncompromising loyalty to the Jerusalem Temple and its authorities, and they want Egyptian Jews to abandon allegiances that compete with this loyalty. Both letters make

---

13. D. Schwartz, *2 Maccabees*, 143; cf. Whitters, "Some New Observations," 280; Harrington, *Maccabean Revolt*, 38; Goldstein, *II Maccabees*, 171.

14. Whitters, "Some New Observations," 280.

15. The celebration of the Septuagint's production was a historical event; Philo speaks of it in *Moses* 2.5–7.

16. Kasher may be correct that the absence of references to Onias's temple in these letters means they may not have intended to undermine that temple's authority. Still, a tone of reproof undergirds these texts. See Kasher, "Political and National Connections," 31.

their arguments by citing liturgical and prophetic traditions that imply that Egyptian Jews are not in good standing with God.[17] While they share the same concerns as those expressed in the Judean response to Jedaniah and his colleagues in the fifth century BCE, these letters employ Hellenistic rhetorical strategies to make their arguments.

2 Maccabees 1:1–9

There is no reason to doubt the integrity of the first letter's dating, which places its composition in 124 or early 123 BCE.[18] The Judean authors of this letter likely knew that Egyptian Jews at this time were experiencing a political juncture. Ptolemy VIII (also known as Physcon, meaning "pot-bellied") was at war against his sister Cleopatra II, and Jews in Egypt were faced with the precarious decision of choosing a claimant to support. These Jews enjoyed protection under the rule of Cleopatra, but Physcon was backed by most native Egyptians and a good portion of the Greek population. Judean leaders paid close attention to this conflict. They wanted Jews in Egypt to take the welfare of their Judean kin into account when making a decision about whom to support. They also believed that by prioritizing Judean holidays over the Greek calendrical cycle, Egyptian Jews could secure God's protection during an uncertain time. Their letter reads:

> [1]To our brothers the Jews of Egypt, greeting, your brothers the Jews in Jerusalem and in the land of Judah. A good peace [2]may God make for you, and may He be good to you, and may He remember His covenant with His faithful servants Abraham, Isaac, and Jacob. [3]May He give you all a heart to revere Him and to do His will wholeheartedly and with a willing spirit. [4]May He open your heart to His Torah and to His commandments. (And may He make peace). [5]May He listen to your prayers and forgive you and not abandon you in an evil time. [6]And now, here we continually offer prayers for you.
> [7]In the reign of Demetrius in the year 169 we Jews wrote you, "In the affliction and in the distress which came upon us in the years from

---

17. It is not clear whether the request for salvation at an "evil time" (2 Macc 1:6; cf. 1:26–28) reflects an actual crisis. Bickerman and Goldstein view the first letter as a critical interpretation of Egyptian Jewish suffering. See Bickerman, *Studies in Jewish and Christian History*, 2:155–56; Goldstein, *II Maccabees*, 142. Schwartz, however, argues that the speakers' request for salvation represents standard liturgical language that includes phrases that appear in other Jewish prayers during this period. Had the Egyptian Jews actually been in distress, the authors would have developed this theme in the body of their letter. See D. Schwartz, *2 Maccabees*, 138; cf. Ps 37:18–19; Jer 2:27–28; 11:12.

18. Goldstein, *II Maccabees*, 24.

the time that Jason and his followers rebelled against the Holy Land and the Kingdom ⁸and set fire to the temple gateway and shed innocent blood, we prayed to the LORD, and He hearkened to us. We brought animal sacrifices and fine flour, and we kindled the lamps and laid out the showbread."

⁹And now we ask you to celebrate the Days of Tabernacles in the Month of Kislev. In the year 188. (2 Macc 1:1–9)[19]

The letter's introductory greeting and wish for peace is common in biblical and postexilic Judean letter writing, as is its reversal of the standard Hellenistic formula, "A to B, Greetings."[20] These features suggest a Hebrew or Aramaic original and perhaps a desire to add Judean flavor to the text.[21] The letter's opening blessing, however, is disarmingly long. Early Jewish and Hellenistic letters often begin with greetings followed by good wishes. This letter, however, devotes half its words—an unusually high proportion—to a prayer that expresses the hope that God will help Egyptian Jewish leaders attain divine favor.[22] Their present behaviors, the writers imply, are precluding them from achieving piety.[23]

The letter's second half references past events that highlight the two communities' common past and shared commitment to their mutual welfare. Knowing that their recipients might not be amenable to their request to observe the Days of Tabernacles holiday, the writers appealed to past precedent to argue that their relationship, and the expectation of reciprocity, were self-evident, ancient, and nonnegotiable. Both communities, the writers implied, had leaned on one another in times of hardship. The letter's opening wishes and offering of prayer indicate that the Egyptian community is in crisis (2 Macc 1:5), while the second half refers to a time of distress when Judeans required the aid of Egyptian Jews (1:7). For the writers, the Egyptian Jewish observance of "the Days of Tabernacles in the month of Kislev" was an expression of support for Judeans that mirrors the support that Judean leaders

---

19. Translations of both letters appemded to 2 Maccabees are taken from Goldstein, *II Maccabees*.
20. Stowers, *Letter Writing*, 21.
21. D. Schwartz, *2 Maccabees*, 132, 139; Fitzmyer, "Some Notes on Aramaic Epistolography," 201–25; Doran, *Temple Propaganda*, 4. The letter likewise uses transitional words such as "and" and "and now," which suggests a Hebrew or Aramaic original. The NRSV reverses the Greek phrasing, perhaps to standardize the letter's opening address so it follows the more typical "from A to B" structure found in Greek letters.
22. Stowers, *Letter Writing*, 20.
23. Goldstein suggests that "and make peace," which does not work with the overall implication that Egyptian Jews have sinned, was added as a later gloss by an editor who picked up on the phrase "a good peace" in 2 Macc 1:1. See Goldstein, *II Maccabees*, 141. For a more cohesive reading, see D. Schwartz, *2 Maccabees*, 137–38.

showed Egyptian Jews in the past. It is also an expression of piety that would help Egyptian Jews atone for their sins and regain God's favor (1:9).[24]

The expressions of friendship that run through this letter are undermined by discursive features that suggest a less than mutual relationship.[25] The writers do not simply wish good tidings upon their audience in accordance with standard epistolary practice. Instead, they wish for Egyptian Jews to bring good tidings *upon themselves*. The writers want to empower their Egyptian Jewish audience with agency to control their own destiny, but they establish the terms by which these Egyptian Jews can enter divine favor. Egyptian Jews will only bring good tidings upon themselves if they accept the authority of their Judean kin and celebrate the Days of Tabernacles.

This letter shares thematic and structural features with Jedaniah's letter to Bagavahya. Like Jedaniah's letter, it follows standard customs of Aramaic letter writing practices by opening with a warm greeting and by citing historical precedent for Egyptian Jewish loyalty to Judea.[26] The Judean writers note that they had already written to Egyptian Jews in 143 or early 142 BCE regarding the events of 167–164 BCE, in the same way that Jedaniah tells Bagavahya that the Judeans of Yeb had already appealed to leaders in Jerusalem for permission to rebuild their temple.

The reference in this letter to earlier correspondence raises the question of why its authors waited twenty years to reach out to Egyptian Jews about commemorating the Judean victory over the Seleucid Empire. Perhaps they were waiting for Cleopatra II's power to wane, since they knew that Egyptian Jews who supported her became increasingly vulnerable as Cleopatra lost her grip over Egypt. Judeans may have reasoned that this vulnerability would make Egyptian Jews amenable to forging ties with them and more receptive to their request.[27]

It is also not clear whether the people who wrote this letter were the same Judeans who made contact with Egyptian Jews a generation earlier. If the Judean Jews who wrote in 143 or 142 BCE were eyewitnesses to the conflict of 167–164 BCE, they would have likely been elderly by 123 BCE. The three generations of Judeans referenced in this letter—the Jews of the Hasmoneans' time, the Jews who wrote to Egyptian Jews a generation later, and the Jews of the

---

24. On the relationship between the Feast of Tabernacles and the Feast of Dedication that commemorated the Hasmonean recovery of the Jerusalem Temple in 164 BCE, see Doran, *Temple Propaganda*, 4–5.

25. Doran reads the letter as one of genuine friendship, since it does not contain "imperatives and threats" as 2 Chr 30:6–9 does (*Temple Propaganda*, 4). Yet it was common for Jewish writers to conceal admonition behind expressions of friendship.

26. Fitzmyer, "Some Notes on Aramaic Epistolography," 214–16; Doran, *Temple Propaganda*, 4.

27. Goldstein, *II Maccabees*, 24, 147–48.

writers' own day—are all joined together in the simple remark that "we Jews wrote to you." This phrase conflates these Judeans, and implies that all three generations of Judean Jews have shared the same relationship with Egyptian Jewry. The letter's ventriloquy suggests a cohesion to Judean thinking that was meant to discourage Egyptian Jews from denying their relationship and their subordination to Judean authorities.

The letter's closing words parallel its greeting, but the request to observe "the Days of Tabernacles in the month of Kislev" comes as a surprise. It seems that the writers saved this request for the end of their letter to clarify that their main interest was the spiritual welfare of their kin. The observance of the Days of Tabernacles holiday was a means for Egyptian Jews to show loyalty to the Jerusalem Temple but was not an end unto itself.

2 Maccabees 1:10–2:18

The second letter appended to 2 Maccabees is attributed to "the people in Jerusalem and in Judaea and the Council of Elders and Judas," and is addressed to "Aristobulus, tutor of King Ptolemy and member of the stock of the anointed priests, and to the Jews in Egypt." This letter, which requests that Egyptian Jews observe the "Purification" holiday, is set in the first half of 163 BCE following the Hasmonean defeat of Antiochus IV Epiphanes in Persia.[28] Historical errors in the letter, however, suggest that it was written at the end of the second century BCE by Judean Jews who wanted to encourage Egyptian Jews to demonstrate their exclusive loyalty to Jerusalem (Josephus, *Ant.* 13.240).

Despite questions about its compositional date, there is no reason to question the letter's claim that it was written in Jerusalem. The work's message correlates with other works that were almost certainly produced in Judea, such as Baruch and the Greek translations of Ben Sira and Esther. It would also have been quite natural for Judean Jews at this time to make a religious appeal to their Egyptian Jewish kin. The young monarchy was threatened by divisive and controversial leadership, and Judean leaders must have wondered why they had not attained the power and independence to which they had aspired. Many concluded that Egyptian Jews could help them to assert the political strength and religious authority that remained aspirational but still within their reach.

As in the first letter appended to 2 Maccabees, the annual commemoration of the Judean victory over the Seleucid Greeks functions in this letter as a discursive Trojan horse, a premise that the authors use to exhort their

---

28. See Wacholder, "Is the Letter Authentic," 131–32.

audience to display loyalty to the Jerusalem Temple and Judean leaders.[29] Each of this letter's three main sections bolsters an argument regarding the centrality of the temple. After an introduction that describes the death of Antiochus IV (2 Macc 1:10b–17), the writers transition to the main body of the letter (1:18–2:15), which also contains three sections. Each of these three subsections focuses on a biblical hero who treats the Jerusalem Temple as the locus of divine worship and who lives in an increasingly distant period. This middle section employs ventriloquy by citing older biblical heroes who pray for the exile to come to an end. The letter's concluding section (2:16–18) repeats the authors' request that Egyptian Jews observe the Purification holiday and asks God to bring Jews who live outside Judea back to their homeland. The letter begins:

> [10]The people in Jerusalem and in Judaea and the Council of Elders and Judas to Aristobulus, tutor of King Ptolemy and member of the stock of the anointed priests, and to the Jews in Egypt, greeting and wishes for health. [11]Having been saved by God from great perils, we thank Him greatly as befits men who war against a king, [12]for God Himself cast away those who made war on the Holy City.
>
> [13]Indeed, when the commander and the apparently irresistible army accompanying him came to Persis, they were massacred in the temple of Nanaia through the trickery of Nanaia's priests. [14]Antiochus came with his Friends to the shrine intending to marry the goddess and thereby acquire the money in her rich treasury as dowry. [15]The priests of Nanaia's temple set the money before him, and Antiochus came with a few of his men into the precinct of the shrine. As soon as Antiochus had entered, the priests locked the temple. [16]Opening the secret trap door in the coffered ceiling, they rained stones down upon the thunderstruck commander. After dismembering and beheading the corpses they threw them out to the men outside. [17]In every way blessed is our God, Who delivered over the evildoers!
>
> [18]Inasmuch as we are about to celebrate, on the twenty-fifth of Kislev, the Purification of the Temple, we thought we ought to let you know,

---

29. Simon-Shoshan reads this letter as part of a constellation of Jewish texts that present the Jerusalem Temple as a continuous locus of the divine presence. The letter's interests are not merely festal but are also tied to the temple's authority ("Past Continuous," 398–431). Cf. Goldstein's comment that both letters "have in common the fact that they devote a surprisingly small part of their content to the festival they are supposed to announce" (*II Maccabees*, 159). Gruen, on the other hand, suggests that this letter aims to encourage "the Judaeans' Egyptian compatriots" to observe the Purification holiday (*Diaspora*, 239).

so that you, too, might celebrate it as Days of Tabernacles and Days of the Fire, as when Nehemiah, the builder of the temple and the altar, brought sacrifices. (2 Macc 1:10–18)

The attribution of this letter to Judas, a council of elders, and "the people in Jerusalem and in Judaea," suggests that this letter was meant to serve as a national declaration of friendship with Egyptian Jewry.[30] The letter likewise addresses a specific leader, the priest Aristobulus, and a general audience, "the Jews in Egypt" (1:10). The specification that Aristobulus comes from a priestly family implies that Egyptian Jews who have priestly lineage should be especially mindful of this letter, since it addresses matters pertaining to the Jerusalem Temple. The identification of Aristobulus as a priest also links him to the Judean priests mentioned in the main body of the letter who played a major role in restoring the community of Yehud following the Babylonian exile (2:19). All of these addressees, but Aristobulus in particular, are meant to understand that they have a personal stake in the story that the Judean writers are about to tell.

The letter opens with a brief blessing and then recounts the miraculous death of Antiochus IV Epiphanes, which occurred when the king traveled to the Temple of Nanaia to engage in a marriage rite with the goddess, where he was assassinated by temple priests.[31] This anecdote reminds the audience of God's disdain for foreign temples and perhaps subtly implicates Egyptian Jews for worshiping in illegal temples themselves. The section closes by imploring Egyptian Jews to observe a holiday so new that it does not yet have a uniform name. The writers refer to this holiday as "the Purification of the Temple" and as "Days of Tabernacles and Days of the Fire" (1:18).

Having established the letter's setting and purpose, the writers proceed to the main narrative, which makes a case for the global Jewish observance of this holiday by describing the commitment of Nehemiah, Jeremiah, and Solomon to the site of the temple:

> [19]When our forefathers were being carried off to Persia, the pious priests of that time secretly took some fire from the altar and hid it in a pit which was like a dry well and shut it up securely so that the place remained unknown to all. [20]Many years went by, and then, in God's own

---

30. Alexandria's *gerousia*, its local Jewish governing body, is mentioned in Philo, *Flaccus* 74–80; *Embassy* 229; Josephus, *J.W.* 7.407–419; 3 Macc 1:8.

31. This account contradicts other ancient accounts of Antiochus's death. See 2 Macc 9:1–9; Polybius, *Histories* 3.19; Appian, *Syrian War* 66.

time, Nehemiah received his commission from the king of Persia and sent the descendants of the priests who had hidden the fire to recover it. ²¹When they reported that ... they had found no fire[32] but a viscous liquid, Nehemiah ordered them to draw it up and bring it to him. After the sacrificial offerings had been placed upon the altar, Nehemiah ordered the priests to sprinkle the liquid over the firewood and over the offerings laid upon it. ²²When that had been done, after a while the sun, which had been covered by clouds, began to shine, and a great fire blazed up, to the astonishment of all.

²³As the sacrifice was being consumed, the priests and the whole assemblage uttered a prayer, in which Jonathan led and the rest, following Nehemiah, responded. ²⁴The prayer was as follows: "LORD, LORD, God, creator of all, awesome and powerful and just and merciful, our sole good king, ²⁵our sole provider, the sole just One Who is almighty and eternal, the preserver of Israel from every evil, the One Who chose and sanctified the patriarchs! ²⁶Accept our sacrifice for the sake of all Your people Israel, and guard Your portion and make it holy. ²⁷Gather together our dispersion. Free those who are enslaved among the nations. Look upon those who have been despised and abominated, and let the nations know that You are our God.

²⁸"Put to torment the oppressors and the arrogant perpetrators of outrage. ²⁹Plant Your people in Your holy Place, as Moses said." ³⁰The priests went on singing hymns to the accompaniment of lyres. ³¹When the sacrificial offerings had been consumed, Nehemiah ordered that they pour the remaining liquid too, ... large boulders. ³²As soon as the command was carried out, a flame blazed up, and when the fire on the altar lit up in turn, ... was consumed.

³³The news of the phenomenon spread. The king of the Persians received the report that the liquid had been found in the place where the priests being led into exile had hidden the fire and that by means of it Nehemiah and his followers had burned the sacrificial offerings. ³⁴After verifying the phenomenon, the king had the place fenced in and declared it holy. ³⁵The king took large sums of money and distributed them to Nehemiah and his followers. ³⁶Nehemiah and his followers called the liquid "nephthar," which means "purification," but it is commonly called "nephthai." (2 Macc 1:19–36)

---

32. The Greek text is literally: "When they reported to us not to have found fire." According to Goldstein, the author certainly "did not imagine the senders as contemporaries of Nehemiah!" Probably the text is slightly corrupt" (*II Maccabees*, 177). The other ellipses in the translation represent other places where the Greek text is corrupt.

This section indicates that the Purification festival has ancient roots that can be traced to the early years of the postexilic period, when the prophet Nehemiah guided Judeans back to Yehud. In this retelling, Nehemiah dispatches priests to obtain fire from the First Temple that had been hidden by Judahites on their way into exile. The priests who search for this fire discover instead a mysterious liquid, which they pour over sacrificial offerings on an altar.[33] After some time, the sacrifice miraculously ignites, which signifies to Nehemiah and the priests that God has accepted their offering.[34] Upon witnessing this miracle, the priest Jonathan utters a lengthy prayer that begs God to gather the scattered people, set free those who are enslaved by foreign nations, and look upon the dejected so that these nations might come to know God (1:27). Jonathan's prayer characterizes the exile as a place of continual suffering for Judeans, whose oppression under a foreign government reminds them that they have failed to remain loyal to God.[35] Though this scene is set in a time when Judeans were permitted to move freely within the empire, Jonathan speaks of the space outside the land of Israel as one where Judeans remain enslaved.

Through Jonathan's prayer, the writers of this letter draw close to non-Judean Jews by showing concern for their welfare and pull away from them by asking God to put an end to life outside Judea. They avoid expressing explicit condemnation of Egyptian Jews, perhaps because such condemnation would undermine their goal of convincing Egyptian Jews to accept Judean authority. Their message, however, is clear: the Jews of Egypt should mimic Nehemiah and other early Judean returnees by yearning for the exile to come to an end and by expressing this yearning through the observance of rituals that connect them to the Temple. Such behaviors might earn the Jews of Egypt the same divine beneficence that Nehemiah and his colleagues once received.

This section closes with the Persian king recognizing the significance of the miraculous kindling by cordoning off the space where it occurred and by declaring it a sacred site. These acts suggest that if the most powerful person in the known world can recognize the significance of what had taken place at Nehemiah's altar, surely Egyptian Jews could do the same. The letter's

---

33. Torrey suggests that Nehemiah's sacrifice takes place in Babylonia, perhaps to solve the question of why Nehemiah is featured in this story rather than Ezra ("Letters," 127–29). If this were so, the story would be of limited use in a text that argues that miraculous events took place at the site of the temple.

34. The notion that tabernacle or temple fire signifies divine favor has biblical precedent; see Lev 9:24; 1 Kgs 18:36–39; and 2 Chr 7:1–3; cf. Grant, "Fire," 139–61; Simone, *Devouring Fire*.

35. Whereas some scholars view this prayer as reflective of the letter's editorial reworking, Wacholder's treatment of the prayer as reflective of a cohesive effort to ascribe theological meaning to the conflict is more compelling. See Wacholder, "Letter from Judah Maccabee," 131–32; Kasher, "Political and National Connections," 39n28.

introduction and conclusion, which implore Egyptian Jews to properly observe their laws, parallel this embedded story.

The next section turns to the prophet Jeremiah who, in the decades leading up to the Babylonian exile, encouraged Judahites to submit to Babylonian rule while maintaining devotion to the Jerusalem Temple:

> ¹In our documents we find that it was Jeremiah the prophet who commanded those who were being led into exile to take some of the fire, as we have just told you. ²They also show that the prophet gave the Torah to those who were being led into exile and admonished them not to forget the LORD's commandments and not to let their minds be led astray when they saw gold and silver images and the ornaments upon them.
>
> ³With other words to the same effect, he exhorted them not to let the Torah depart from their hearts.
>
> ⁴The text also said that the prophet, on receiving a divine revelation, ordered that the tabernacle and the ark should go with him. It went on to say that Jeremiah went out of the mountain which Moses ascended to see the heritage promised by God. ⁵There, Jeremiah found a cave chamber and brought into it the tabernacle and the ark and the incense altar and blocked up the entrance. ⁶Some of those who had come along went back to mark the path, but they could not find it. ⁷When Jeremiah found out, he rebuked them, saying, "the place will remain unknown until God gathers His people together in the Age of Mercy. ⁸At that time the LORD will bring these things to light again, and the glory of the LORD and the cloud will be seen, as they were over Moses and as Solomon, too, requested, in order that the Place should be greatly sanctified." (2 Macc 2:1–8)

The writers claim to possess a document that identifies the person who took charge of hiding the fire found by Nehemiah's priests as Jeremiah (2:1), a prophet who was known to associate the people's exile with God's rejection.[36] The document that the writers allude to may be the Letter of Jeremiah, in which Jeremiah warns the exiled people "to avoid the idolatrous practices of their host culture."[37] That letter, whose message is reminiscent of this one,

---

36. In 2 Macc 1:19, the Judeans who hide the fire are also identified as priests.

37. The letter does not reference fire that was taken from the temple and consequently hidden. However, 2 Baruch 6:4–7 depicts an angel descending from heaven into the holy of holies, taking its ark, tables, priestly vestments, altar, and other precious objects, and hiding them until the time of Jerusalem's future deliverance. Four angels stand at four corners of the city, each holding a torch of fire, as the fifth angel descends into the temple. This angel then instructs the other four to destroy the city, a detail that indicates that the author of this text may have been aware of an ancient legend that associated sacred fire with the temple's destruction.

develops themes that appear in yet another letter attributed to Jeremiah, preserved in Jeremiah 29, which predicts that a restoration will take place following seventy years of exile. In Jeremiah 29, the prophet levies an ancient curse upon false prophets that compares them to "Zedekiah and Ahab, whom the king of Babylonia roasted in the fire" (Jer 29:22).[38] Our letter, then, draws upon ancient epistolary traditions that attribute words of condemnation and comfort to the prophet Jeremiah. By producing historical layers that retroject a message into the biblical past, the writers of this letter convey a sense of continuous Judean authority over Jews who live outside the land of Israel. This authority is embodied in the messages of prophets who were committed to advancing the exceptional status of the land of Israel, but who had close ties to Judeans who lived elsewhere.

Like the prior section concerning Nehemiah, this section ventriloquizes a biblical hero who asks God's followers—and by implication, the letter's audience—"not to let the Torah depart from their hearts" (2 Macc 2:3). Jeremiah's prayer, and its reference to God's ancient promise to gather the exiled people to Zion, parallels Jonathan's prayer in the earlier section. And just as Jeremiah hid fire from the temple in the letter's first section, Jeremiah again hides something precious: he stores the tabernacle and its ark in a cave on Mount Nebo, where Moses "ascended to see the heritage promised by God" (2:4). When Judeans start to make note of the location of these treasures, Jeremiah prevents them, insisting that the place will only be revealed again when "God gathers his people together." At this time, the cloud representing the divine presence would reappear, "as they were over Moses and as Solomon, too, requested" (2:8). This description produces a sense of connection between Moses, who received God's revelation, and the administrators of the Jerusalem Temple.

Both Jonathan's prayer and Jeremiah's prayer reflect the writers' desire that Egyptian Jews should imitate their ancestors by asking God to put an end to Jewish life outside Judea, even if their ancestors' petitions had gone unanswered. One crucial difference, however, distinguishes these prayers. Whereas Jeremiah anticipates that all exiled people will soon return to Judea, Jonathan's prayer clarifies that a complete ingathering did not occur after the exile. By the time the authors wrote this letter, the idea of restoration was an abstract concept that Judeans prayed for but was far from a reality. The letter as a whole suggests that these prayers have gone unanswered because Jews have chosen to remain in exile.

The letter's third section, which does not survive in its complete form, opens by citing what seems to be a biblical verse:

---

38. Cf. Dan 3:19–23, where Nebuchadnezzar attempts to burn Shadrach, Meshach, and Abednego in fire.

> ⁹We are also told that Solomon in his wisdom offered a sacrifice in honor of the dedication and completion of the temple. ¹⁰Just as Moses prayed to the LORD and fire came down from heaven and devoured the sacrifices, so Solomon prayed, and fire came down and consumed the burnt offerings.... ¹¹(And Moses said, "On account of... the sin offering... was consumed.") ¹²... So, too, Solomon celebrated the eight days. (2 Macc 2:9–12)³⁹

This section cites a tradition that Solomon's prayer at the temple culminated in a heavenly fire that descended onto his sacrificial offering to signify God's approval. The event resembles a prayer uttered by Moses that likewise culminated in heavenly fire. These prayers also parallel the prayer of the high priest Jonathan mentioned in the letter's earlier section, which in turn references Moses.⁴⁰ All of these figures guided the people of Israel at watershed moments in their history, and their prayers at the Temple Mount culminated in the descent of heavenly fire. The earlier figures portend the later ones, and the later figures imitate the earlier ones. Egyptian Jews, the writers suggest, could participate in this multidirectional chain of imitation by observing the Purification holiday.

The narrative layering of prayers and fires at the site of the temple correlates with the narrative layering of the preservation of documents during pivotal moments of the people's history. In the next section, the writers note that the tradition about Solomon's prayer was preserved in Nehemiah's library:

> ¹³The same account is given also in the records and the memoirs of the time of Nehemiah, and also that Nehemiah founded a library and collected the books about the kings and those of prophets and the books of David and the letters of Persian kings on dedicatory gifts to the temple. ¹⁴In the same manner, Judas reassembled for us the books scattered in the course of the recent war, and we have them. ¹⁵If you have need of them, send messengers to fetch them. (2 Macc 2:13–15)

The collection of writings mentioned here may be the same collection that the writers allude to in 2 Macc 2:1 and 2:4, which recall how Jeremiah hid fire from the temple as Judahites were forced into exile ("In our documents we find... The text also said"; 2:1, 4). Nehemiah's preservation of documents that derive from the time of Solomon mirrors the actions of Judas, who "reassembled for

---

39. The ellipses here represent places where the Greek text is corrupted.
40. Jonathan's prayer asks God to "plant Your people in Your holy Place, as Moses said" (2 Macc 1:29).

us the books scattered in the course of the recent war" (2:14). The writers' offer to send these documents to Egyptian Jews suggests that Judeans are inheritors of a chain of transmission that authorizes them to instruct all Jews on the matter of how to properly worship God. The offer also gives Egyptian Jews a chance to participate in this chain of transmission by reading these texts and sharing them with others (2:15).[41] The letter's references to a Jewish library may have also served to supersede well-known Greek libraries, such as those assembled by Ptolemy I Soter and by Eumenes II of Pergamum, which were viewed at this time as competing symbols of political power. The existence of an ancient Judean library indicates that Jews, too, possessed an authoritative collection of texts, and this collection was housed in Jerusalem, the central gathering place of the Jewish people.

The letter's body thus comprises a set of stories about the sanctity of the Temple Mount as well as a series of references to the transmission of sacred texts. Jews in the Hellenistic era treated both mediums of worship as legitimate, but Judean Jews clearly worried that Jews in Egypt would presume that access to their written tradition was sufficient, and that they did not need to lean on Judean authority for guidance. Judean Jews rebutted this attitude with stories about the Temple Mount and the connection between its administrators and the preservation of sacred texts. These sacred texts were not meant to enable Jews to settle outside the land of Israel. They were meant to bring Jews back to the land of Israel. Both modes of worship, the Judeans insisted, pointed Jews back to Jerusalem.

The letter's coda clarifies that the events described therein are especially relevant to the Egyptian Jewish community:

> [16]As we said, we write you inasmuch as we are about to celebrate the Purification. Please celebrate the days. [17]God, Who saved His entire people and restored the heritage to us all ... also ... the kingdom and the priesthood and the sanctification, [18]as He promised in the Torah. For we hope in God, that He will speedily have mercy upon us and gather us together from the lands under the heavens to His holy Place, for He has indeed delivered us from great evils and has purified His Place. (2 Macc 2:16–18)[42]

The juxtaposition between the main section's closing reference to the Temple's dedication and the coda's request that Egyptian Jews observe the Purification

---

41. Haran, "Archives," 59.
42. The coda seems to be missing a verb, but Goldstein restores it to "God, Who saved His entire people and restored the heritage to us all will also restore the kingdom and the priesthood and the sanctification" (*II Maccabees*, 187).

holiday suggests a connection between Solomon's dedication of the First Temple, which took place on the Tabernacles holiday, and the Hasmoneans' restoration of the temple and consequent celebration of the Tabernacles holiday (1 Kgs 8:2; 2 Macc 10:6). The letter writers viewed the Hasmoneans' holiday as a replication of the Days of Tabernacles and as a replication of the First Temple's dedication. Both events were celebrations that united the people at the site of the temple.

The closing affirmation that God "delivered us from great evils and has purified His Place" parallels the first section's argument that God has "delivered over the evildoers." Both blessings imply that the story of God's salvation of the Judean returnees holds a message that impacts all Jews. Even those Jews who did not witness the Hasmonean restoration, therefore, should observe the Purification holiday (2 Macc 1:17–18; 2:18). The universal Jewish observance of this holiday would symbolize widespread Jewish support for the Jerusalem Temple and its leaders, and it would also signify regret on the part of those who remain outside Judea. The conclusion's prayer, which asks God to restore all Jews to Judea, parallels similar sentiments in Jonathan's and Jeremiah's prayers.[43] All three prayers indicate that the Jerusalem Temple is not operating in its proper capacity. As long as Jews live outside Judea, total Jewish participation in temple worship is impossible.

Some scholars argue that this letter contains no evidence of a negative attitude toward the Egyptian Jews who were meant to read it. My close reading, however, indicates otherwise.[44] The speeches and prayers attributed to Judean leaders in this letter express the hope that Jewish life outside of Judea will come to a permanent end.[45] They portray the Jerusalem Temple as the locus of Jewish worship and call upon Jews in Egypt to affirm the same ideas. The letter's opening and closing petitions, moreover, are presented as outgrowths of ideas first articulated by Solomon, Jeremiah, and Nehemiah, who produced or preserved authoritative written works that highlight the centrality of the temple. By linking the First Temple period to the writers' own contexts, this letter invites its Egyptian Jewish readers to complete the association by intuiting that Nehemiah's ancient mission to gather all exiled Judeans remains

---

43. Wacholder, "Letter from Judah Maccabee," 130.

44. Doran insists that this letter contains no critique of Egyptian Jews (*Temple Propaganda*, 11). Gruen likewise suggests that the letter's references to the Jerusalem Temple and to the ingathering of the Jews comprise a "dramatic plea with scriptural resonance, not a mirror of contemporary longings by diaspora Jews" (*Diaspora*, 238–39; cf. Bunge, "Untersuchungen," 583–94). The letter does not, however, read like a dramatic plea. Nor would a mirror of diasporic longings be possible, since there is scant evidence that such longings existed. What the letter does express is *Judean* longing for Jews outside Judea to submit to the authority of its leadership.

45. Doran sees "eschatological expectation" in this letter but does not address what kind of role the writers expect their Egyptian Jewish readers to play in this expectation (*Temple Propaganda*, 10).

TABLE 1. *Mise en Abyme* in 2 Maccabees 1:17–2:18

	Nehemiah	Jeremiah	Solomon	Judah
Protects or recovers temple objects	1:20	2:4–6		
Fire consumes a sacrifice	1:22, 32		2:10	
Utters prayer	1:24–30		2:10	2:18
Expresses concern for the audience's piety		2:2–3	[lines missing]	2:16–17
Wishes for an ingathering of exiles	1:27–29	2:7	[lines missing]	2:18
Refers to Moses in liturgical context	1:29	2:8	2:10–11	
Establishes holiday	1:36			2:16
Reference to written text	2:13	2:1	2:9, 13	2:14

unfulfilled.[46] Each section of the letter shares the same structure and themes and thus effectively argues for a continuous line of divine intervention stretching back to the earliest period of Israelite history (see table 1).

The examination of the rhetorical strategies used by both of the letters in this chapter reveals that the main objective of their authors was to strengthen ties between Judean and Egyptian Jewish communities while asking Egyptian Jews to affirm the notion of Judean exceptionalism. The observance of the Purification holiday was not their focal point but a pretense for writing. Judean writers pulled Egyptian Jews into their orbit by encouraging them to observe practices that had been established by Judean authorities. But they also used rhetorical devices to keep these same Jews at arm's length. They especially relied on the practice of ventriloquy to speak in the voices of ancient heroes who underscored the unique status of the Jerusalem Temple.

Not all Judean writers who wanted to convey these ideas composed letters to Egyptian Jews. Some of them refurbished popular Judean works that were already in circulation by making small changes and reframing them as Judean missives to the Jews of Egypt. These writers reworked documents that could be interpreted as messages about the theological significance of exile. The next chapter will explore two such documents.

---

46. Nehemiah in particular was recognized as an inspirational steward of ancient archives. Bergren, "Nehemiah in 2 Maccabees," 252–60; Doran, *Temple Propaganda*, 7–8.

CHAPTER 6

"For Those Living Abroad Who Wish to Gain Learning": The Transformations of Esther and Ben Sira into Judean Correspondence

---

JUDEAN JEWISH WRITERS in the Hellenistic era recognized that letters to Egyptian Jews that used layering techniques could strengthen their bond with Egyptian Jews and simultaneously enforce their own authority. They also realized that these strategies could be applied to other kinds of documents. In addition to writing letters to Egyptian Jews, they began to transform well-known texts into documents that looked like personal letters by translating them into Greek, adding introductory and concluding frames, and making changes to accommodate an Egyptian Jewish audience. Two such texts, a Greek version of the book of Esther and a Greek version of the wisdom book Ben Sira, were probably produced about fifty years apart. This Greek version of Esther was probably written in the early first century BCE, while the Greek version of Ben Sira was produced in the late second century BCE. The translator of Esther made more extensive use of ventriloquy than the translator of Ben Sira, but both translators framed their works as letters to Jews living in Egypt.

The Hebrew versions of these two works are markedly different. The Hebrew book of Esther was written sometime during the Persian period, but a more precise date of composition is difficult to determine. The book recalls how two exiled Judeans, Mordecai and Esther, save their people from annihilation. Esther's story is one of several Jewish novellas written in the Second Temple period that features a woman whose extraordinary piety in the face of adversity is presented as a model of behavior to inspire all Jews.[1] Ben Sira, in contrast, was composed in the early second century BCE, about a century and a half after the Persian Empire was conquered by Alexander the Great. This book speaks of women as temptresses whose sensuality threatens to undermine men's observance of Jewish laws. Whereas Esther takes place in

---

1. The story may have been associated with the novellas of Susanna, Judith, and Joseph and Aseneth, and with the legend preserved in 2 Maccabees 7, which recalls a Judean woman encouraging her sons to be martyred at the hands of Antiochus IV Epiphanes rather than violate her ancestral dietary laws. This story likely derives from an independent narrative tradition. Wills, *Jewish Novel*; Ilan, *Integrating Women*.

the Persian city of Susa and makes no mention of Judea, Jerusalem, or the Jerusalem Temple, Ben Sira highlights the Jerusalem Temple and the authority of its priests (45:6–22; 50:1–21, inter alia).

Judean Jews who read these texts in Hebrew might have been perplexed by both works. Esther makes no mention of God and contains almost no religious content. Esther and Mordecai participate in court life and express no anxiety over attending royal parties, where their ancestral dietary laws would not have been observed. Even more problematically, they express no anxiety over the story's resolution, which closes with the union of Esther and the king. Ben Sira presents other challenges. The book is oriented toward male readers who want to achieve piety and observe Jewish practice, but it advocates for a level of stringency that most Jewish men would have been unable, or unwilling, to adopt.

Neither Esther nor Ben Sira treats Jewish life outside the land of Israel as a problem that requires resolution. While the writer of Esther could have easily incorporated a critique of Persian Jews into his work, his story uncritically valorizes Persian Jews who participate in local affairs without expressing attachment to their ancestral land. Ben Sira, meanwhile, says little about Jews outside the land of Israel and does not contrast Judean Jews who worship at the Jerusalem Temple with Jews who live abroad. One can imagine a Judean Jew reading one of these works and looking for such details, wondering how its author could have missed the opportunity to say something meaningful about life outside Judea.

Despite these difficulties, both Esther and Ben Sira seem to have been popular among Judeans. By the second century BCE, the holiday of Purim was celebrated by most Jews in Judea, and the story of Esther clarified its origins. Ben Sira, likewise, was revered as a manual for Judeans who wanted to maintain devotion to their traditions in the face of increasing access to Hellenistic culture. Ben Sira may have been the more popular of the two works. Surviving fragments of Ben Sira have been found at Qumran, a site that was home to a tiny community of sectarian Jews who lived near the northwestern corner of the Dead Sea. Fragments of Ben Sira were also found at Masada, a mountaintop fortress in the Judean desert where a group of Jews hid from the Romans during the Jewish War of 66–73 CE. The Qumran library, moreover, included copies of every book that would become canonized in the Hebrew Bible except, apparently, the book of Esther. Despite its connection to Purim, Esther may have had a more ambiguous role than Ben Sira due to its lack of religious content.

The Judeans who translated Esther and Ben Sira into Greek wanted to make these works more palatable to an Egyptian Jewish audience. They also sought to resolve perceived deficiencies in the works they were translating. For the translator of Esther, this meant inserting passages about God's role into the story and presenting its heroes as observant of Jewish practices. For the translator of Ben Sira, this meant raising the profile of biblical heroes mentioned in the book who lived outside the land of Israel. Both translators added Hellenistic flourishes that would have appealed to Jews living in Egypt at this time. They also framed their works as documents meant for Jews living in Egypt.

The epistolary framing of these translated works holds the key to their interpretation. As letters, the Greek versions of Esther and Ben Sira bear a polemical message that positions Judean Jews as authoritative disseminators of their ancestral traditions. The Judean Jews who wrote these translations were reacting to the successes of Egyptian Jews and their connections with Judean Jewry. They knew that both communities found themselves in the middle of long-standing conflicts between the Ptolemaic and Seleucid Kingdoms. Both communities had to cultivate personal relationships with these kingdoms while being attentive to how these relationships impacted Jews across the diasporic line. Judean Jews were also sensitive to local political disappointments that took place after the Hasmonean uprising, which included two decades of subservience to the Seleucid Kingdom, threats of a Ptolemaic attack and annexation, and weak Judean leadership that failed to enforce the observance of Jewish laws. Faced with these challenges, Judean Jews looked for opportunities to present themselves to their Egyptian kin as being in control rather than being vanquished, of being proud of their ancestral heritage rather than being ashamed of their political failures, and of being authorized to disseminate their traditions rather than being helpless to control their destinies.

Rather than explicitly denying the legitimacy of life outside the land of Israel, the Greek versions of Esther and Ben Sira chart a course of influence that moves from Jerusalem to farther reaches of the Hellenistic world. In these revised texts, the center of the world is neither Susa nor Alexandria but the city of Jerusalem. To make their case, the translators constructed a dialogical framework that transformed their documents into personal messages about God's role—and by extension, about Judea's role—in the lives of the Jews of Egypt.

The Wisdom of Ben Sira

The author of the Hebrew version of Ben Sira addressed elite Jewish students in Judea who were familiar with their biblical scriptures and oral traditions. He reminded them of the Jerusalem Temple's vital importance, stressed the authority of the priesthood, and gave special attention to Aaron and his priestly descendants. He insisted that his readers show obedience to priests, who embodied the authority of divine law and steered the people away from error and injustice.[2] He also asserted that Jews should accept the authority of their judges, elders, and kings (Sir 10:1–5, 14–17; 11:5–6).[3] The book reads like a wisdom text that aims to assist readers in their pursuit of piety, but it was likely motivated by a desire to protect its readers from assimilation into Hellenistic life.[4]

The author's grandson who translated Ben Sira into Greek also hoped that his work would help his audience resist the temptations of Hellenistic culture. Instead of addressing a small community of elite Judean Jews, however, the translator wanted to reach a wide swath of Jews in Egypt, and perhaps Jews who lived elsewhere in the Greek-speaking world.[5] He accommodated this new audience by adding a prologue and making adjustments to his text.[6] The prologue's Greek is more sophisticated than the Greek in the main body of Ben Sira, and it is possible that the work continued to be revised after it arrived in Egypt.[7] Such interpolation cannot be discounted, but the Greek version of Ben Sira should nevertheless be read as a Judean dispatch to Egypt, since its prologue was almost certainly produced by a Judean Jew.[8]

The Prologue of Ben Sira

In the prologue to his Greek version of Ben Sira, the translator clarifies the purpose of his grandfather's project and explains the purpose of his own translation. He explains that he writes not for the Jews of Judea but for the Jews of Egypt and implies that this new audience will transform the meaning of the entire work:

---

2. On the connection between ritual law and moral perfection, see Sir 34:21–23; 35:1–13.

3. Ben Sira also presumes that his audience has proximity to the Jerusalem Temple: "Fear the Lord and honor the priest, and give him his portion, as you have been commanded: the first fruits, the guilt-offering, the gift of the shoulders, the sacrifice of sanctification, and the first fruits of the holy things" (Sir 7:31).

4. Mélèze Modrzejewski, *Jews of Egypt*, 123.

5. Satlow, "Ben Sira," 428.

6. Wright, "Translation Greek in Sirach," 75–94; Toury, *Descriptive Translation Studies*.

7. Perhaps the Judean translator produced the whole work but reduced the quality of the Greek in the document's main body to maintain its Judean flavor. Alternatively, Jewish scribes in Egypt who received this version made changes to accommodate the tastes of their local Jewish communities. See Wright, *No Small Difference*; Wright, "Translation Greek in Sirach," 75–94.

8. Some Hebrew versions of Ben Sira may postdate rather than predate the Greek version of Ben Sira. Fragments from the Cairo Genizah may correspond to an original text or to an alternate version that circulated later. Fragments of Hebrew Ben Sira have also been discovered at Masada, but the only complete ancient version of the work survives in Greek. See Mélèze Modrzejewski, *Jews of Egypt*, 123.

¹Many great teachings have been given to us through the Law and the Prophets ²and the others that followed them, ³and for these we should praise Israel for instruction and wisdom. ⁴Now, those who read the scriptures must not only themselves understand them, ⁵but must also as lovers of learning be able through ⁶the spoken and written word to help the outsiders. ⁷So my grandfather Jesus, who had devoted himself especially ⁸to the reading of the Law ⁹and the Prophets ¹⁰and the other books of our ancestors, ¹¹and had acquired considerable proficiency in them, ¹²was himself also led to write something pertaining to instruction and wisdom, ¹³so that by becoming familiar also with his book those who love learning ¹⁴might make even greater progress in living according to the law. (Sir prol. 1–14)

As an expert in the "Law and the Prophets and the other books of our ancestors," the translator's grandfather was well suited to compose a document aimed to help Judeans "make even greater progress in living according to the law" (prol. 14). Like the Jews' scriptural traditions, which provide "learning and wisdom," the original version of Ben Sira provides "instruction and wisdom" to those who are devoted to these scriptures and their laws. By using similar language to describe Jewish scriptural tradition and his grandfather's work, the translator links this tradition to Ben Sira's book and, by extension, to his own project as well. Jews who accept the authority of their scriptures, the translator suggests, should also accept the authority of both versions of Ben Sira.[9] The prologue's middle section asks readers to study the present translation even while recognizing its inferiority to the original:

¹⁵You are invited therefore ¹⁶to read it ¹⁷with goodwill and attention, ¹⁸and to be indulgent ¹⁹in cases where, despite our diligent labor in translating, we may seem ²⁰to have rendered some phrases imperfectly. ²¹For what was originally expressed in Hebrew ²²does not have exactly the same sense when translated into another language. ²³Not only this book, ²⁴but even the Law itself, the Prophecies, ²⁵and the rest of the books ²⁶differ not a little when read in the original. (Sir prol. 15–26)

The translator's disclaimer that his work cannot capture the exact meaning of certain portions of the original version paradoxically granted the translator license to make adjustments that he believed would resonate with an Egyptian Jewish audience. His declaration that all translated works are imperfect, moreover, established a link between his project and translations of Jewish

---

9. Wright, "Translation Greek in Sirach," 84.

scriptures that were circulating at this time. The Egyptian Jews' lack of access to texts in their original Hebrew versions, he implied, has produced an impermeable barrier between their communities and those of Hebrew-speaking Jews. Because Greek-speaking Jews in Egypt read an inferior form of the scriptures, they practice an inferior form of Judaism. Egyptian Jews will never attain the same levels of piety as Jews who live in the land of Israel and will be continually dependent upon their Judean Jewish kin to produce quality translations. The translator closed his prologue with an autobiographical note about his experiences in Egypt:

> ²⁷When I came to Egypt in the thirty-eighth year of the reign of Euergetes ²⁸and stayed for some time, ²⁹I found opportunity for no little instruction. ³⁰It seemed highly necessary that I should myself devote some diligence and labor to the translation of this book. ³¹During that time I have applied my skill ³²day and night ³³to complete and publish the book ³⁴for those living abroad who wished to gain learning ³⁵and are disposed ³⁶to live according to the law. (Sir prol. 27–36)

The author's comment that he went to Egypt "in the thirty-eighth year of the reign of Euergetes" dates his arrival to 132 BCE (prol. 27).[10] Once in Egypt, he "found opportunity for no little instruction," and discerned that local Jews were in urgent need of his grandfather's work (prol. 29). Unlike his grandfather's Judean Jewish readers, who are described as "lovers of learning" who desire to "make even greater progress in living according to the law," the translator's audience merely wish to "gain learning and are *disposed* to live according to the law" (prol. 34–36).[11] This difference distinguishes Judean Jews from Jews outside the land of Israel, who cannot perfect their knowledge because they require translations. The translator's reference to all Jews "living abroad" clarifies that he was not writing exclusively for Jews in Egypt (prol. 34).[12] Though his experiences in Egypt motivated him to embark on his project, the translator viewed his work as beneficial to all Jews who live outside the land of Israel.

---

10. The translator's use of the aorist participle *synchronisas*, which suggests that Euergetes's reign had ended when he began his work, indicates that he produced his translation in 117 BCE or shortly afterward. See Skehan and Di Lella, *Wisdom of Ben Sira*, 134.

11. Wright understands the phrase as a reference to Jews who lived outside the circle of Ben Sira's scholarship, even those in Judea. See Wright, "Translation Greek in Sirach," 83; Hart, "Prologue to Ecclesiasticus," 290.

12. More literal renderings of the Greek *paroikia* are "to reside as a stranger" or "to be away from home." These meanings enforce the sense that the Jews of Egypt have left their true home of Judea.

The translator's prologue treats Jews who live outside Judea and have no direct access to the Hebrew scriptures as occupants of a monolithic space that is distinct from Judea. It then pulls these Jews into a Judean orbit by expressing a desire for Jewish cohesion. By framing his work as a document for Egyptian Jews, the translator hoped that these Jews would read Ben Sira as personally addressed to them, even while acknowledging the chasm that separated them from its original Judean audience.

The Translation of Ben Sira

Ben Sira's translator believed that certain passages in his grandfather's work had potential to convey a distinctive message to Egyptian Jews that concerned their loyalty to Judea. To make this message appealing to Egyptian Jews, the translator had to make it clear that his text was meant for them. One way to do this was to change prayers in the text to include all Jews. The translator rendered the Hebrew phrase, "Fill Zion with your majesty, and your temple with your glory" (36:14 MS B), for instance, as "Fill Zion with the celebration of your wondrous deeds, and your people with your glory" (Sir 36:19 LXX). This change implies that it is the Jewish people, and not the Jerusalem Temple, that can be filled with divine glory. Such a prayer would have been pleasing to Egyptian Jews who cherished the idea that the universal God could be worshiped anywhere, and who considered this idea to be complementary to the central role that the Jerusalem Temple played in their religious imagination. The translated version of this prayer highlights the land of Israel as a place where God's intercessory behavior is celebrated but clarifies that the Jewish people can be filled with God's glory, wherever they are.

The translator also made changes that suggest that Egyptian Jews have a personal stake in Judean leadership. In a verse that appears toward the end of a long section about biblical heroes, the Hebrew version of Ben Sira praises Simon the son of Yohanan (50:1 MS B). The Greek translation of this passage, however, identifies Simon's father as Onias and praises Simon as "the leader of his brothers and the pride of his people," who "repaired the house, and in his time fortified the temple" (50:1 LXX). Most scholars believe that this is a reference to Simon II, who served as high priest of the Jerusalem Temple from 220 to 195 BCE, and his father Onias II.[13] Simon II was succeeded as high priest

---

13. Askin, "Beyond Encomium or Eulogy," 344–65; Collins, "Ecclesiasticus," 108. George Foot Moore, however, argues that this Simon was Simon I, father of Onias who founded the temple at Leontopolis ("Simon the Righteous," 348–64). For a review of the scholarly debates, see Brutti, *Development of the High Priesthood*, 79–84. Simon II may be the same Simon mentioned in 3 Maccabees who prays on behalf of the people when Ptolemy IV Philopator (244–204 BCE) tries to enter the Jerusalem temple (3 Macc 2:1–20).

by Onias III, who in turn was replaced by Jason. Onias III's son, Onias IV, fled to Egypt after clashing with the pro-Hellenist Alcimus and built a Jewish temple in Leontopolis. Onias IV, then, was the descendent of esteemed priests, including the former high priest Simon II. The praise lavished upon this family in Ben Sira's translated version would have reminded Egyptian readers that their beloved leader Onias had elite Judean lineage. It was Onias's Judean pedigree that legitimized him as a leader, the translator indicated, and not his role as an iconoclast who paved the way for Judean Jews to migrate and settle in Egypt.

Some passages in Ben Sira's Greek version suggest an increased effort to celebrate biblical heroes who were known to have lived in Egypt. The reference to Joseph in the Hebrew version, for example, praises him for being uniquely righteous and states that "nor was anyone ever born like Joseph; even his bones were cared for" (49:15 MS B), whereas the Greek version expands this praise by adding that Joseph was "the leader of his brothers, the support of the people" (49:15 LXX). This phrase borrows from the description of Simon in Ben Sira's Hebrew version (50:1 MS B). The translator seems to have moved the phrase up two verses, modified it slightly, and applied it to Joseph in order to present him as a Jew par excellence. The figure of Joseph was famous among Greek-speaking Jews at this time, who celebrated him for being a model of loyalty to his ancestral traditions and host government.[14] Knowing that an Egyptian Jewish audience was more likely to venerate Joseph over the Jerusalem Temple's high priest, the translator borrowed language about the priesthood to demonstrate that Ben Sira recognized Joseph's substantial legacy. Loyalty to Judea, the translator implied, does not require Egyptian Jews to give up their veneration of beloved heroes. The translator also omitted a line in the Hebrew version of Ben Sira that asks God to ensure that the children of Simon observe "the covenant of Phinehas," grandson of the high priest Aaron (50:24; cf. Num 25:1–18; Sir 45:23–26 MS B). The translator seems to have felt that this line would not resonate with Jews who did not associate temple leaders with global religious authority. It is possible that these changes were made by an Egyptian Jewish editor after the translated version of Ben Sira began to circulate in Egypt, but these changes are also consonant with the work of a Judean translator who was attuned to the sensibilities of an Egyptian Jewish audience.

The Greek version of Ben Sira also lacks a psalm of thanksgiving that appears in the Hebrew version. Each verse of this psalm, which seems to be a version of Psalm 136 preserved in the Hebrew Bible, opens with a call to thank God for mercy bestowed upon the people of Israel. Included among these mercies is the divine capacity to gather the exiled people:

---

14. See Joseph and Aseneth, the Testament of Joseph, and later rabbinic traditions in Gen. Rab. 87:5–7; Tanḥuma Vayeshev 5, inter alia.

> Give thanks to him who gathers the dispersed of Israel,
> for his mercy endures forever;
> Give thanks to him who rebuilt his city and his sanctuary,
> for his mercy endures forever; . . .
> Give thanks to him who has chosen Zion,
> for his mercy endures forever.[15]

The translator may have known that Jewish readers outside the land of Israel were not accustomed to praying for a divine ingathering of all Jews to the land of Israel. His omission of the psalm reflects a sensitivity toward these readers. The fact that the psalm was likely not composed by Ben Sira, moreover, but was an older prayer that Ben Sira incorporated likely contributed to the translator's decision to abandon it.[16]

Even passages that appear unchanged in Hebrew and Greek versions of Ben Sira were probably interpreted differently by their audiences. Verses about the Jerusalem Temple and its priests, for instance, would have been read by Judean Jews as affirmations of their good behavior. These Judean readers may have visited the temple regularly and tithed their income to priests and Levites. In Ben Sira's Greek version, however, passages that praise the temple read as subtle admonitions to Egyptian Jews for living outside Judea.[17] This may explain why the translator made no major changes to Ben Sira's extensive encomia of the priests Aaron and Phinehas. Such passages could have served as gentle encouragements to Egyptian Jews to cultivate a sense of connection to Jerusalem and its temple (45:6–22; 50:1–21 MS B; LXX). Other passages that associate exile with disobedience and sin are also unchanged. Given the translator's personal interest in the piety of Egyptian Jews, these passages may have been intended as hints that Egyptian Jews inhabited the extended biblical exile but could improve their circumstances by turning to Judeans for guidance.[18]

---

15. This psalm appears following Sir 51:12 in MS B. Sir 51:13–30 may have comprised the original ending of the book, with the original version comprising 1:1–23:27 and 51:13–30. A Hebrew version of these verses found in the Cairo Genizah may not reflect the original version but a translation of the Syriac version of the book. See Corley, "Searching for Structure and Redaction," 21–47; van Peursen, "Sirach 51:13–30," 357–74. The first half of chapter 51 appears in Hebrew in the Psalms Scroll of Qumran (11Q5 XXI, 11–XXII, 1).

16. Reymond, "Sirach 51:13–30," 208. On connections between this poem and demotic wisdom that infiltrates early Jewish thinking, see Koller, "Self-Referential Coda," 2–25.

17. On loyalty to the Jerusalem priesthood as a key message of the work, see Wright, "Fear the Lord," 192–93; Olyan, "Ben Sira's Relationship to the Priesthood," 264–66; Himmelfarb, "Wisdom of the Scribe," 65–76.

18. See, for example, "their sins increased more and more, until they were exiled from their land" (Sir 47:24 LXX, MS B) and "despite all this the people did not repent, nor did they forsake their sins, until they were carried off as plunder from their land, and were scattered over all the earth" (48:15 LXX, MS B). Ben Sira's Septuagint version mentions Jerusalem as the domain of

Another example of how the translator's audience impacts its tenor appears in a poem attributed to Lady Wisdom, who declares that the universal God takes a special interest in the affairs of Israel (24:1–22 LXX).[19] The personification of wisdom as a woman was a well-known practice in Greek traditions. Here, however, Lady Wisdom's poem functions to supersede this trope by suggesting that true wisdom lies in the Jews' Hebrew scriptures (24:8–12 LXX). In Ben Sira's Hebrew original, the contrast between Lady Wisdom and Greek traditions would have been clear. In the translator's Greek version, however, the contrast is less apparent, and the poem reads as an attempt to syncretize Jewish and Hellenistic wisdom traditions. Perhaps the translator understood that Egyptian Jews reading this poem would interpret it not as a rejection of Hellenistic traditions but as a respectful incorporation of literary norms.

Liturgical passages also read differently with an Egyptian Jewish audience in mind. The following passage asks God to bring exiled Jewish back to Jerusalem:

> [1]Have mercy upon us, O God of all, [2]and put all the nations in fear of you. [3]Lift up your hand against foreign nations and let them see your might. [4]As you have used us to show your holiness to them, so use them to show your glory to us.... [12]Crush the heads of hostile rulers who say, "There is no one but ourselves." [13]Gather all the tribes of Jacob, [16]and give them their inheritance, as at the beginning. [17]Have mercy, O Lord, on the people called by your name, on Israel, whom you have named your firstborn, [18]Have pity on the city of your sanctuary, Jerusalem, the place of your dwelling. [19]Fill Zion with your majesty, and your temple with your glory. [20]Bear witness to those whom you created in the beginning, and fulfill the prophecies spoken in your name. [21]Reward those who wait for you and let your prophets be found trustworthy. [22]Hear, O Lord, the prayer of your servants, according to your goodwill towards your people, and all who are on the earth will know that you are the Lord, the God of the ages. (Sir 36:1–4, 12–22 MS B)

This prayer asks God to restore all Jews to the land of Israel but does not anchor this request in the author's present reality. Instead, it draws from biblical passages that speak of the eschatological end-time. The author's request that God "gather all the tribes of Jacob, and give them their inheritance, as at

---

God's resting place in 24:11 and 36:19 (corresponding with 36:14 in MS B) and uses the term "Zion" (*Siōn*) in Sir 24:10; 36:19; 48:18, 24 and "temple" (*naos* or *oikos*) in 45:9; 49:12; 50:1–2, 7; 51:14.

19. Cf. Sir 17:1–17, especially 17:17's "He appointed a ruler for every nation, but Israel is the Lord's own portion." The Hebrew version of this poem is not extant; only the Greek version survives.

the beginning" anticipates a transformative event that will be experienced as a return to the First Temple era before 722 BCE, when the ten tribes of Israel were exiled by the Neo-Assyrian Empire (36:13, 16 MS B).[20] The prayer's biblical language suggests that those who recite it do so as part of a global community of Jews. Hebrew and Greek versions of Ben Sira refer to this community as *Israel*, a term that connotes a polity that has existed since ancient times rather than an ethnogeographic population.[21] Hebrew and Greek versions of Ben Sira also refer to the land of Israel as *Zion* rather than as *Judea* (36:19 LXX; 36:14 MS B). Like *Israel*, *Zion* is not merely a political entity in biblical prophetic literature but an abstract ideal whose fulfillment requires a restoration to the land of Israel.

Ben Sira and his grandson probably hoped that their readers would not only study this prayer but would recite it as a personal affirmation. As a Hebrew text that was read by Judeans, the prayer affirms that all Jews, wherever they live, hope for a restoration that will transform the political state of Judea into the ideal of Zion. These Judean readers would have been comforted by the idea that God would reunite them with their exiled kin. Ben Sira's plea that God "hasten the day, and remember the appointed time ... gather all the tribes of Jacob, and give them their inheritance, as at the beginning" (36:10, 13–16) parallels other Judean liturgical material produced in the Hellenistic era, which likewise offered inspiration to a Judean audience.[22] As a Greek text that was read by Jews in Egypt, however, the prayer serves as a reminder that the anticipated restoration must culminate in the shuttering of Egyptian Jewish communities. Perhaps Ben Sira's translator hoped that Egyptian Jews would take comfort in the prediction that those who are presently subject to divine wrath are guaranteed to become future beneficiaries of divine forgiveness.

The translator of Ben Sira was not the only Judean writer who sought to bring the idea of Judean authority to an Egyptian audience by translating a popular Judean work. The translator of the Hebrew book of Esther similarly rendered this novella into Greek and had it delivered to Egyptian Jews for the purpose of enforcing Judean authority. Unlike Ben Sira, which reads as a highminded wisdom text meant for a learned audience, Esther records extraordinary events meant to capture the imaginations of all Jewish readers.

20. These verses are juxtaposed in Hebrew Ben Sira. Most scholars do not believe that text is missing here, though these verses are dislocated in Greek manuscripts. See Satlow, "Ben Sira," 475.
21. Staples, *Idea of Israel*.
22. See, for example, the Psalms of Solomon: "Bring together the dispersed of Israel with mercy and goodness.... May (you) be pleased with us and our children forever; Lord, our savior, we will not be troubled at the end of time" (Pss. Sol. 8:28, 33), and Tobit's deathbed prediction that the people of Israel will be "taken as captives from the good land.... But God will again have mercy on them.... [T]hey all will return from their exile and will rebuild Jerusalem in splendor... then the nations in the whole world will all be converted and worship God in truth" (Tob 14:4–6 [G^i]). Tobit survives in two recensions, known as G^i and G^{ii}, and both versions express this hope.

Greek Esther

The Greek version of Esther survives in two editions. One is a straightforward translation of the original Hebrew.[23] The other includes six sections that are absent in the Hebrew version. These additions strive to "improve" the Hebrew original with Hellenistic flourishes that resolve difficulties in the Hebrew version, which makes no mention of God or of Jewish ancestral laws. By supplementing Esther's story with pietistic material, the author of this Greek version brought it in line with what he perceived to be a scriptural norm.[24]

In addition to its lack of pietistic material, the Hebrew version of Esther was also considered problematic because it does not mention the land of Israel.[25] The story's celebration of the Persian Jews' salvation, therefore, could have been read as proof that God always saves Jewish people from annihilation, even if they live outside the land of Israel. The Judean translator of Esther addressed this concern by inserting prayers that connect the exiled people to their Judean heritage. He also added closing information that identifies the Judeans involved in the book's dispatch to Jewish communities in Egypt. In its translated version, Greek Esther reads as a Judean message to the Egyptian Jewish community about the perils of life in exile.[26]

The additions to Esther form a chiastic structure. The first and last additions mirror one another, the second and penultimate additions mirror one another, and the middle two additions mirror one another. In Addition A, which opens the story, Mordecai has a dream about two dueling dragons. After one dragon defeats the other, Mordecai identifies the triumphant dragon as the people of Israel, who will soon be threatened by a powerful enemy. In the book's closing section, Addition F, Mordecai interprets his dream in detail and clarifies that the dragon threatening Israel signifies the evil Haman. Additions B and E comprise royal edicts concerning the Jews. In the first edict, the Persian king declares that all Jews in the empire will be annihilated.[27] In the second edict, the king permits the Jews to defend themselves against

---

23. This Greek version is known as the Alpha Text (GEA). On the manuscript traditions of Greek Esther, see Fox, "Three Esthers," 50–59.

24. Clines, *Esther Scroll*; Koller, *Esther*, 118–19.

25. On the dating of the Hebrew book of Esther, see Moore, *Esther*, lvii.

26. According to Bickerman, Egyptian Jews read Greek Esther as a tale that helped them cope with local anti-Judaism by reminding them that their aspirations of independence and nationalism could only take place in Judea. The colophon thus reflects tension between Jews and Greeks in Judea but also reflects the differences between Judeans Jews and Egyptian Jews. Tcherikover similarly associates Judean festal writings with Egyptian Jewish loyalty to Judea. See Bickerman, "Colophon," 361–62; Tcherikover, *Hellenistic Civilization*, 355–56.

27. This edict is referred to in Esth 3:12–13, and this addition follows Esth 3:13.

their enemies.[28] Additions C and D comprise the prayers that Mordecai and Esther utter prior to Esther's appearance before the king and Esther's fateful meeting with the king. These sections mark the dramatic climax of the book.[29]

This Greek version of Esther also includes a signatory line at the end of the work, known as a colophon, which Hellenistic writers used to provide readers with information about their text's provenance.[30] According to its colophon, this version of Esther was produced in Jerusalem by a Jew named Lysimachus during the reign of Ptolemy and Cleopatra, a detail that probably dates the work to 77–76 BCE.[31] The historical information provided in the colophon has been challenged on the basis that the colophon is a Hellenistic technique and therefore must have been written outside the land of Israel.[32] Yet talented Judean writers were aware of Hellenistic rhetorical styles and were capable of imitating them. The Hellenistic features of Greek Esther serve not to masquerade Esther's story as a Hellenized tale but to make Esther's religious message appealing to Egyptian Jews.[33]

Most scholars believe that Lysimachus produced all the additions in this Greek version of Esther besides Additions B and E, which do not cohere with the rest of the book's language and tone. These additions were probably written in Judea at a later time, or in Egypt shortly after the book arrived there.[34] We will not study Additions B and E in this chapter, but it is worth noting that the writer who penned these additions produced yet another layered voice that mimics the enemy. I will begin my analysis of Greek Esther by studying the colophon as its outer frame. The colophon reads:

---

28. This edict is referred to in Esth 8:9–12, and this addition falls between Esth 8:9–10 and 8:13. See Crawford, "Additions to Esther," 426–27.

29. Additions C and D fall consecutively between Esth 4:17 and 5:1.

30. Some scholars refer to the colophon as a *subscriptio*; see White and Keddie, *Jewish Fictional Letters*, 317–19.

31. The colophon's reference to the Egyptian king Ptolemy and his wife Cleopatra could place the work in 114–113 BCE, but it more likely refers to Cleopatra V and Ptolemy XII Auletes, whose reign began in 80 BCE. Based on this colophon, Bickerman dates the dispatch of Greek Esther to Egypt in 78–77 BCE. See Bickerman, "Notes on the Greek Book of Esther," 108; Bickerman, "Colophon," 361; cf. Levenson, *Esther*, 27. Bickerman's dating has been corrected to 77–76 BCE in Bar-Kochva, "Festival of Purim," 389–90. This dating is accepted by Koller, *Esther*, 121; White and Keddie, *Jewish Fictional Letters*, 319.

32. Bickerman, "Colophon," 349–50; Gregg, "Additions to Esther," 1:668. For a rebuttal, see White and Keddie, *Jewish Fictional Letters*, 319.

33. White and Keddie, *Jewish Fictional Letters*, 320; Burns, "Special Purim," 18; Levenson, *Esther*, 29; Martin, "Syntax Criticism," 65–72.

34. Dell'Acqua, "Liberation Decree," 72–88; Koller, *Esther*, 118–23; Moore, *Daniel, Esther and Jeremiah*, 165–66; Torrey, "Older Book of Esther," 1–40. According to Koller, the goal of Additions B and E "appears to be primarily literary, since the current fashion in Greek historiography was to quote documents verbatim." Koller, *Esther*, 123; cf. Bickerman, "Notes on the Greek Book of Esther," 119–20.

> In the fourth year of the reign of Ptolemy and Cleopatra, Dositheus, who said he was a priest and a Levite, and Ptolemy his son, brought in [to Egypt] the foregoing letter [*epistolēn*] concerning the Phrourae [Purim], saying that it was authentic and that Lysimachus, son of Ptolemy, a resident of Jerusalem, had translated it. (Add Esth F 11:1)[35]

The colophon's note that Esther's dispatchers to Egypt were priest and Levites suggests that these roles provide the necessary credentials to sanction the revised text and transmit it to Egyptian Jews. The identities of these individuals also reverse the transmissional direction of authority that takes place within Esther's story. Mordecai and Esther, who live in exile, establish a holiday to commemorate the Persian Jews' salvation for perpetuity. Whereas in the Hebrew version of Esther the Persian city of Susa displaces Judea as the locus of Judean leadership, the Greek colophon reinstates Judean authority by specifying that a Judean scribe in Jerusalem recorded and dispatched the work to two priests and Levites, who in turn brought it to Jews living in Egypt with instructions to observe the holiday of Purim.[36]

The colophon also transforms Esther's story into a Judean epistle whose sanctioning of the Purim holiday depends upon its Judean origins.[37] Whereas the translator used the word *biblion* to describe the document that Mordecai writes (Esth 9:20 LXX), the colophon refers to the dispatch of an *epistolē*, which suggests that the letter in question is not Mordecai's document but the entire story. By referring to the novella as a letter, the translator indicated that his Egyptian Jewish readers held a personal stake in the story of God's salvation of Persian Jewry. For the Judean authorities who sanctioned this document, every Jewish holiday, even one that seems to celebrate God's protection of Jews in exile, should be observed as an act of loyalty to Judea.[38]

---

35. Translated in Whitters, "Some New Observations," 275. The NRSV reads "brought to Egypt," though "Egypt" does not appear in the Greek. The NRSV's capitalization of "Letter" implies that the letter has almost canonical authority.

36. Hebrew Esther closes with a section about the Jews' celebration and their establishment of the Purim festival that commemorated their salvation (Esth 9:1–10:3). This section includes either one or two letters instructing Persian Jews to observe the holiday of Purim (9:20–32) and closes with a conclusion about the success of the Persian Empire under Mordecai's advisement (10:1–3).

37. On the connection between the Greek *epistolē* and the Hebrew *'iggeret*, "letter," as well as the later rabbinic term *məkiltā'*, see Tg. Sheni to Esth 9:26, 29; Levenson, *Esther*, 136.

38. Bickerman suggests that Purim may have been relatively unknown at this time, but 2 Maccabees, which was likely written some decades before Greek Esther, refers to the holiday as Mordecai's day (2 Macc 15:36). This appellate suggests some knowledge of a festival commemorating the story ("Colophon," 349–51). For the theory that the holiday was known but not the story behind it, see Torrey, "Older Book of Esther," 26–27.

The colophon's division of transmission into two stages, translation and dissemination, mimics the transmission process of Esther's original story, which was recorded by Mordecai and dispatched under Esther's authority.[39] Yet even this similarity breaks from Esther's Hebrew version. Esther's authorization and dissemination does not distinguish between Jews who live within and without Judea. In the existential battle between Persians and Jews, the Jews scattered throughout the Persian Empire all unite against the threat of their Persian enemy. Greek Esther's colophon, however, adds a secondary distinction to this primary one: it separates Jews living in Judea from Jews living in Egypt.[40] As a Judean letter to Egyptian Jews, the Greek version of Esther reminds Egyptian Jews not to lose sight of their ancestral origins. Mordecai and Esther's prayers in Addition C drive this point home. The prayers ask for salvation, express concern over assimilation, and highlight the Jews' dependence upon God for survival.

The Prayers of Mordecai and Esther

The prayers of Mordecai and Esther affirm God's control over the universe and imply that the fates of all Jews lie entirely in God's hands. Addition C, which cites Mordecai's prayer, reads as follows:

> [8]Then Mordecai prayed to the Lord, calling to remembrance all the works of the Lord. [9]He said, "O Lord, Lord, you rule as King over all things, for the universe is in your power and there is no one who can oppose you when it is your will to save Israel, [10]for you have made heaven and earth and every wonderful thing under heaven. [11]You are Lord of all, and there is no one who can resist you, the Lord. [12]You know all things; you know, O Lord, that it was not in insolence or pride or for any love of glory that I did this, and refused to bow down to this proud Haman; [13]for I would have been willing to kiss the soles of his feet to save Israel! [14]But I did this so that I might not set human glory above the glory of God, and I will not bow down to anyone but you, who are my Lord; and I will not do these things in pride.

---

39. Mordecai records the story onto a scroll that is disseminated to "the Jews in the kingdom of Artaxerxes both near and far" who are to observe Purim "in every city, family, and country" (Esth 9:20, 27). The Greek "in every city, family, and country" (*kai polin kai patrian kai choran*) in Greek Esther 9:27 diverges from the Hebrew version's Persian-specific "every family, province, and city" (*mišpāḥâ ûmišpāḥâ mədînâ ûmədînâ wəʿîr wāʿîr*) in Esth 9:28, perhaps because the Greek version seeks to make the story more applicable to all Jews.

40. Bickerman, "Colophon," 361.

> [15]"And now, O Lord God and King, God of Abraham, spare your people; for the eyes of our foes are upon us to annihilate us, and they desire to destroy the inheritance that has been yours from the beginning. [16]Do not neglect your portion, which you redeemed for yourself out of the land of Egypt. [17]Hear my prayer, and have mercy upon your inheritance; turn our mourning into feasting, that we may live and sing praise to your name, O Lord; do not destroy the lips of those who praise you." (Add Esth C 13:8–17)

Mordecai's emphasis on God's past interventions to save the Israelites reminded Egyptian Jewish readers that God went to great lengths, so to speak, to take the Israelites out of Egypt and bring them to the land of Israel. Egyptian Jewish readers were invited to make a simple inference. If the exodus from Egypt was the primary sign of God's covenantal love, then the decision made by the Israelites' descendants to return to the land of Egypt and settle there was a rejection of this love. The Judean author of this addition comforted his Egyptian Jewish readers by using Mordecai's voice to ask God to overlook this shortcoming by reminding God that all Jews, even those in exile, recognize the significance of the exodus from Egypt.

Esther's prayer develops the closing lines of Mordecai's prayer, which ask God to grant him the ability to be articulate in the face of the people's enemies. The first half of Esther's prayer, which asks God to imbue her with proper speech when she approaches the king, emphasizes God's merciful listening. The second half addresses the present crisis and highlights the people's petitionary speech. Esther's prayer begins:

> [3]"O my Lord, you only are our king; help me, who am alone and have no helper but you, [4]for my danger is in my hand. [5]Ever since I was born I have heard in the tribe of my family that you, O Lord, took Israel out of all the nations, and our ancestors from among all their forebears, for an everlasting inheritance, and that you did for them all that you promised. [6]And now we have sinned before you, and you have handed us over to our enemies [7]because we glorified their gods. You are righteous, O Lord! [8]And now they are not satisfied that we are in bitter slavery, but they have covenanted with their idols [9]to abolish what your mouth has ordained, and to destroy your inheritance, to stop the mouths of those who praise you and to quench your altar and the glory of your house, [10]to open the mouths of the nations for the praise of vain idols, and to magnify forever a mortal king. [11]O Lord, do not surrender your scepter to what has no being; and do not let them laugh at our downfall; but turn their plan

against them, and make an example of him who began this against us."
(Add Esth C 14:3–11)

Like Mordecai, Esther alludes to the biblical promise that Israel will remain in an everlasting covenantal relationship with God, and that a time will come when all people will recognize God's universal power. Both Mordecai and Esther draw upon images related to speech. Mordecai asks God to save Israel, lest God "destroy the lips" of those who praise God. Esther, likewise, asks God to prevent the silencing of Jews who praise God, noting that their enemies seek to "abolish what your mouth has ordained" and hope to "stop the mouths of those who praise you." These enemies want to stymie the speech of God's followers in order "to open the mouths of the nations for the praise of vain idols." If successful, they will put an end to the transmission of the divine word that travels from God to the Jews and from the Jews to other nations.

In the second half of her prayer, Esther begs God to save the people on account of her piety. Once again, she praises God for granting speech to the pious:

> [12]Remember, O Lord; make yourself known in this time of our affliction, and give me courage, O King of the gods and Master of all dominion! [13]Put eloquent speech in my mouth before the lion, and turn his heart to hate the man who is fighting against us, so that there may be an end of him and those who agree with him. [14]But save us by your hand, and help me, who am alone and have no helper but you, O Lord. [15]You have knowledge of all things, and you know that I hate the splendor of the wicked and abhor the bed of the uncircumcised and of any alien. [16]You know my necessity—that I abhor the sign of my proud position, which is upon my head on days when I appear in public. I abhor it like a filthy rag, and I do not wear it on the days when I am at leisure. [17]And your servant has not eaten at Haman's table, and I have not honored the king's feast or drunk the wine of libations. [18]Your servant has had no joy since the day that I was brought here until now, except in you, O Lord God of Abraham. [19]O God, whose might is over all, hear the voice of the despairing, and save us from the hands of evildoers. And save me from my fear!
> (Add Esth C 14:12–19)

Esther's confidence in God's salvation transforms her—and this text—into an embodiment of divine transmission. She needs God to imbue her with inspired speech to save her people from enemies who want to undermine her ability to receive and transmit the divine word. From the perspective of the reader, Esther's petition becomes a triumphant transmission of the divine word itself.

The author of Greek Esther used ventriloquy in Mordecai's and Esther's prayers to remind Egyptian Jewish readers that only the God of Israel can decide whose voices will ultimately prevail. Egyptian Jewish readers who read these prayers would have appreciated them as declarations of loyalty to a God that protects all Jewish people. The Judean translator, however, likely hoped that these readers understood the deeper subtext of the speeches: God's protective message, for which Mordecai and Esther so deeply yearn, comes not from exile but from Jerusalem.

The Judean translators who transformed Ben Sira and Esther into letters for Egyptian Jewish readers were witnesses to extreme political instability. Seleucid subjugation was an embarrassing thorn in the side of Judeans, who worried that Egyptian Jews would compare their own circumstances, which were marked by relatively successful diplomacy, to the Judeans' political failures. Judean writers probably knew that Egyptian Jews had taken significant risks by supporting peaceful Egyptian relations with Judea. For some Judean writers, however, such shows of loyalty were not enough. They needed to know that Egyptian Jews not only cared for them as distant cousins but also looked up to them as leaders who safeguarded and disseminated authoritative material and who inspired them to remain devoted to their heritage and homeland. The people who translated Ben Sira and Esther were participants in a broader project to reclaim Judea's position as the central hub of global Jewry. This project trained its attention on the Jews of Egypt, since many of them descended from families who had fled Judea or were brought to Egypt by force.

Having so far limited my focus to correspondence from Judea to Egypt, I have not yet addressed an essential question: was the Judean fascination with the behavior of Egyptian Jewry specific to that particular relationship, or was it representative of an exceptionalist view of Judea that applied to all Jews living outside the homeland? To answer this question, I will turn to a popular Judean document that was written for a local audience.

CHAPTER 7

"There Is Open Shame upon Us": Fantasies of Exile in the Letter of Baruch

JUDEAN LETTERS TO EGYPTIAN JEWS that express concern for the piety of their kin tell us little about whether Jews in Judea felt responsible for the welfare of all Jews outside the land of Israel. Judean documents produced for local readers, however, shed light on this question. One such document is the book of Baruch, which purports to recall the teachings of Jeremiah's scribe in the early sixth century BCE. The book opens with Baruch delivering a speech to Judahites in Babylonian exile that is then dispatched to Judahite authorities in Jerusalem.

The author of Baruch dated this speech to "the fifth year, on the seventh day of the month" following Jerusalem's destruction, which set his story in 581 BCE (Bar 1:2). If the month in question is the fifth Hebrew month of Ab, Baruch's speech took place five years to the day after the Jerusalem Temple's destruction (2 Kgs 25:8–9). Such a date would suggest that Baruch's speech was intended to memorialize the temple's catastrophic fall.[1] The historical details provided here, however, are unreliable. Baruch was almost certainly not in Babylonia in 581 BCE. According to the book of Jeremiah, Baruch and Jeremiah had fled to Egypt by this time.[2] And while Baruch's letter asks Jerusalem leaders to bring sacrifices on the exiled Judahites' behalf, it is unlikely that Judahites who remained in Jerusalem in 581 BCE had the authority to offer sacrifices at the site of the temple (Bar 1:10). These inaccuracies, and the fact that the speech uses phrases that appear in the book of Daniel and the Greek version of Jeremiah, indicate that the opening section of Baruch (1:1–3:8) was produced well after the Babylonian exile, in the second century BCE or later.[3]

---

1. Alternatively, the month in question may be the third month of Sivan, which is referenced when Baruch gathers the temple vessels in preparation to return them to Yehud (Bar 1:8).
2. See Jer 43:1–7, especially 43:6.
3. Henderson, *Second Temple Songs*, 176–77. Goldstein sets the text to around 163 BCE in Judea, drawing parallels between 581 BCE and 163 BCE. In 163 BCE, "Jews knew of a king who perpetrated ruinous acts in Jerusalem and knew also of his son. Then, as in the imagined time, four

Other parallels between epistolary features in Baruch's first section and contemporaneous Judean documents suggest that this section, though it survives in Greek, was originally composed in Hebrew or Aramaic.[4]

Despite having a sense of its provenance and original language, scholars are not certain of Baruch's intended purpose.[5] The work may have been written around 163 BCE as propaganda to support Alcimus, a Hellenized Jew who was loyal to the Seleucid government and who opposed the Maccabean rebellion. According to this view, Baruch's insistence that exiled Judahites should be loyal to the Babylonian Empire was a veiled message that the Hasmonean victory over the Seleucids did not move the Jewish people toward a period of redemption.[6] Alternatively, Baruch may have been written as an expansion of ancient prophecies attributed to Jeremiah.[7] If so, Baruch seeks to resolve Jeremiah's condemnations of the Judahites by appending a promise of restoration to his prophetic oeuvre. Baruch can also be read as an entreaty to all Jews, wherever they live, to repent of their sins and place their trust in God's covenantal promises.[8] These theories all presume that Baruch's Judean author attributed theological meaning to the experience of exile. But they do not account for the question of why Baruch's author and his Judean readers would have cared so much about the exile. To fully appreciate why a Judean writer would have wanted to produce a work that takes place in the Babylonian exile,

---

years had elapsed since the ruinous acts of the king" ("Apocryphal Book of Baruch," 199). Goldstein also notes parallels between Bar 1:15–3:8 and Dan 9:5–19, especially between Bar 1:15–16 and Dan 9:7–8 (179–99). The author's misidentification of Belshazzar son of Nabonidus as Belshazzar son of Nebuchadnezzar parallels a similar misidentification in Dan 5:2.

4. See Emanuel Tov's Hebrew retroversion of the first section of Baruch based on its Semitisms in *Book of Baruch*. Baruch's prose sections were probably translated into Greek by the same scholar who produced the LXX translation of Jeremiah. See Tov, *Septuagint Translation*, 111–33. Henderson similarly treats these sections as originating from separate authors that were later assembled by an active editor. She detects editorial reworking in the contrast between the book's opening attitude toward the triumphant Babylon over the defeated Jerusalem and the reversed dynamic in the closing poem of Baruch where Jerusalem triumphs over Babylonia. See Henderson, *Second Temple Songs*, 177; cf. Pfeiffer, *History of New Testament Times*, 412–13; Moore, *Daniel*, 303–4. Hogan, however, notes that Baruch may be the work of a single author who wrote in different genres and styles but expressed a cohesive message throughout the work ("Baruch," 315). If this is the case, then Baruch was likely originally composed in Greek. Goldstein also suggests that the distinctive tones that separate Baruch's two halves reflect the work of one versatile author who had the facility to translate Hebrew prose and poetry into different styles of Greek ("Apocryphal Book of 1 Baruch," 198). Had the book derived from a single author, however, one would expect to see a consistent attitude toward whether the people could hope for a return to their homeland. Instead, see Bar 4:21–23, 36–37; 5:5–9.

5. Henderson, *Second Temple Songs*, 180.
6. Goldstein, "Apocryphal Book of 1 Baruch," 179–99; Nickelsburg, "Bible Rewritten," 145.
7. Steck, Kratz, and Kottsieper, *Das Buch Baruch*, 20–21.
8. Saldarini, *Book of Baruch*, 934.

we must take a closer look at political events taking place in Judea toward the end of the second century BCE.

As we noted in earlier chapters, Judeans at this time may have expected a mass return of Jews to Judea that would signify the beginning of a restoration process and reunite the Jewish people. The failure of this event to materialize prompted questions about when prophetic promises of redemption would be fulfilled. These questions turned into crises when Hasmonean leaders began to adopt Hellenistic practices, which many Jews perceived as betrayals of their heritage. Faced with increasing sectarianism and partisanship, Judean Jews may have wondered whether Judea was truly destined to become the epicenter of Jewish life once again. Baruch's opening section responds to this question by presenting the land of Israel as the locus of the Judahites' religious leadership. The return of all exiles to the land, according to Baruch, would mark the beginning of a new era characterized by peace and divine favor. Until then, Judahites and their descendants would continue to be afflicted in exile by suffering and divine rejection. Authorities in Jerusalem, meanwhile, would continue to await their return.

The author of Bar 1:1–3:8 believed that the story of the exiled Judahites, who were forced into Babylonia four centuries before he composed his work, bore contemporary resonance. Jews who lived outside of Judea in the second century BCE had the capacity to return to Judea but expressed little interest in doing so. Baruch's author believed that this stasis aligned these Jews with the Judahites of old, whose sins led to exile and divine disfavor. Unlike the author's contemporaries, however, the Judahites of the sixth century BCE were embittered by their exile. Baruch's author produced a negative comparison between these Judahites and his Jewish contemporaries. If the Judahite exiles paid obeisance to Jerusalem authorities because they recognized that life outside the land of Israel was meant to be experienced as a divine punishment, could not the Jews of his present day acknowledge the connection between exile and sin and recognize the authority of Judean leaders? To draw this comparison, the author depicted Baruch as a respected leader who encouraged the exiled Judahites to express fealty to both Judea and their captors. The author thus implied that Jews outside Judea in the second century BCE could likewise show loyalty to both their host country and motherland, but only with the understanding that life in their host country was a sobering catalyst for repentance rather than an exciting opportunity for integration and success.

Baruch's closing poems also address the dissonance between prophetic predictions of restoration and the reality that a full restoration had not occurred. These poems assure the Judahite community that ancient promises of restoration would soon be fulfilled. Scholars have dated the composition of these poems to a time of turbulence and instability for Jews living outside Judea.

As rhetorical texts, however, the poems may not allude to a specific crisis at all.[9] Rather than reflecting a historical reality, the poems' depiction of suffering in exile only reflects the projected Judean view of Jewish life outside the land of Israel as fundamentally negative. While the poems' authors viewed Jewish suffering outside the land as inevitable, they also viewed this suffering as an opportunity for Jews to embrace the leadership and guidance of authorities in Judea. This section of Baruch functions identically to the letters appended to 2 Maccabees, which were composed at around the same time, and to the Greek versions of Ben Sira and Esther, which oriented Egyptian Jews toward Jerusalem and its temple.

Both sections of Baruch respond to a Judean concern that arose in the wake of the Hasmoneans' victory over the Seleucid Kingdom. Given the robust population of Jews who did not return to the land of Israel after the war, did the Hasmoneans' extraordinary victory mark a theologically significant restoration? Baruch's authors responded to this question by asserting that while Jerusalem remained the locus of Jewish life, a full restoration of the people had not yet taken place. The absence of this event, however, did not reflect God's failure to fulfill ancient promises. Instead, it reflected the Jews' failure to fully repent of their sins. The message that unifies both halves of Baruch is that God remains eager to accept the people's repentance and to restore them to their homeland. This repentance requires Jews who live outside Judea to acknowledge that their choice to live in the place of their ancestors' exile is a grave sin as well as a perpetuation of divine punishment.

Pseudepigraphy and Ventriloquy in Baruch

Baruch's outer frame casts the text as an ancient work produced by the scribe of Jeremiah, a revered prophet who devoted his career to warning Judahites about the imminent Babylonian exile. This pseudepigraphic framing authorizes the text to speak in the voices of biblical heroes whom the author viewed as representative of his own community. The book's inner frame, meanwhile, makes extensive use of ventriloquy, a strategy used to speak in the voices of people outside the author's community. Baruch's first section speaks in the voices of exiled Judahites who send a message to leaders in Jerusalem asking them to pray to God on their behalf. The poems that comprise the second half of Baruch also employ ventriloquy. Speaking in the voices of Zion, Jerusalem, and God vwho in turn invoke traditions from the written scriptures, the poems offer comfort to exiled Judahites and assure them that God's promise of

---

9. Contra Floyd, "Penitential Prayer," 51–81; Henderson, *Second Temple Songs*, 179.

restoration will soon be fulfilled.[10] The speeches in both halves of Baruch imagine God as the restorer of all Jews rather than as the cause of their suffering. In Baruch's first half, Judahites in exile treat Judahites in Jerusalem as intercessors between God and the exile and take responsibility for their own suffering. In Baruch's second half, Zion and Jerusalem beg God to bring the exile to a permanent end and express longing for the people who crave to return to them.

Like other Judean Jewish letters, monologues, and speeches produced in the Hellenistic era, the speeches in Baruch ground the attachment between Jews within and without Judea in ancient scriptural traditions. Unlike other Judean letters we have studied, however, these speeches were meant to be read by Judean Jews rather than Egyptian Jews. Such Judean Jews would have identified not with the story's penitent exiled Judahites but with the Judahite leaders who receive the exiled Judahites' request to appeal to God on their behalf. Baruch's authors knew that their Judean readers would probably not identify with the people suffering from divine wrath in their text. They nevertheless hoped that their work would raise their audience's anticipation of a widespread Jewish return to the land of Israel.

The Structure of Baruch

Baruch is divisible into four sections. The introduction establishes the book's setting by dating Baruch's speech to the fifth year following the destruction of Jerusalem (1:1–9). The next section is a confessional prayer made by Judahites in exile, who attribute their circumstances to past sins and who promise loyalty to Judahite leaders (1:10–3:8). The third section is a poem that depicts the people's exile as a just divine response to their abandonment of the Torah (3:9–4:4). The fourth section is a poem of consolation that promises restoration (4:4–5:9).

The rhetorical and linguistic features that distinguish Bar 1:1–3:8 and 3:9–5:9 indicate that these sections were composed by different writers. The most significant distinction between these sections is that they convey different messages about how the exile will end. In the book's first half, the people accept the exile as an ongoing divine punishment that will continue indefinitely unless God forgives the people.[11] Baruch's closing poems, however,

---

10. Jerusalem "speaks with the authority of the written scrolls of the Law and Prophets, which have been collected and stored within the city" (Henderson, "Baruch's Jerusalem," 554–55; cf. Henderson, *Second Temple Songs*, 294–99).

11. See the petition in Bar 2:11–18, which does not ask God to restore the exiled Judahites to their homeland.

console the people by guaranteeing that God will provide an unconditional restoration.

Both sections of Baruch draw language and themes from the book of Jeremiah and its Greek translation in particular, which the authors mined for clues about the prophet's message.[12] This Greek version features Baruch more prominently than the Hebrew version, which shows more attention to Baruch's brother Seraiah.[13] The authors of Baruch assumed that their Judean readers admired Jeremiah and his scribe Baruch as key figures in the story of the Judahites' exile who understood that the exile was catastrophic to the spiritual health of the people. Similar presumptions about Jeremiah's central role in interpreting the exile undergird the second letter appended to 2 Maccabees, which praises Jeremiah for understanding that the exiled Jehudites were destined to return to the land of Israel. Perhaps the image of Jeremiah as a heroic visionary who understood the symbolic import of political events in Judea was well known to Judeans at this time. Like Nehemiah, Jeremiah was probably revered by Judean Jews in the Hellenistic era because he was credited with preserving precious written scriptures that ensured the continuity of Jewish traditions.

As a cohesive work, Baruch conveys two messages. First, Judean Jews should grieve for the suffering of Jews who live abroad. Second, Judean Jews are qualitatively different from Jews who live abroad because they do not experience the shame of public punishment that exposes them to other nations. A closer reading of Baruch's two main sections demonstrates how these messages wend their way through the text.

---

12. Parallels between Bar 1:1–3:8 and the Greek version of Jeremiah have led Tov to suggest that the scribe who produced Bar 1:1–3:8 was the same scribe who reworked the Greek version of Jeremiah 29–52. See Tov, *Septuagint Translation*, 6, 111–33; Tov, "Literary History," 211–37. Alternatively, the author of Bar 1:1–3:8 used language from Jeremiah's Greek version to produce a sense of cohesion that presents Baruch as part of an ancient scriptural tradition.

13. The Hebrew version of Jeremiah differs substantially from the Greek version of Jeremiah in the Septuagint. Both versions close with the assassinations of Judean leaders in the final stages of exile. In the Hebrew version, however, one of the assassinated individuals is Baruch's brother, Seraiah ben Neriah (Jer 52:24). The Greek account does not mention Seraiah (51:31–35 LXX), and its description of the executions is preceded with a passage in which Jeremiah comforts Baruch as he prepares to accept the mantle of leadership. The Greek version also treats Baruch as the principal inheritor of Jeremiah's dual mission to encourage exiled Judahites to stay connected to Judah but loyal to their captors (Jer 27:9–15). This account may reflect an older version of Jeremiah that highlights Baruch's role. Perhaps it was later reworked into a Hebrew version by Seraiah or one of his followers who minimized Baruch's role. See Lundbom, "Baruch, Seraiah," 89–114; Steiner, "Two Sons of Neriah," 74–84; contra Eichhorn's theory that Jeremiah produced a second edition of his book in "Bemerkungen über den Text," 167–68.

Baruch 1:1–3:8

The opening section of Baruch comprises a layered Judean fantasy that imagines the Judahite community in exile asking authorities in Jerusalem to pray on their behalf. Embedded into their request are citations of earlier prophets who warned Judahites and Israelites that God would reject the people by expelling them from the land of Israel. The effect of all these voices is a dizzying set of multivocal layers that derive from different times and places but all agree that exiled Judahites should accept the authority of leaders in Jerusalem.

Baruch's opening verses, which describe Baruch's public recitation, establish two directions of correspondence: one from Baruch to the exiled Judahite community and one from the exiled Judahite community to Jerusalem authorities. The Judahites' acknowledgment that their exile is a just consequence of wrongdoing, and their pledge to send money to Jerusalem authorities to be used toward offering sacrifices, is a wish-fulfillment visualization that reveals how Judean Jews wanted Jews who lived abroad to relate to them (1:5).[14] The exiled Judahites in this scene, therefore, express feelings of closeness and deference toward Judahites who have remained in the land of Israel:

> ¹These are the words of the book that Baruch son of Neriah son of Mahseiah son of Zedekiah son of Hasadiah son of Hilkiah wrote in Babylon, ²in the fifth year, on the seventh day of the month, at the time when the Chaldeans took Jerusalem and burned it with fire. ³Baruch read the words of this book to Jeconiah son of Jehoiakim, king of Judah, and to all the people who came to hear the book, ⁴and to the nobles and the princes, and to the elders, and to all the people, small and great, all who lived in Babylon by the river Sud. (Bar 1:1–4)

The book of Baruch opens by dating Baruch's words in relation to the Babylonian razing of Jerusalem and by referencing leaders who are identified according to the roles they once held in Judah. Their royal titles, once indicative of social and religious authority, are now reminders of what the exiled people have lost. By orienting the exiled protagonists toward the land of Israel, the author orients his Judean readers toward the land of Israel as well. The scene continues:

> ⁵Then they wept, and fasted, and prayed before the Lord; ⁶they collected as much money as each could give, ⁷and sent it to Jerusalem to the high

---

14. White and Keddie, *Jewish Fictional Letters*, 5.

priest Jehoiakim son of Hilkiah son of Shallum, and to the priests, and to all the people who were present with him in Jerusalem. ⁸At the same time, on the tenth day of Sivan, Baruch took the vessels of the house of the Lord, which had been carried away from the temple, to return them to the land of Judah—the silver vessels that Zedekiah son of Josiah, king of Judah, had made, ⁹after King Nebuchadnezzar of Babylon had carried away from Jerusalem Jeconiah and the princes and the prisoners and the nobles and the people of the land, and brought them to Babylon. (Bar 1:5–9)

The exiled Judahites respond to Baruch's public reading by crying, repenting, and acknowledging that they have no right to expect delivery from their captors. They also send funds to leaders in Jerusalem and state their intention to return the temple vessels. This plan evokes the account preserved in the book of Ezra that recalls how Ezra brings the original set of vessels to Jerusalem (Ezra 8:24–34). It thus presents Baruch, who was a scribe with connections to the priesthood, as a precursor to Ezra, who was both a priest and a scribe. The author of Baruch must have also known that scriptural traditions about Jeremiah were influential not only to his work but to the book of Ezra as well, which opens by recounting events that fulfill Jeremiah's prophetic visions about how the exile would end (Ezra 1:1–4).

The Judahites' repentant behavior in Baruch's opening scene contrasts with the grim image in Jeremiah of Baruch reading a scroll to king Jehoiakim, who tears the scroll panel by panel and tosses it into a fire (Jer 36:4, 22–25 [43:4, 27–28 LXX]). While this and other stories in Jeremiah present Judahites who live on the cusp of exile as blithely unrepentant, Baruch imagines the Judahites in exile as being painfully aware of their shortcomings. Baruch's goal is not to develop Jeremiah's denigrating image of Judahites who were later forced into exile but to provide local Judean readers with a comforting fantasy that imagines how exiled Judahites repented and became deserving of restoration. Wholly dependent upon Judahite leadership to shepherd them through the crisis of exile, these exiled Judahites in Baruch confirm their obeisance to Jerusalem authorities by sending their leaders a message declaring their loyalty, along with funds that are to be used toward the purchase of goods necessary for temple sacrifice:

¹⁰They said: Here we send you money; so buy with the money burnt-offerings and sin-offerings and incense, and prepare a grain-offering, and offer them on the altar of the Lord our God; ¹¹and pray for the life of King Nebuchadnezzar of Babylon, and for the life of his son Belshazzar, so that their days on earth may be like the days of heaven. ¹²The Lord will

give us strength, and light to our eyes; we shall live under the protection of King Nebuchadnezzar of Babylon, and under the protection of his son Belshazzar, and we shall serve them for many days and find favor in their sight. ¹³Pray also for us to the Lord our God, for we have sinned against the Lord our God, and to this day the anger of the Lord and his wrath have not turned away from us. ¹⁴And you shall read aloud this scroll that we are sending you, to make your confession in the house of the Lord on the days of the festivals and at appointed seasons. (Bar 1:10–14)

The Judahites' request that Jerusalem authorities pray for the Babylonian royal family parallels passages in Jeremiah that insist that the people must accept their subjugation to Babylonian rule as a divine punishment for their sins.[15] In Baruch, however, submission to Babylonian rule is not merely a reflection of loyalty to God. It is also a reflection of loyalty to Judahite leaders, whose sacrifices on behalf of Babylonian rulers signify that true authority lies in Jerusalem.[16] The author's desire for widespread Jewish recognition of Judean exceptionalism and the authority of Jerusalem-based leaders becomes explicit in the prayer that the exiled Judahites ask these leaders to utter on their behalf:

¹⁵The Lord our God is in the right, but there is open shame on us today, on the people of Judah, on the inhabitants of Jerusalem, ¹⁶and on our kings, our rulers, our priests, our prophets, and our ancestors, ¹⁷because we have sinned before the Lord. ¹⁸We have disobeyed him, and have not heeded the voice of the Lord our God, to walk in the statutes of the Lord that he set before us. ¹⁹From the time when the Lord brought our ancestors out of the land of Egypt until today, we have been disobedient to the Lord our God, and we have been negligent, in not heeding his voice. ²⁰So to this day there have clung to us the calamities and the curse that the Lord declared through his servant Moses at the time when he brought our ancestors out of the land of Egypt to give to us a land flowing with milk and honey. ²¹We did not listen to the voice of the Lord our God in all the words of the prophets whom he sent to us, ²²but all of us followed the intent of our own wicked hearts by serving other gods and doing what is evil in the sight of the Lord our God. (Bar 1:15–22)

---

15. Compare language in the first section of the prayer with Jer 7:34; 27:9–12; and 48:9, and language in the second section with Jer 9:16; 32:40; and 42:4.

16. The community's request that the Jerusalem leaders offer a confession on its behalf is obfuscated in the NRSV's rendering of verse 14's *exagoreusai* as "your confession," which implies that by engaging in the ritual, Judahites in Jerusalem will equally partake in confession. The NETS rendering of the verse as "And you shall read aloud this book, which we sent to you to declare in the house of the Lord on a feast day and on days of a season" is preferable.

By conferring shame onto all the "people of Judah" and the "inhabitants of Jerusalem," the letter initially elides any difference between Judahites in the land of Israel and Judahites in exile. As the letter progresses, however, the speakers establish a link between their own lives and the experience of shame, and the gap between these communities expands. Their reference to the "calamities and the curse that the Lord declared through his servant Moses" likely alludes to the curse of exile predicted in Deut 28:15–68, which in its Greek version associates shame with exile by rendering the word for horror (*zaʿăwâ*) as *diaspora*.[17] Abandoned by God and mocked by the foreign nations, the people's shame is more painful than the threat of physical annihilation:

> ¹So the Lord carried out the threat he spoke against us: against our judges who ruled Israel, and against our kings and our rulers and the people of Israel and Judah. ²Under the whole heaven there has not been done the like of what he has done in Jerusalem, in accordance with the threats that were written in the law of Moses. ³Some of us ate the flesh of their sons and others the flesh of their daughters. ⁴He made them subject to all the kingdoms around us, to be an object of scorn and a desolation among all the surrounding peoples, where the Lord has scattered them. ⁵They were brought down and not raised up, because our nation sinned against the Lord our God, in not heeding his voice.
> ⁶The Lord our God is in the right, but there is open shame on us and our ancestors this very day. ⁷All those calamities with which the Lord threatened us have come upon us. ⁸Yet we have not entreated the favor of the Lord by turning away, each of us, from the thoughts of our wicked hearts. ⁹And the Lord has kept the calamities ready, and the Lord has brought them upon us, for the Lord is just in all the works that he has commanded us to do. ¹⁰Yet we have not obeyed his voice, to walk in the statutes of the Lord that he set before us. (Bar 2:1–10)

This prayer suggests that the most painful aspect of God's abandonment is the consequent experience of shame, and that shame is specific to exile. The people's shame is the natural result of their recognition that God's punishment is justified because collective repentance has yet to take place. The Judahites'

---

17. The association between shame and exile ("there is open shame"; *aischunē tōn prosōpōn*) parallels similar associations in Daniel and Ezra, which suggests that the association was well known when the author composed this prayer. See Dan 9:11; Ezra 9:7 (1 Esd 8:74, 77). Similarities between this prayer and Daniel's prayer in Dan 9:7–14 may also suggest that Daniel 9 had direct influence on this text. See Moore, "Toward the Dating," 312–20; Venter, "Penitential Prayers," 406–25. On how the author uses Daniel 9 but changes his message, see Goldstein, "Apocryphal Book of Baruch," 191–207.

admission of guilt segues into the next section, which asks God to deliver the people from more suffering:

> "And now, O Lord God of Israel, who brought your people out of the land of Egypt with a mighty hand and with signs and wonders and with great power and outstretched arm, and made yourself a name that continues to this day, we have sinned, we have been ungodly, ¹²we have done wrong, O Lord our God, against all your ordinances. ¹³Let your anger turn away from us, for we are left, few in number, among the nations where you have scattered us. ¹⁴Hear, O Lord, our prayer and our supplication, and for your own sake deliver us, and grant us favor in the sight of those who have carried us into exile; ¹⁵so that all the earth may know that you are the Lord our God, for Israel and his descendants are called by your name. ¹⁶O Lord, look down from your holy dwelling, and consider us. Incline your ear, O Lord, and hear; ¹⁷open your eyes, O Lord, and see, for the dead who are in Hades, whose spirit has been taken from their bodies, will not ascribe glory or justice to the Lord; ¹⁸but the person who is deeply grieved, who walks bowed and feeble, with failing eyes and famished soul, will declare your glory and righteousness, O Lord. (Bar 2:11–18)

The exiled Judahites are so overwhelmed with shame that they can barely bring themselves to ask God to restore them to their homeland. They allude to the Israelites' exodus from Egypt to highlight God's omnipotence but stop short of drawing an explicit parallel between their circumstances and the exodus story by asking God to take them out of exile. Instead, their prayer segues into an admission of sin and an acceptance of their fate: "we have sinned, we have been ungodly, we have done wrong, O Lord our God, against all your ordinances" (2:12). Because the present community is undeserving, the speakers can ask for mercy but not for restoration.

After admitting their sins, the Judahites recount divine punishments that they have recently incurred (2:19–26). They then reference God's ancient promises (2:27–35) and close with another petition for restoration (3:1–8). Each of these sections speaks in the voices of outsiders to the Judahite community residing in the land of Israel, which is the community with which Baruch's author identifies. The first section cites prophets, who speak in the voice of God and warn the people of impending exile. The second section cites God's assurance to Moses that, should the exiled people repent, they will be restored to their land. The third section speaks in the voices of the exiled Judahites, who ask God to remember ancient promises that assure them of survival. The generality of language in the first two sections, which make no reference to Babylonian exile, indicates that Baruch's author sought to make his message applicable to multiple scenarios that extended into his contemporary reality. Like exiled Judahites of old, the author suggested, Jews living abroad in his own day should turn to Judean Jewish leaders for guidance.

Narrative elements of the Judahites' letter parallel the letter preserved in 2 Macc 1:10–2:18. Both texts allude to Jeremiah and Nehemiah as key figures who, at the very beginning and very end of the exile, ensure that the exiled people maintain loyalty to their homeland. Both texts are also structured identically. They open with references to a document that recounts the crisis surrounding the Babylonian exile (Bar 1:3–4; 2 Macc 2:1–8). They then turn back to the ancient Israelite period, when God and biblical heroes conferred with one another regarding the people's sins (Bar 1:15–22; 2 Macc 2:9–12). Both draw connections between those earlier events and a present day crisis (Bar 2:1–5; 2 Macc 2:13–15). Finally, both texts pray for a restoration (Bar 2:6– 3:8; 2 Macc 2:16–18). This structure, which does not appear in contemporaneous documents produced outside of Judea, implies that the Babylonian exile is the central event in the people's history. It also treats leaders stationed in the land of Israel as the sole source of the people's hope for deliverance.

Baruch's opening scene similarly shows awareness of Nehemiah 8, which recalls how Ezra publicly reads from a Torah scroll to Judeans who have recently returned from Babylonian exile. Baruch's references to the scribe's writings as a book (*biblon*) rather than a letter (*epistolē*) evokes Ezra's reading of the Torah in Nehemiah (*sēper tôrat Mōšeh*; LXX: *to biblion nomou Mōusē*) and his efforts to reinstate the Judeans' ancestral practices (Bar 1:3; Neh 8:1). Baruch also follows the plotline of Nehemiah 8. Both stories open with a public reading of an authoritative scroll that leads to communal weeping, penitence, and fasting, and both close with expressions of repentance and hope. Although Baruch was written well after Nehemiah, Baruch's evocation of Ezra's dramatic recitation of the Torah transforms Baruch's story into a precursor to the scene of Ezra's recitation. Just as Ezra and Nehemiah helped Judeans resettle the land of Israel and reminded them to repent of past sins, Baruch helped an earlier generation of Judahites vocalize their desire to repent and return to their homeland.[18] Like Ezra and Nehemiah, Jeremiah and his collaborator Baruch were viewed by Jews in the Hellenistic era as participants in a chain of leaders who protected and transmitted the people's authoritative written scriptures.

---

18. This passage also parallels the account in 2 Kings 22–23 and 2 Chronicles 34 about the discovery of a scroll in the Jerusalem Temple during the time of King Josiah's reign that prompts a national reform. A similar scene of communal gathering is recounted in 1 Kings 8 concerning Solomon's dedication of the Jerusalem Temple.

Baruch's image of exiled Judahites, however, is not quite identical to the image of Judean returnees in Nehemiah 8. Unlike Nehemiah, Baruch creates distance between the people and their leaders. Whereas Nehemiah identifies Ezra as a priest and scribe who has returned from exile with the Judean people and has inspired them to repent, Baruch' eponymous hero works in exile, where he recites a confessional statement that he attributes to the people.[19] And while Ezra and Nehemiah instruct Judeans to cease their mourning and prepare for the Tabernacles holiday, Baruch encourages the Judahites' confession and asks leaders in Jerusalem to facilitate a reconciliation between them and God.

Nehemiah 8, 2 Macc 1:10–2:18, and Baruch's opening scene each feature a Judean or Judahite leader who acts as the conservator of written texts that contain the authoritative word of God. Suffering in exile, the people admire this figure and look to him for inspiration. The familiarity that this leader has with the written text, moreover, helps him to chart a course of repentance that can bring the people into right relationship with God. The message of all these Judean texts is that Jews living outside of the land of Israel should *want* to return to their homeland. The absence of a desire to return to Judea is the greatest obstacle to the people's restoration.

Baruch 4:5–5:9

Baruch's closing poems comprise consolation speeches that can be read as answers to the Judahites' petition in the first half of Baruch.[20] The structural and thematic similarities between these poems and the book's first half highlight their complementarity. Both sections attribute the people's exile to their sins, and both sections present the exile as a source of shame.[21] Like Baruch's opening scene, which employs multilayered ventriloquy to speak in the voices of the exiled Judahites, the prophets, and God, this section speaks in the voices

---

19. Ezra is referred to as a scribe in Neh 8:1, 4, 13; as a priest in Neh 8:2; and as a priest and scribe in Neh 8:9. Baruch is referred to as a scribe (*sōpēr*) in Jer 36:26–32. A Baruch is also mentioned in Neh 10:7 (cf. 2 Esd 20:6) in the list of priests and Levites who sign a covenantal confession. If this Baruch is Jeremiah's scribe, it suggests that he was from a prominent Jerusalemite family that returned to the land of Israel after the exile. Indeed, Josephus refers to Baruch as one "who came from a very distinguished family, and was exceptionally well instructed in his native tongue" (*Ant.* 10.155–158). Later rabbinic traditions suggest that Jeremiah and Baruch were both exiled to Babylonia (S. 'Olam Rab. 26).

20. The literary connections between Bar 4:5–5:9 and the Septuagint could indicate that this section was originally written in Greek, or that the person who translated the Hebrew poem into Greek knew the Septuagint. See Henderson, *Second Temple Songs*, 178–79; Schürer, "Book of Baruch," 3.2:736–38; Moore, *Daniel, Esther, and Jeremiah*, 260.

21. Compare Bar 2:14–15 with 4:21–24, 36–37; 5:5–9.

of the bereft figure of Jerusalem, a prophet, and God. Both halves also presume a Judean audience and should be read as conveyors of comfort to Jews in Judea.

The first main poem in this section (4:9b–29) speaks in the voice of Jerusalem, who imagines herself as a grieving mother that invites other nations to witness her grief.[22] Jerusalem's address to these nations is despairing and critical, but her address to Israel is consoling:

> [21]Take courage, my children, cry to God, and he will deliver you from the power and hand of the enemy. [22]For I have put my hope in the Everlasting to save you, and joy has come to me from the Holy One, because of the mercy that will soon come to you from your everlasting savior. [23]For I sent you out with sorrow and weeping, but God will give you back to me with joy and gladness forever. [24]For as the neighbors of Zion have now seen your capture, so they soon will see your salvation by God, which will come to you with great glory and with the splendor of the Everlasting. (Bar 4:21–24)

Jerusalem's assurance that her people will soon return to her is based on the untested assumption that all displaced Judahites desire this return. Like the speakers in Baruch's opening section, Jerusalem cannot fathom that the exiled people do not want to return, since their displacement has brought them extraordinary shame. She is grieved by her children's sins, their punishment, and their humiliation, but she assures them that their exposure to oppression and mockery will soon come to an end (4:25). Jerusalem's promises of restoration, however, are conditional: the Judahites must repent by acknowledging the sins that have led to their suffering (4:28). The reminder that exile is a punishment that derives from sin and results in humiliation would have comforted Judean readers of this poem, who were witnesses to their own hardships in the land of Israel. These readers might have been consoled by the fact that Jews outside the land of Israel who seemed to be thriving were experiencing punishment and shame, even if they were tragically unaware of it.

In the next poem (4:30–5:9), God assures Jerusalem that the exiled Judahites will return to their homeland.[23] The section's opening phrase, "Take

---

22. Henderson divides this section into four poems: (1) Bar 4:5–9a, a prologue that invokes Moses's Song in Deut 32; (2) Bar 4:9b–16, a lament sung by Jerusalem, who is personified as a mother and whose song is resonant of Lam 1:12–22; (3) Bar 4:17–29, a song uttered by Jerusalem that encourages her people and is resonant of Lam 2–3; and (4) Bar 4:30–5:9, a song uttered by the prophet who consoles Jerusalem. See Henderson, "Baruch's Jerusalem," 543. The poem is also divisible into sections that open with the phrase "take courage" (Bar 4:5, 21, 27, 30). Henderson reviews other possible structures in *Second Temple Songs*, 181–84.

23. Henderson, "Baruch's Jerusalem," 554.

courage, O Jerusalem" (4:30) parallels the refrains of the earlier poem—"take courage, my people" (4:5) and "take courage, my children" (4:21, 27)—and brings the two poems into conversation. Here, however, Jerusalem moves from being the consoler to being the consoled, as God supplants Jerusalem as the facilitator of redemption. This redemption is no longer imagined as an event that will take place in the distant future. Instead, it is imagined as a phenomenon that is developing in the present:

> [36] Look towards the east, O Jerusalem, and see the joy that is coming to you from God. [37] Look, your children are coming, whom you sent away; they are coming, gathered from east and west, at the word of the Holy One, rejoicing in the glory of God....
> [5:5] Arise, O Jerusalem, stand upon the height; look toward the east, and see your children gathered from west and east at the word of the Holy One, rejoicing that God has remembered them. [6] For they went out from you on foot, led away by their enemies; but God will bring them back to you, carried in glory, as on a royal throne. [7] For God has ordered that every high mountain and the everlasting hills be made low and the valleys filled up, to make level ground, so that Israel may walk safely in the glory of God. [8] The woods and every fragrant tree have shaded Israel at God's command. [9] For God will lead Israel with joy, in the light of his glory, with the mercy and righteousness that come from him. (Bar 4:36–37; 5:5–9)

Whereas Baruch's opening scene has exiled Judahites making contact with leaders in Jerusalem, this poem reads as if the land is completely empty of Judahites. The image of upheaval and restoration in this poem suggests that any Judahite presence in the land is inconsequential compared to the great restoration that lies on the horizon (5:5). Judean readers of this poem would have inferred that their presence in the land of Israel signified the beginning stages of restoration and an encouraging step toward the fulfillment of prophetic promises. At the same time, a new era marked by reconciliation between God and the people could not truly begin as long as other Jewish people remained scattered. A full restoration could only take place when the remainder of their kin returned to their homeland.

Baruch's closing poems adopt strategies of ventriloquy to remind their Judean readers of the bond that all Jews share with one another through their common connection with the land of Israel. By speaking in the voices of Jerusalem and God, who make no distinction between Jews in Judea and Jews who live elsewhere, the authors of these poems bring all Jewish people into a single polity. At the same time, these poems carve out a distinctive role for Judean readers, who would have read the poems from the perspective of pious Judahites that embodied the fulfillment of God's promises. The association between exile and shame would have functioned as a comforting redress to Judeans Jews who noted the disparity between the upheaval in their own lives following the Hasmonean rebellion and the peaceful lives that many of their kin enjoyed elsewhere. They would have also noted the poems' repeated instruction to take courage, which implies that living in a foreign land was a frightening experience that generated a desire to return to the homeland (4:5, 21, 27, 30).[24] Judean readers must have been encouraged by the idea that when the time came for Jews who lived abroad to finally return, they would happily live under the authority of leaders in Jerusalem.

Baruch opens with exiled Judahites expressing their anguish about being in exile, and it closes with Jerusalem and God offering these Judahites words of comfort. Both sections of Baruch ventriloquize outsiders who negatively assess the experience of exile. The first half of Baruch cites exiled Judahites who write to leaders in Jerusalem asking them to pray on their behalf, and the second half speaks in the voices of Jerusalem and God who both predict that the exiled people will return to their homeland. By having all participants of the covenantal relationship—God, the people, and even the land—denigrate the exile, Baruch's Judean author suggests that life outside Judea is marked by estrangement and shame. The story of Baruch, however, operates against a historical reality rather than within it. No surviving text produced outside Judea in the Hellenistic era begs God to restore Jews to their homeland in order to put an end to the Jews' extraordinary shame.

The difference between Baruch and other Judean letters we have studied lies in their intended audiences but not in their message. Like Judean letters to Egypt, Baruch attributes meaning to the idea of a diaspora, that is, the idea that life outside Judea holds monolithic theological significance that symbolically opposes life in Judea. To make their arguments, Judean authors looked for common ground upon which all Jews could agree. The Jews' shared scriptural traditions and common devotion to the Jerusalem Temple were, for these authors, mutually enforcing modes of worship that brought Jews together by orienting them toward the land of Israel.

Judean Jewish images of the suffering that their ancestors endured in exile tell us nothing about what Jews living outside Judea actually thought

---

24. The Greek imperative plural verb used in the first three verses is *tharseite*. In Bar 4:30, which addresses not the people but Jerusalem, the imperative singular form, *tharsei*, is used. The parallel Hebrew verbal command *'al tîrā'*, "do not fear," appears as a mandate to Israel in Deut 1:21; 3:2; Josh 8:1; 10:8; 11:6; inter alia. Cf. Neh 8:9, 11, when Levites twice instruct Judeans who have returned from exile to stop weeping.

about their own lives. Only the literature produced by these Jews can tell us whether they engaged with Judean overtures that asked them to accept Judean leadership. In the next section, I will turn to two Jewish novellas produced in Egypt that shed light on this question. Both novellas develop the notion of a universal God who cares equally for all people, wherever they live. They also use the same layering techniques found in Judean documents, though they use them to dissolve emerging concepts of the diaspora. Both novellas, moreover, express a close connection to Judean Jewry but betray no desire for their own communities to meet their end. Finally, whereas Judean documents present the relationship between Judean and Egyptian Jews as connected but unequal, these novellas present this relationship as founded upon mutuality and respect.

PART 3

The Dissolution of Diaspora in Diasporic Letters

CHAPTER 8

"A Sign of Friendship and Love": Fantasies of Judea in the Letter of Aristeas

JUDEAN JEWISH AUTHORS USED PSEUDEPIGRAPHY, the attribution of texts to vaunted heroes, and ventriloquy, the citation of people who represent an outside community, to produce an effect of infinitude that projected and amplified their views. Egyptian Jewish writers employed the same strategies in novellas that may have been composed in regions of Egypt where Jews received letters from Judean authorities. Perhaps the writers of these novellas knew of these letters or of similar dispatches that have not survived. Like their Judean kin, Egyptian Jewish writers believed that the relationship between Judean and Egyptian Jews was special. Rather than producing texts that accept the supervisory position of Judean Jews over Egyptian Jews, however, Egyptian Jewish writers brought themselves into mutual relationship with Judean Jews in stories that argue for the integrity of Jewish life outside their ancestral land.

One such novella recalls the process by which the first five books of the Hebrew Bible were translated into Greek under the direction of Ptolemy II Philadelphus (r. 283–246 BCE). This novella, known as the Letter of Aristeas, is framed as a letter written by a Greek courtier to his brother Philocrates. In his letter, Aristeas describes how King Ptolemy and Eleazar, the high priest of the Jerusalem Temple, enthusiastically collaborate with one another by arranging for seventy-two Judean scholars to travel to Alexandria, where they feast with the king at a seven-day long symposium and embark upon the Torah's translation on the nearby island of Pharos. Aristeas's author was not especially interested in the details of the Torah's translation. His aim was to convince Jewish readers, and perhaps Greek readers as well, that the Hebrew Bible and the Jews who revere it uphold values that correlate with Greek ideas.[1] The

---

1. Some scholars suggest that the author of Aristeas wanted to establish the Septuagint's authority in comparison to competing Greek translations of the Hebrew Bible, while others claim that he wanted to legitimize the Septuagint's status in comparison to the Hebrew Bible. The general existence of such translations is alluded to in Ben Sira's prologue, but the more specific theory that a competing translation of the Torah originated in the Jewish community of Leontopolis is unsubstantiated. See Jellicoe, "Occasion and Purpose," 158–59; Hadas, *Aristeas to Philocrates*, 28.

author therefore punctuated his novella with lengthy asides that defend the integrity of Jewish ancestral practice. He also highlighted the friendly interactions between Judean Jews and Greeks that took place prior to the Torah's translation.

Most scholars date Aristeas to the second half of the second century BCE.[2] The text bears linguistic parallels to other Jewish texts written in Greek that can be confidently dated to this period, and the late second century BCE was a period of growth for Jews in Egypt, who were taking advantage of their access to Hellenistic learning. Many of these Jews, who studied Hellenistic philosophical wisdom while continuing to observe their ancestral laws, probably did not speak or read Hebrew. Numerous versions of the Torah were circulating in Greek by this time, and some Jews must have felt that a single, agreed-upon Greek version of their scriptures was necessary in order to preserve the integrity of their scriptural tradition.

Aristeas's insistence that relations between Jews and Greeks were overwhelmingly positive during the time of Ptolemy II (and by extension, during the time of Aristeas's writing) is inconsistent with the complex political realities of Egyptian Jewish life. Like Judean authors, the author of Aristeas pushed against a historical reality rather than reflected it. He did not want to describe what relations between Egyptian Jews and Greeks were like but wanted to imagine how relations between Egyptian Jews and Greeks could transform. The reality was that, at some points during the second century BCE, the delicate rapport between Jews and Greeks in Egypt was on the verge of collapse. Egyptian Jews at this time enjoyed significant political influence, which helped them to secure the right to practice their ancestral laws and to obtain exemptions from their participation in public festivals. But the Jews' political influence also exposed them to higher risks, especially when their Greek allies became mired in civil conflict.

One such conflict took place during the reign of Ptolemy VI Philometor (r. 180–164; 163–145 BCE). According to Josephus, Philometor's army was

---

The author likely wanted to argue that the Septuagint was as legitimate as the Hebrew Bible, and superior to other existent Greek translations. Scholars who presume that Aristeas is primarily concerned with the Septuagint's status miss key features of the story. The Torah's translation is part of Aristeas's broader project to nurture the Jewish-Greek relationship on the basis that Judaism complements but does not threaten the integrity of Greek wisdom.

2. Hadas suggests that Aristeas was written sometime after 132 BCE based on his dating of Ben Sira and his argument that Aristeas postdates Ben Sira's translation into Greek (*Aristeas to Philocrates*, 43). Bickerman also makes a case for a late second-century BCE date but bases his dating on parallel epistolary phrases in 3 Maccabees. A review of this debate appears in White and Keddie, *Jewish Fictional Letters*, 34–38; cf. Wright, *Letter of Aristeas*.

headed by two Jewish generals, Onias and Dositheus (*Ant.* 12.224; *J.W.* 1.31–33).[3] Over the course of Philometor's reign, the king's brother Ptolemy VIII (also known as Physcon) tried to wrest control of the kingdom. When Philometor died in 145 BCE, Physcon clashed with his sister (and Philometor's wife) Cleopatra II over control of the kingdom (*Ag. Ap.* 2.49–56).[4] Josephus reports that Philometor's former Jewish general, Onias, marched into Alexandria with a military force to support Cleopatra.[5] This invasion committed Onias to Cleopatra's side. It also suggested to the broader public that all Egyptian Jews, who were linked to Onias by association, likewise supported Cleopatra. Onias's offensive placed these Jews in a precarious position, since most Greeks supported Physcon. When Physcon took the reins of the kingdom as Euergetes II later that year, the Jews' good standing in the Egyptian court and with their neighbors became gravely endangered. The crisis was averted when Physcon and Cleopatra put an end to the conflict by marrying one another. The perception that Jews had supported Cleopatra, however, did lasting damage to their relationship with local Greeks and Egyptians.[6]

Jews continued to occupy significant governmental positions in Egypt even after this episode.[7] They also continued to find themselves caught in dynastic conflicts. When Physcon's son Ptolemy IX Soter (r. 116–107, 88–81 BCE) was ousted by his mother Cleopatra III, the Jews once again took the side of the queen. As I noted in chapter 5, the queen was supported by two high-ranking Jewish generals, Onias's sons Chelkias and Ananias (Josephus, *Ant.* 13.287, 349). Josephus writes that when Cleopatra prevented Soter from annexing Judea into his kingdom, some of her advisors tried to persuade her to invade the region. Chelkias and Ananias, however, dissuaded the queen, insisting that an invasion of Judea would imperil her relationship with the Hasmonean king Alexander Jannaeus and would decimate her Jewish support base in Egypt (*Ant.* 13.354). Cleopatra assented to the advice of her Jewish generals and formed an alliance with Alexander, which prompted public fallout. Local Egyptians and Greeks were especially resentful that the queen's Jewish

---

3. Josephus may have overstated the position of these officials; perhaps they served in the army but were not top generals.

4. Barclay, *Jews in the Mediterranean Diaspora*, 37.

5. Some scholars assume that the Onias to whom Josephus refers is Onias IV, the priest who fled Jerusalem after clashing with Judean Hellenizers and built a Jewish temple at Leontopolis. See Tcherikover, *Hellenistic Civilization*, 276–79; Goldstein, *I Maccabees*, 35. Gruen questions this identification, noting that Josephus identifies the Onias who built the temple in Leontopolis as the son of Simon the high priest—that is, Onias III—and Onias IV would have been young to assume such an exalted position ("Origins and Objectives," 53).

6. Later Roman historians such as Apion treated this incident as evidence of the Jews' disloyalty to Egypt. See Barclay, *Jews in the Mediterranean Diaspora*, 39.

7. Josephus, for instance, highlights the Jews' positions as river guards (*J.W.* 1.175).

advisors prioritized the interests of their Judean kin above the welfare of the queen's own kingdom (*Ant.* 13.352–355).[8]

Questions regarding the loyalty of Egyptian Jews extended into the first century BCE as Jews continued to ally with claimants to power who were unpopular among the Greek populace in Egypt. While Greeks were suspicious of a Roman takeover, for instance, the Judean leaders Antipater and Hyrcanus, along with the Jewish guard at Pelusium, helped the Roman puppet king Ptolemy XII Auletes (r. 80–58, 55–51 BCE) enter Egypt in 55 BCE.[9] Another incident that cemented the Jews' reputation of advancing outside interests took place in 48 BCE, when Jews from Onias's district, once again with the encouragement of Antipater and Hyrcanus, provided safe passage to Julius Caesar's troops and armed them with supplies as they moved from Pelusium to Memphis. The support of these Jews for Judean (and Roman) interests put them at odds with local Greeks and Egyptians, who broadly opposed Roman annexation.[10]

The Egyptian Jews' attitude that their fates were intertwined with the fates of Judean Jews pervaded both elite Jewish circles and lower classes. Inscriptional evidence of Hebrew names discovered in Egypt suggests that the rate at which Jews gave their children Hebrew rather than Greek names rose significantly in the mid-second century BCE.[11] This increase may reflect rising support among Egyptian Jews for the Hasmonean rebellion against the Seleucid Greeks in Judea. Support for this rebellion, even in the form of name giving, was not without risks. The Ptolemies of Egypt were bitter rivals of the Seleucid dynasty, but they were nevertheless skeptical of Jews who refused to accept the Seleucid yoke. Perhaps they feared that Jews would incite a similar rebellion in Egypt. Jews in Egypt, meanwhile, may have worried that their Egyptian Greek rulers would become inspired by Antiochus IV Epiphanes's oppression of Judean Jews and would punish the Egyptian Jews' loyalty to Judea by issuing prohibitions against the observance of the Jews' ancestral laws. As I will show in the next chapter, an Egyptian Jewish novella known as 3 Maccabees imagines a similar scenario.

Jewish fears about potential repercussions for the Jews' loyalty to Judea were confirmed in the late first century BCE when Cleopatra VII (r. 51–30 BCE) refused to provide Alexandrian Jews with corn rations. Like other incidents, the Jews barely avoided disaster. Cleopatra died in 30 BCE, and Rome annexed Egypt shortly thereafter (Josephus, *Ag. Ap.* 2.60). Egyptian Jews came under

---

8. Stern, "Relations Between the Hasmoneans," 101–2.
9. Barclay, *Jews in the Mediterranean Diaspora*, 40.
10. Barclay, *Jews in the Mediterranean Diaspora*, 39; Gruen, "Diaspora and Homeland," 308–9.
11. Honigman, "Birth of a Diaspora," 93–128.

attack once again in 38 CE, when anti-Jewish violence spread throughout Alexandria after the Judean leader Herod Agrippa passed through the city.

The author of Aristeas was sensitive to the delicate social position of Egyptian Jewry and wanted to clarify that Jewish loyalty to Judea did not compromise Jewish loyalty to the Ptolemaic dynasty. Rather than highlighting Egyptian Jewish loyalty to Egyptian Greeks, however, he highlighted Judean Jewish friendship with Egyptian Greeks.[12] Aristeas's letter opens with Ptolemy and his chief librarian, Demetrius, asking Jewish authorities in Jerusalem to collaborate with them on producing a translation of the Hebrew scriptures. These authorities, in turn, enthusiastically dispatch Judean scholars to Egypt, where they produce the work. Egyptian Jews, meanwhile, are nearly absent in this story. What are we to make of the fact that Aristeas makes Egyptian Jews disappear? Why would an Egyptian Jewish author take his Egyptian Jewish community, and himself, out of his own story?

The absence of Egyptian Jews in Aristeas is best understood as an expression of the author's desire to present all Jews as united in friendship with Greeks. To achieve this goal, the author used pseudepigraphic and ventriloquizing techniques that portray all Jews as unified and harmonious. Only then could he argue that Greeks respect and admire all Jews and not only Jews who are properly acculturated into Hellenistic life. Treating Egyptian Jews and Judean Jews as part of a single population was, in fact, a very "Greek" thing to do. Greeks valued unity in language, culture, and tradition, and Greek writers went to substantial lengths to present their customs as consistent. The fifth-century BCE Greek writer Herodotus, for instance, insisted that Greeks have "one and the same blood," "one and the same tongue," and the same cults and customs (*Hist.* 8.44).[13] This idea gained momentum over the course of the Hellenistic era, despite the ethnic diversity of the millions of people who lived under Hellenistic rule. By framing his story as one of equanimity between Jews and Greeks, the author of Aristeas implied that all Jews enjoy the same unity of mind, spirit, and national pride as the Greeks. Since the Jews unanimously celebrate a corpus of literature that rivals the greatest wisdom traditions produced by Greeks, moreover, all Jews deserve acceptance and respect.

Placing Judean Jews into direct conversation with Egyptian Greeks had other advantages as well. This strategy centered Egyptian Jews in Greek and

---

12. Trotter suggests that Aristeas seeks to legitimize Jewish settlements outside Judea by replacing narratives about forced Jewish migrations that were in circulation at this time with a single "corporate" migration that was commissioned by a king who brought Judean scholars to Alexandria. The theory that the scholars' journey functions as a praiseworthy migration from Judea misrepresents Aristeas's attitude toward Judea, which is overwhelmingly positive. See Trotter, "Homeland," 93–124.

13. See Mélèze Modrzejewski, "How to Be a Jew," 76–77.

Judean Jewish consciousness by making Egyptian Jews the principal commonality that Greeks and Judean Jews shared.[14] The author's focus on Judean Jewry also enabled him to defend the legitimacy of Egyptian Jewry without having Egyptian Jews shoulder the burden of legitimization. The involvement of Judean Jews in Egyptian Jewish affairs, coupled with Ptolemy's endorsement of his Jewish subjects' devotion to the Jerusalem Temple, suggest that Egyptian Jews were so widely embraced by their host community and ancestral community that they did not need to speak up for themselves. Such legitimization responded to Greek accusations of Egyptian Jewish misanthropy. It also responded to Judean Jewish accusations of Egyptian Jewish impiety. Both kinds of accusations amounted to the same suspicion that Egyptian Jews were showing loyalty to the wrong community. Aristeas's marginalization of Egyptian Jewry, then, is part of a broader strategy to treat Egyptian Jews as legitimate members of a cohesive population that enjoyed divine approval and protection. The absence of Egyptian Jews in this story, along with the ventriloquy that dissolves communal boundaries and presents all relationships as interconnected, transforms Egyptian Jewry from being a doubly marginalized population into the keystone group that brings Greeks and Judeans into positive contact.

In summary, Aristeas's message can be distilled into three theses:

1. Egyptian Jews and Judean Jews enjoy a harmonious relationship that is based on common values and mutual respect. All Jews are united by common reverence for their sacred scriptures and traditions.
2. Jews and Greeks have much to admire in one another. The Jewish scriptures reflect a sophisticated form of philosophical wisdom, which is based on rational reasoning that corroborates Greek teachings.
3. Humanity, as represented by Jews and Greeks, can unite in common worship of the universal God. The Jewish wisdom tradition has universal value because it affirms the dominion of the one true God.

According to Aristeas, Judean Jewish and Egyptian Jewish communities are so aligned in values that they act as one. Aristeas's idealized notion of the relationship between Egyptian Jews and Judean Jews forms the basis upon which the author scaffolds his idealized notion of the Jew-Greek relationship. This relationship, in turn, forms the basis upon which the author argues for a united

---

14. Drawing on Homi Bhabha's work on postcolonial identity, Charles suggests that Aristeas was a "hybrid project" that sought to construct a "third space" between the Jews' homeland and host empire, which risked being rejected by both Jews and Greeks. Charles nicely highlights the interconnections between the Jewish-Greek relationship and the Egyptian-Judean relationship. See Charles, "Hybridity," 243–44; Bhabha, *Location of Culture*, 170.

humanity that lives in a cosmological system structured as a set of concentric circles with diasporic Jewry in the innermost circle, global Jewry in the second, humanity in the third, and God in the outermost.

In this system, the Jews' written scriptures function as a centripetal force that unites humanity. The Torah's translation will benefit Greek readers who want access to the Jewish scriptures in order to gain greater wisdom and knowledge of God. Yet all Jews, too, will benefit from the translation, since they will now have access to the best version of their scriptures, regardless of the language that they speak. The Torah's translation, moreover, only takes place because Judean leaders want to invest in the future of Greek-speaking Jewry outside the land of Israel. Rather than pushing Egyptian Jews out of a Judean Jewish orbit, the Torah's translation will bring Egyptian Jews and Judean Jews closer together by ensuring that they will have access to equally authoritative texts.

Aristeas's Pseudepigraphic Frame

Aristeas is framed as a letter and includes letters within it. By framing the text pseudepigraphically, the author suggests that Egyptian Greeks are so sincere in their admiration for Jews that they speak about this admiration privately among themselves. And by using ventriloquy to cite Greek and Judean officials who affectionately correspond with one another in public documents, the author implies that the Greeks' affection for Jews is conveyed out in the open without self-consciousness or fear.[15] Aristeas's multiple layers of ventriloquy parallel similar layers in Judean letters to Jews in Egypt, such as those that were appended to 2 Maccabees. While the letters appended to 2 Maccabees were sent to Egyptian Jews to argue for Judean exceptionalism, the Letter of Aristeas was composed to assure Egyptian Jews of the legitimacy of their scriptures and their practices. Egyptian Jews, therefore, were recipients of two kinds of competing documents: dispatches from Judean leaders and novellas written by members of their own communities. Aristeas is considered to be a fictional work, but Egyptian Jewish readers would have taken its message as seriously as the competing message found in letters sent to them by leaders in Jerusalem.

The intimate and informal tone of Aristeas's opening lines, along with unexplained references to earlier correspondence, convey the impression that the novella begins in the middle of a conversation. It is unlikely, however, that

---

15. Framing the text as a letter implies a "certain candidness, importance, and authenticity." White and Keddie, *Jewish Fictional Letters*, 41.

the text as we have it once included a longer introduction. Instead, these opening lines throw the reader into a personal conversation that casts the friendship between Jews and Greeks as self-evident. The introduction reads:

> ¹Now that a noteworthy narrative has been compiled, O Philocrates, *concerning the audience afforded us with Eleazar the high priest of the Jews*, because you place such value on hearing point by point concerning what topics and why we undertook the mission, I have attempted to give a clear exposition of the matter for you, since I perceive what a disposition you possess for love of learning, ²which is the greatest (type of disposition) for a person (to have)—"*ever to learn something more and make progress*"—whether through the study of history or by actually experiencing the events themselves. For in this way the soul's disposition is rendered pure, by taking up the noblest things, and, having fixed its aim on reverence as the noblest goal of all, it lives by adopting an unerring rule.
>
> ³Since we possess a set purpose of gaining extensive knowledge of divine matters, we offered ourselves for an embassy to the aforementioned man [the high priest Eleazar], who was held in the highest esteem by his own citizens and by others both for his virtue and his majesty, since he was in full possession of documents of the highest value to his (fellow) citizens, both those (dwelling) with him and those in foreign lands, with regard to the interpretation of the divine law; for their laws are written on leather parchments in Hebraic characters.
>
> ⁴This embassy we have now accomplished with earnest zeal, having first of all found an opportunity of pleading with the king on behalf of the Jewish captives who had been transported from Judea to Egypt by the king's father, when he first took possession of this city and succeeded to (the rule of) the land of Egypt. It is also worthwhile that I should clarify these matters for you. ⁵For I am convinced that, with your inclination toward holiness and toward the disposition of men living in accordance with the holy legislation, you will all the more readily follow the account that I propose to set forth, since you yourself have lately come to us from the island and wish to understand all that it provides for equipping the soul.
>
> ⁶Now formerly, too, I sent you a record of those things I thought worthy of mention *Concerning the Race of the Jews*—the record that I had obtained from the most learned high priests of the most learned land of Egypt. ⁷For since you possess a love of learning for those things that are able to benefit the mind, it is incumbent upon me to share these things, especially with all who have the same disposition, but all the more so

with you, since you possess such noble principles of conduct and since you by kinship are not only my brother with respect to character but also are the selfsame with me in the impulse toward goodness. ⁸For neither the pleasure derived from gold nor any other trappings of the possessions that are prized by shallow minds confers the same benefit as the pursuit of culture and the study that we expend in securing it. But lest we make idle chatter by prolonging these introductory matters, we shall proceed at once to the substance of our narrative. (Let. Aris. 1–8.)[16]

Aristeas provides no historical setting that explains his reason for writing. Instead, he gives the impression that his story is part of a larger set of documents devoted to the same topic by borrowing phrases from other well-known texts. He praises Philocrates for wanting "to learn something more and make progress," which seems to have been a popular axiom in Greek circles.[17] He also alludes to a work called *Concerning the Race of the Jews*, which may be a reference to the work of another Jew named Aristeas (known among scholars as Aristeas the Exegete).[18] The citation of older texts immediately situates Aristeas's work within the sphere of authoritative tradition and begins the process of creating a "surround-sound" effect of unanimity.

Aristeas's introduction seems to serve a similar purpose as the prologue of Ben Sira's Greek translation. Ben Sira's translator states that his aim is to "publish the book for those living abroad who wished to gain learning and are disposed to live according to the law" (Sir prol. 34–36). Aristeas similarly flatters Philocrates and, by extension, the Egyptian Jewish readers of his book by noting that he is writing to satiate Philocrates's thirst for knowledge.[19] The different origins of these two works, however, impact their polemical valances. Whereas the Greek version of Ben Sira transforms an older Judean text into a personal work that asks Egyptian Jews to fashion their piety according to Judean standards, Aristeas's address to Philocrates lends an air of objectivity to the story because it frames the text as a private correspondence between Greeks.

---

16. Translations of Aristeas are from White and Keddie, *Jewish Fictional Letters*, 40–172 (italics original).

17. The phrase is in iambic trimeter and shares parallels with other Greek fragments, including two attributed to Sophocles, although it is not attested to in earlier writings in this precise form. See White and Keddie, *Jewish Fictional Letters*, 58n6.

18. The author of this text may have intentionally posed as this older Aristeas. See Alexander Polyhistor *apud* Eusebius, *Preparation for the Gospel* 9.25.1–4; White and Keddie, *Jewish Fictional Letters*, 60n8.

19. Philocrates is praised as desiring "to learn something more and make progress" and bears "inclination toward holiness and toward the disposition of men living in accordance with the holy legislation" (Let. Aris. 2, 5).

Aristeas's praise of Philocrates avoids drawing a contrast between Jews and Greeks and between Egyptian and Judean Jewry. His praise of Philocrates parallels his praise for the Jerusalem high priest Eleazar, "who was held in the highest esteem by his own citizens and by others both for his virtue and his majesty" (Let. Aris. 3). Aristeas presents both Judean Jews and Ptolemaic Greeks as bearers of wisdom and upholds Eleazar's virtue as emblematic of collective Jewish virtue that is comparable to the wisdom of virtuous Greeks. This positive orientation toward Jews and Greeks and, by extension, toward Aristeas's Jewish readers differs from the Greek version of Ben Sira, whose prologue contrasts Judean Jews who read the original Hebrew version of Ben Sira to make "even greater progress" in their pursuit of piety with Egyptian Jews, who will read the translated version and are merely disposed to live according to the law. The translator of Ben Sira believed that Judean scholars were models of intellectual mastery, and he therefore distinguished between the intellectual dispositions of Judean Jews and Egyptian Jews.

Aristeas's positive attitude toward the translated scriptures is another distinguishing factor between his story and the Greek version of Ben Sira, which expresses an unequivocally negative attitude toward the translated scriptures. Aristeas admiringly describes how prominent and pious Judean leaders celebrated the Septuagint as a source of blessing to all Jewish people. The translator of Ben Sira, however, insists that his version is inferior to his grandfather's original work because "what was originally expressed in Hebrew does not have exactly the same sense when translated into another language" (Sir prol. 21–22). His observation that "not only this book, but even the Law itself, the Prophecies, and the rest of the books differ not a little when read in the original" (Sir prol. 23–26) refers to the Septuagint or to another Greek version of the Torah to which the author had access. For this writer, such translations undermined the integrity of the Hebrew scriptures and were a necessary evil in order to keep Egyptian Jews within the fold of observant Jewish life.

Aristeas and Divine Universality

Aristeas argues that worship of the universal God is a powerful binding agent that can bring Jews and Greeks together in social harmony. He expresses this idea to the king just before the translation project is initiated in a speech that requests the manumission of Jewish captives as a gesture of goodwill to local Jews:

> [12] And now I for my part, thinking it to be timely for the matters concerning which I had frequently entreated Sosibius of Tarentum and Andreas,

the chief bodyguards, namely, concerning the release of the Jews who had been carried off from Judea by the king's father—For when by a combination of good fortune and courage the latter had invaded the whole region of Coele-Syria and Phoenicia, in bringing everyone into subjection by fear, he resettled some (of the inhabitants) but reduced others to captivity. The number of those whom he carried off from the country of the Jews to Egypt amounted to no less than a hundred thousand. ¹³Of these he armed thirty thousand picked men and settled them in garrisons in the country districts. (Now even before this time large numbers of Jews had come into Egypt with the Persian [king], and in an earlier period still others had been sent to Egypt to fight as allies of Psammetichus in his campaign against the king of the Ethiopians. But these were nothing like so numerous as the captives whom Ptolemy the son of Lagus carried off). ¹⁴As I have already said, Ptolemy selected the best of these, those in prime of age and bodily strength, and armed them, but the rest, a great crowd of older and younger men and even the women, he reduced to slavery, not that he was so disposed in soul by his set purpose, but he was compelled by his soldiers as a reward for the services they had rendered in military campaigns—and since, as has already been stated, we had obtained such an opportunity for securing their emancipation, we addressed the king with the following arguments. (Let. Aris. 12–14)

Aristeas's optimism that Ptolemy will free Jews who were captured in prior military conflicts suggests that the Jews' captivity is not evidence of the king's personal animosity toward the Jewish people. Their capture is merely unfortunate fallout of political conflict and therefore easily reversible. To make his case, Aristeas refers to three waves of Judean emigration to Egypt. He mentions one hundred thousand Judeans who were taken captive by Ptolemy II's father, Ptolemy I Soter (r. 305/304–282 BCE), whom he refers to as Lagus (Let. Aris. 13). These Judeans were likely captured in the battle of Gaza in 312 BCE, when Ptolemy and Seleucus I Nicator attacked and defeated the Macedonian king Demetrius following Alexander the Great's death.[20] According to Aristeas, thirty thousand of these Judeans were taken captive and forced to work as soldiers in garrisons throughout Egypt. Seventy thousand elderly people, women, and children were taken into slavery. Aristeas then mentions an earlier wave of migration to Egypt that took place under the rule of "the

---

20. Ptolemy I Soter also made excursions into Syria in 320 and 302 BCE, at which time he could have taken Judeans back to Egypt as well. See White and Keddie, *Jewish Fictional Letters*, 63.

Persian" (*tō Persē*; Let. Aris. 13).[21] This enigmatic allusion may refer to Cambyses, the Persian king who conquered Egypt in 525 BCE. Aristeas goes on to state that Judahites were brought to Egypt to fight Psammetichus in his campaign against the Ethiopians. This may be a reference to Psammetichus I (r. 664–610 BCE), who was possibly the first Egyptian king to employ Greek mercenaries.[22] Alternatively, Aristeas could be alluding to Psammetichus II (r. 595–589 BCE), whose conflict with Ethiopia also necessitated the use of mercenaries.[23]

Aristeas's description of migration waves represents a form of *mise en abyme* that reaches back into the Jews' history and gives the impression of continuous motion. Like the second Judean letter appended to 2 Maccabees, which reaches into incrementally earlier periods to give the impression that Jews have been continually devoted to Jerusalem and its temple, Aristeas produces historical layers to give the impression that Jews have continually lived in Egypt since ancient times. The authors of these texts employed *mise en abyme* toward different ends. Whereas the letter appended to 2 Maccabees seeks to create an effect of continual Judean *return* to the land of Israel, Aristeas seeks to create an effect of continual Judean *departure* from the land of Israel.

Aristeas's claim that Judeans and their ancestors were brought to Egypt against their will obfuscates the probability that the majority of them probably came to Egypt of their own volition.[24] The book of Jeremiah mentions voluntary migration to Egypt that took place in the early sixth century BCE, and Josephus cites the fourth-century BCE Greek historian Hecataeus of Abdera, who wrote that Judeans voluntarily left Judea for Egypt during the reign of Ptolemy I (*Ag. Ap.* 1.183–186).[25] Onias IV and his followers, moreover, selected Egypt as a refuge from Judea in the second century BCE, and there were likely many other voluntary migrations contemporaneous with the author of Aristeas's own time.[26] By presenting Judean migration to Egypt as forced, Aristeas gives the impression that most Jews living in Egypt remain emotionally

21. Thackeray, "Translation of the Letter of Aristeas," 344n1.
22. Whether Aristeas is referencing Psammetichus I or Psammetichus II is unclear, though Psammetichus I is more likely. See Kahn, "Judean Auxiliaries in Egypt's Wars," 507–16, and our discussion in chapter 5.
23. Many of the mercenaries employed by Psammetichus I and his son Necho II settled in the region; see p. 19, n. 1.
24. As Mélèze Modrzejewski writes, "voluntary immigration was by far the principal source of the Jewish establishment in the Ptolemaic kingdom" ("How to Be a Jew," 76).
25. See the *prostagma* of Ptolemy II (PER 24552 = C.Ord.Ptol. 21–22); Mélèze Modrzejewski, "How to Be a Jew," 75–76; Biezunska-Malowist, *L'esclavage dans l'Égypte gréco-romaine*, 19–21.
26. See Jer 44:1–30, which records a letter dispatched by Jeremiah to a Judahite community that had settled in Egypt. On whether the Onias who fled Judea is Onias III or Onias IV, see Josephus, *J.W.* 1.31–33; *Ant.* 12:43, 157, and my discussion of these sources in chapter 3.

attached to the land of their ancestors and should not be accused of disloyalty to Judea. He also implies that the Jewish presence in Egypt derives from political events and has nothing to do with divine rejection. The Jews of Egypt, therefore, remain part of a cohesive and legitimate community of Jews who live throughout the Hellenistic world.

Aristeas's overview of Judean migration to Egypt suggests that Jews and Greeks, as well as Judean Jews and Egyptian Jews, are interconnected and therefore naturally invested in one another's welfare. All Jews are united, Aristeas insists, and all Jews are bound in friendship with Greeks who worship the universal God. The concept of diaspora, which treats the space outside the land of Israel as a monolith that signifies God's displeasure, serves no purpose to Aristeas. The second half of Aristeas's speech to Ptolemy indicates that God takes equal interest in all people:

> ¹⁵Let us not be so unreasonable, O King, as to be put to shame by these actions of ours. For since the legislation that we intend not only to transcribe but also to translate was established for all Jews, what justification shall we claim for an embassy while such vast numbers of them remain in slavery in your kingdom? Rather, with perfect and rich soul release those who are held in such miserable bondage, since, as I have been at pains to discover, the God who has given them their law is the one who guides your kingdom aright. ¹⁶For they themselves worship the God who is Overseer and Creator of all, as do all other people and we ourselves, O King, although naming him differently Zeus and Dis (i.e., life and first cause). This name was quite properly bestowed upon him by our first ancestors, in order to signify that this One, through whom all things are given life and come into being, rules and governs the universe. Now you will surpass all humankind in magnanimity by granting freedom to those being kept in slavery. (Let. Aris. 15–16)

Aristeas's claim that Jews and Greeks worship the same God is pivotal to his argument that Jews and Greeks are equals.[27] In the context of this argument, the release of Jewish captives is not simply a gesture of goodwill. It is a

---

27. White and Keddie explain the connection between Zeus and Dis as an etymological play on words: "Δία (from archaic Δίς, Latin *Dis*) was used as the regular accusative of Zeus (Ζεύς), while Ζῆνα (the accusative of the old poetic form Ζήν) was carried over in poetic and dialectal usage for the same; hence, both variations were typical accusative forms for Zeus. The combined reference here comes from Stoic etymologies on the divine names, according to which Δία (by assimilation to the preposition διά, meaning 'through') suggested the source or cause of all things, while Ζῆνα (by assimilation to ζῆν, the infinitive form of ζάω) means 'to live'" (*Jewish Fictional Letters*, 64n16).

recognition that a collaboration of such magnitude cannot proceed amid social imbalance between two equal partners.

Ptolemy's Letter to Eleazar

The first embedded letter within Aristeas's letter is a personal note from Ptolemy II Philadelphus to Eleazar, the high priest of Jerusalem. Ptolemy asks Eleazar to participate in the Torah's translation project and requests that Eleazar personally select Judean translators who will work under Ptolemy's supervision. Ptolemy begins his letter by assuring Eleazar that he bears no ill will toward Jews who live in Egypt:

> [35]King Ptolemy to Eleazar the high priest: *Greetings and be well.* Since it has come to pass that many Jews were settled in our realm, having been carried off from Jerusalem by the Persians at the time of their power and many more who came into Egypt as captives with my father [36]— of whom he placed large numbers in the army and paid them higher wages than usual, and when he had proved the loyalty of their leaders he built fortresses and placed them in their charge that the native Egyptians might [not] be intimidated by them. And we, when we ascended the throne, adopted a kindly attitude toward all (our subjects), and more particularly to your fellow-citizens—[37]we have set at liberty more than a hundred thousand captives, paying their owners the appropriate market price for them, and if ever evil has been done to your people through the passions of the mob, we have made them reparation, intending to act reverently and rendering unto the supreme God a thank offering for maintaining my kingdom in peace and great glory in all the world. Moreover, those of your people who were in the prime of life we have drafted into our army, and those who were fit to be in our circle and worthy of trust at our court, we have established in official positions. (Let. Aris. 35–37; italics original)

Ptolemy declares that the Jews' captivity and forced emigration to Egypt has not impacted his positive view of Jews. He has long recognized the Jews' talents and has rewarded their loyalty by appointing Jews to his military and court. Ptolemy praises the Jews of Egypt for being devoted to his interests but nevertheless does not challenge the reality that these Jews, having come to Egypt not by choice but through war, are loyal to Judea as well. Ptolemy then turns to the topic at hand:

> Now since I am anxious to show my gratitude to these men and to the Jews throughout the world and to the generations yet to come, we have determined that your law shall be translated from the Hebrew tongue that is in use among you into the Greek language, that these books, too, may be ready to hand with us in the library along with the other royal books. (Let. Aris. 38)

The king's reward to the Jews for their loyalty is measure for measure. Since the Jews have proven their fidelity to his court, Ptolemy will ensure that these Jews have the means to maintain fidelity to their ancestral heritage, which requires access to their written scriptures. Ptolemy also clarifies that he has an ulterior motive in initiating the Torah's translation. In addition to being a gesture of appreciation for the Jews' loyalty, the translation will provide Ptolemy with personal gain:

> Therefore, you will do well and (act) in a manner worthy of our earnest zeal by selecting elders, men who have lived nobly and who are well-versed in your law and able to interpret it, six from each tribe, so that from their greater number harmony may be found, for the investigation is of the highest possible importance. We hope to win great renown by the accomplishment of this work. (Let. Aris. 39)

Motivated by the idea that the Torah's translation will bring him "great renown," Ptolemy asks Eleazar to select six men from each Israelite tribe to embark on the translation. His request implies that the participation of a large number of scholars who proportionately represent all Judean Jewish communities will ensure maximal accuracy. By the Hellenistic era, however, ten of the twelve Israelite tribes were no longer traceable. Five hundred years earlier, in 722 BCE, the Neo-Assyrian king Shalmaneser V exiled inhabitants of the northern Israelite Kingdom following their conquest. While the author of Aristeas would have known that a reference to Israelite tribes was anachronistic, he nevertheless had Ptolemy make this request to convey Ptolemy's desire for Jewish consensus on his project. Such consensus would leave no room to suggest that Jews did not support the project or considered it controversial. Ptolemy closes by praising Andreas and Aristeas, the emissaries who delivered his letter, and by requesting a response:

> We have sent Andreas, of the chief bodyguard, and Aristeas—men whom we hold in high esteem—to lay the matter before you and present you with the firstfruits of dedications for the temple and for the

sacrifices yet another hundred talents of silver. And you will indeed favor us, and do something worthy of our friendship, by writing to us concerning whatever you wish, so that your wishes may be carried out as speedily as possible. Fare thee well. (Let. Aris. 40)

Ptolemy's praise for Aristeas authorizes his letter to Eleazar and legitimizes Aristeas's entire letter to Philocrates. His reference to a long-standing friendship with Eleazar, which suggests that the Greek-Jewish friendship is well established, recalls Aristeas's opening words of friendship to Philocrates. These elements resurface in Eleazar's response to the king.

Eleazar's Response to Ptolemy

Eleazar's answer to Ptolemy matches the king's enthusiasm. He indicates that all Jews support the project, but he makes no mention of the Egyptian Jews who are to be primary beneficiaries of the Torah's translation. Instead, Eleazar speaks on behalf of all Judean Jews, who extol the collaboration that Ptolemy proposes. He also makes it clear that the Torah's translation is not merely politically beneficial. It is also religiously significant.[28] The opening words of Eleazar's introduction follow the standards of typical royal correspondence produced in the Hellenistic period:[29]

> Eleazar the high priest to King Ptolemy, his true Friend: Greetings. My highest wishes are for your welfare and the well-being of your sister, Queen Arsinoe, and your children. We ourselves are also well. (Let. Aris. 41)

Eleazar begins by warmly expressing personal interest in the welfare of Ptolemy and his family. The tonal effect is an easy intimacy, which suggests that Eleazar is a political insider in the geopolitical arena. Because the friendship between Eleazar and Ptolemy extends to the people whom they represent, Eleazar takes care to describe his public reading of Ptolemy's letter to local Jews:

> [42]Having received your letter we rejoiced greatly on account of your set purpose and your noble counsel. And assembling the whole people,

---

28. White and Keddie, *Jewish Fictional Letters*, 41.
29. The style of royal correspondence in this text parallels royal letters found in Eupolemus, 2 Maccabees, Greek Esther, and 3 Maccabees. See White and Keddie, *Jewish Fictional Letters*, 42.

we read it to them that they might know what reverence you hold toward our God. We also showed them the cups that you sent, twenty of gold and thirty of silver, the five bowls and the table for a dedication, and the hundred talents of silver for the offering of sacrifices and for repairs as might be needed for the temple. ⁴³These gifts were brought (to us) by Andreas, one of those honored by you, and by Aristeas, both good men and true, distinguished by their learning and altogether worthy of your high principles and righteous purposes. These men shared your words with us and heard from us an answer in accordance with what you wrote. (Let. Aris. 42–43)

Eleazar's reading of Ptolemy's letter employs a form of *mise en abyme*. When the reader reaches this point of the novella, they encounter a text framed as Aristeas's letter to Philocrates, which cites a letter from Eleazar to Ptolemy, which refers to a letter from Ptolemy to Eleazar, which is recited aloud to Judeans. All of these layers create an effect of multiple voices that proclaim the good relations between Jews and Greeks, whose expressions of kinship are entirely mutual.

Eleazar's recitation of Ptolemy's letter evokes biblical scenes of Israelites and Judeans gathering to hear a public reading of the Torah.[30] It also evokes the letter of Baruch, which recounts how the scribe reads a public letter to exiled Judahites that was later dispatched to Jerusalem authorities on their behalf. Baruch and Aristeas both layer multiple voices into their scenes but deploy these voices toward opposing ends. Baruch's letter beseeches Jerusalem authorities to ask God for forgiveness of the Judahites' sins. Eleazar's reading, however, seeks to legitimize Egyptian Jewry and does not treat the presence of Jews outside the land of Israel as theologically meaningful.

After thanking Ptolemy for the gifts that he has sent for the Jerusalem Temple, Eleazar praises Andreas and Aristeas, the emissaries who brought Ptolemy's written letter and relayed an oral message of personal friendship. Unlike Ptolemy's written letter, which represents the kingdom's official communication, this oral message is alluded to but not cited. The two modes of communication, however, were not entirely distinct. They were both part of a continuous process of transmission that held a coherent message. The author may have understood that both modes of communication enforced one another in his story in the same way that Jews transmitted complementary written and oral traditions. By indicating that Ptolemy conveyed written

---

30. One example appears in Neh 8:1–12 when Nehemiah and Ezra gather Judeans who have returned from Babylonian exile and Ezra reads the Torah to the people, who respond with tearful repentance; see my analysis of this scene in chapter 1.

and oral communications to Eleazar, the author presents Ptolemy as showing recognition that Jews use both kinds of authoritative transmission.

The second half of Eleazar's letter addresses the Jews' devotion to Ptolemy:

> ⁴⁴To all those things that are beneficial for you, even though they are contrary to nature, we will consent. For this is a token of our friendship and love. For you have bestowed upon our citizens great and never-to-be-forgotten benefits in many ways. ⁴⁵Immediately, therefore, I offered sacrifices on behalf of you, your sister, your children, and your Friends, and all the people prayed that your plans might prosper continually and that Almighty God might preserve your kingdom in peace with glory and that the translation of the holy law be carried out beneficially for you and with (all) surety. ⁴⁶In the presence of all the people I selected elders who were good men and true, six from each tribe, and I have sent them to you with a copy of our law. You will do well, then, O just King, by ordering that as soon as the translation of the books is completed, the men shall be restored to us in safety. Fare thee well. (Let. Aris. 44–46)

Eleazar's declaration that "to all those things that are beneficial for you, even though they are contrary to nature, we will consent" is opaque, since the reader is not told what these unnatural acts are. Perhaps Eleazar is implying that the translation of the Torah carries significant risk. Reading the Torah in translation could lead to misinterpretation. It could also make Egyptian Jews vulnerable to outsiders, who could more easily access and critique these translated scriptures or even claim them for themselves. Such concerns, some of which find expression in other Judean texts such as the Greek translation of Ben Sira, would not have been out of place in the writings of a Judean high priest. But whereas Ben Sira's translator suggests that scriptural translations are inferior and misleading, the author of Aristeas has Eleazar mitigate such concerns by expressing faith in his trustworthy friend Ptolemy.[31] Eleazar's commitment to Ptolemy is so steadfast, and his trust in Egyptian Jewry so firm, that the potential negative consequences of producing a Greek Torah are overridden.

Eleazar closes his letter by asking Ptolemy to ensure that the Judean translators are given safe passage back to Judea. Without proper security, the scholars will be susceptible to bandits and thieves. Eleazar is not only alluding to the

---

31. The awkward *kai ei para phusin estin* (Let. Aris. 44) is avoided in Evans's translation, which renders the phrase as "We will consent to everything that is advantageous to you even though your request is very unusual." See Evans and Zacharias, *Old Testament Pseudepigrapha*; cf. Shutt's translation in Charlesworth, *Old Testament Pseudepigrapha*, 2:16: "Everything which is to your advantage, even if it is unnatural, we will carry out; this is a sign of friendship and love."

standard dangers of ancient desert travel. He is also concerned about how the scholars' new roles will throw them into the public limelight. By juxtaposing his request for protection with a description of the scholars' selection process, Eleazar implies that the qualities which make the scholars popular among Judeans, and their devotion to Jewish ancestral traditions in particular, might be the same qualities that make them vulnerable to Egyptian Greeks. His seemingly benign request may allude to the possibility that these Greeks would resent Judean Jews for bringing their foreign laws and scriptures into the Greeks' Hellenistic environment. Aristeas only hints at this potential discord to maintain the veneer of a smooth process that will encounter no friction.

Eleazar's intimation that Judean Jews and Egyptian Greeks will both personally benefit from the Torah's translation is, of course, an Egyptian Jewish fantasy. As we have seen, actual Judean letters to Egyptian Jews express grave concern about Egyptian Jewish loyalty to Judea and implore Egyptian Jews to tether themselves to Judean authority.

The Worldliness of the Judean Translators

Eleazar's enthusiastic willingness to collaborate with Ptolemy on the Torah's translation dissolves the boundaries that separate Egyptian Jews from Judean Jews and implies that Judean Jews perceive Egyptian Jews as their equals. The scholars' mastery of Greek and Jewish wisdom texts, moreover, suggests that they have undergone a training similar to the training that many Jews in Egypt pursued:

> [120b]Now that I have signified to you, my brother Philocrates, what was required concerning these matters under their headings, in what follows I shall now describe the matter of the translation. [121]For he [Eleazar] selected men of the finest character and the highest culture, in view of the fact that they had noble parents. They were men who had not only achieved mastery of Jewish writings but had also studied in no cursory manner the proper style of the Greek writings. [122]Therefore, they were well qualified for embassies, and they fulfilled this duty whenever it was necessary. They possessed a great facility for lectures and questions connected with the law. They strove for the middle condition, for this is always the finest, abjuring rough and barbarous thoughts; but they were likewise above conceitedness and believing that they could look down at others, and in conversation they were ready to listen and give an answer to each person appropriately. And all of them carefully observed these

practices and wished to excel each other most of all in them, and they were all worthy of their teacher [Eleazar] and of his virtue. ¹²³And one could observe how they loved Eleazar by their unwillingness to be torn away from him and how he loved them. For besides what he wrote to the king concerning their return, he also frequently urged Andreas to make it happen, urging me to be of assistance, in whatever way we should be able. (Let. Aris. 120b–123)

Aristeas's emphasis on the Judean scholars' impressive knowledge of Greek and Jewish traditions indicates that Egyptian Jews, who are about to gain access to Jewish written traditions, will soon have the capacity to attain these same levels of scholarship. The potential of Egyptian Jews to reach the greatest heights of erudition subverts the Judean notion that Egyptian Jews lack the tools necessary to achieve religious piety. Egyptian Jews, in fact, are more well-positioned than most of their Judean counterparts to attain piety and wisdom. Eleazar presents the Judean translators' knowledge of Greek scholarship as impressive because such knowledge was atypical among Judean Jews. Egyptian Jews, however, have access to both Greek and Jewish traditions and thus have an advantage over Judean Jews, who do not know Greek and have no access to Greek wisdom texts.

The Judean Symposium

Aristeas's climactic scene is a seven-day symposium during which Ptolemy assembles the Judean scholars and questions them about wisdom and leadership.[32] The king reacts with amazement as each scholar showcases his unyielding devotion to Jewish ancestral tradition and attunement to Hellenistic philosophical wisdom. The scholars' responses to the king's queries suggest that Jewish values correlate with Greek teachings. They therefore function as affirmations of Aristeas's earlier statement that Jews and Greeks worship the same God.[33] Indeed, the king and his philosopher, Menedemus of Eritrea,

---

32. Referring to the symposium as "week-long," as Gruen does, is anachronistic since Ptolemaic Greeks did not use this unit of time. The seven-day period would have been considered a whole unit not because it was a week long, but because it provided symmetry for twelve of the scholars to respond to the king's questions each day. Twelve and seven may have been regarded as significant numbers in Jewish tradition by this time. See Gruen, "Letter of Aristeas," 424.
33. Note the following declarations: "the cause of good things to all is God, whom it is necessary to follow" (Let. Aris. 205); "God draws all humans to himself by his clemency" (207); "God constantly operates and knows all things in the universe" (210); "God imparts on all kings glory as well as great wealth, and no one is king from himself alone" (224).

praise the scholars at the end of the symposium's first day for making God the focus of their responses (Let. Aris. 201).

Egyptian Jews make no appearance at the king's symposium. Once again, they stand in the story's background, awaiting the completion of a project that will provide them with access to their scriptural traditions. The Judean scholars, meanwhile, are front and center, articulating universalist ideas that impress their Greek hosts with their worldliness. This role reversal suggests that Egyptian Jews and Judean Jews are not separated by a massive gap after all. Hints that the author of Aristeas wanted to dissolve cultural differences between Egyptian and Judean Jews appear in many of the scholars' responses. When the king asks, for example, "How can one be a patriot?" one scholar replies:

> The king said that he had spoken well and then asked another, How might he be a lover of his country? "By committing to the proposition," he replied, "that it is good to live and die in one's own country. The status of foreigner causes contempt for the poor and shame for the rich, as though they had been banished for a crime. Therefore, by bestowing benefits upon all, as you do continually, God will give you favor with all, and you will be manifestly a lover of country." (Let. Aris. 249)

The scholar's negative description of living as a foreigner can be read as an indictment against Jews who immigrated to Egypt from Judea. For the author, however, the Jews of Egypt do not fall into this category. Aristeas begins his letter by clarifying that Egyptian Jews arrived in Egypt as forced immigrants, not as willing settlers. The Jews of Egypt have long established legitimate communities by virtue of their ancient origins and forced migration. Like Judean Jews, Egyptian Jews enjoy permanent residence in their land. Relocation to their homeland of Judea, the scholar implies, would be an act of impiety rather than an act of virtue, since it would turn Egyptian Jews into foreigners.

The Judeans' responses to Ptolemy parallel Eleazar's letter to Ptolemy in their emphasis on the relationship between Jews and Greeks and their disinterest in the relationship between Judean Jews and Egyptian Jews. Ptolemy's questions, and the scholars' answers, indicate that the Torah's translation is to be celebrated because it will bring together two groups of people that worship the same God. The relationship between Egyptian Jews and Judean Jews, however, sits just below the surface of their speeches. Consider the following questions and answers:

> [190][Ptolemy] asked another, How could he have friends like himself? And he replied, "If they see you showing great forethought for the multitudes over whom you rule; you will do this if you observe how God

bestows benefits on the human race, providing for them health and food and all other things in due season."

...

¹⁹⁵This man the king praised and then said to the next, What would be the most excellent thing for him to live his life? And he answered, "To know that God rules all things and that in our finest actions it is not we who achieve what we have planned; rather, God who rules brings all things to fulfillment and guides us."

...

¹⁹⁷The king expressed his agreement with this and after this enquired of the next, How might he bear whatever befell him with moderation? And that one said, "If you grasp the concept that all humans have been created by God share the greatest evils as well as the greatest goods and that it is impossible for a human to be exempt from these. But God, whom we must supplicate, grants courage." ¹⁹⁸Being kindly disposed toward this one, too, the king said that all had spoken well. (Let. Aris. 190, 195, 197–98)

The scholars' answers suggest that the Jews' wisdom traditions offer a blueprint with which to build a society based on the pursuit of a common good for all humanity. Ptolemy's questions concern how a king should rule his subjects, but the scholars provide answers that are widely applicable to any person who desires to attain virtue. Their emphasis on moderation and collaboration indicates that piety can be attained by anyone, provided that they worship the one true God. All Jews, therefore, must not humiliate themselves by becoming an economic drain to their Greek neighbors. Nor should they outperform their neighbors by accumulating excessive wealth that could lead to corruption. Such worthy Jews, especially those who can spread this kind of piety to others, deserve admiration. After the king has asked each scholar a question, he thanks the group and declares that "the greatest good has come to me from your presence" (Let. Aris. 293). The scholars' answers, Aristeas suggests, are evidence of the fact that the Jewish people, despite their distinctive identities that separate them from Greeks, make extraordinary contributions to Greek society.

Aristeas closes his letter by praising Philocrates's desire to better understand the circumstances surrounding the Torah's translation. He also promises to record other material that will help Philocrates attain more learning:

And now, Philocrates, you yourself have my narrative, just as I promised. For I think that you will delight in these books more than in those of the mythologists. For you are inclined toward an intense pursuit of those

things that can benefit the mind and spend much time in them. Now I
shall also attempt to record the rest of the noteworthy things, in order
that, by going through them thoroughly you may win the noblest prize
for your aims. (Let. Aris. 322)

Aristeas's expressions of reverence for older writings in his closing words to
Philocrates parallel the speeches of heroes in his story, who lovingly transmit
cherished writings to their friends. The connection between Aristeas's story
and his literary frame are comparable to contemporaneous Judean letters that
use similar layering techniques. Ben Sira's prologue is also framed as a dispatch
to readers who desire to increase their knowledge of the written scriptures,
and material within the work highlights the authority of the written Torah.
The closing lines of the Judean letter to Egyptian Jews in 2 Macc 1:10–2:18,
moreover, offer to send more literature that support the writers' arguments
(2:13–15) and parallel the accounts within the body of the letter concerning
the preservation of ancient scriptures. Allusions to a seemingly endless supply of ancient texts that reach farther back in time is a form of *mise en abyme*
that gives all these letters, which in their written form can seem stagnant and
constrained, the quality of expansive infinitude.

The Message of Aristeas

The Jewish author of Aristeas lived during a time when Jews in Egypt were
being accused of disloyalty by some of their Egyptian Greek neighbors. These
Greeks resented that Jews practiced their Sabbath, holy days, dietary laws, and
other ancestral traditions at the expense of integrating into Hellenistic society. Rather than responding to these critiques by shrinking into their communities, Jews in Egypt found representation in high-ranking Jewish officials
who attained powerful positions in the courts of Ptolemaic rulers. Some of
these rulers did not enjoy the support of most of the population, and the Jews'
power in their courts contributed to an atmosphere of suspicion toward all
Jews, from the influential to the powerless. The author of Aristeas addressed
these matters by producing a story that seeks to instill pride in Egyptian Jews
and to allay Greek concerns about Jewish disloyalty. Aristeas's author was not
only concerned with the Jewish-Greek relationship. He also wanted to address
Judean complaints that Egyptian Jews were improperly practicing their ancestral laws. Such critiques, which find expression in Judean letters to Egyptian
Jews, are rebutted in Aristeas's presentation of Judean leaders as concerned for
the welfare and integrity of Jews in Egypt. The Judean leaders' support for the
Torah's translation suggest that these leaders endorse the notion that all Jews,

regardless of where they live, can proudly devote themselves to the worship of a universal God and can collaborate with outsiders to share their traditions. The author of Aristeas presents Egyptian Jews as mutual partners in their relationships with both Judean Jews and Egyptian Greeks by writing in the voices of these outsiders, who unite to ensure that Egyptian Jewish life will remain successful and long-lasting.

The Letter of Aristeas is not the only Alexandrian Jewish text that presents Judean Jews and Egyptian Jews as united in mind and spirit. Another text, 3 Maccabees, also seeks to bond Egyptian Jews to the Jews of Judea. Unlike Aristeas, 3 Maccabees is darkly pessimistic about the relationship between Greeks and Jews. Rather than grounding the unshakable bond between Egyptian and Judean Jews in a shared love for the Torah, 3 Maccabees grounds this bond in a shared vulnerability to the forces that seek to annihilate the Jewish people.

CHAPTER 9

"Boundless and Immeasurable Earth": The Prayers of 3 Maccabees

EGYPTIAN JEWS BELIEVED THEMSELVES to be legitimate members of two societies that the first-century Alexandrian Jewish philosopher Philo referred to as a motherland and a fatherland (*Flaccus* 46–47).[1] These Jews likely knew that Judean Jews perceived them as outsiders to Judean Jewish life, and Egyptian Greeks perceived them as outsiders to Egyptian Greek society. Egyptian Jews were not deterred by these attitudes. Instead, they wrote texts that speak in the voices of people who imbue Egyptian Jews with dignity and legitimacy. Some of these texts, like the Letter of Aristeas, sought to establish positive connections with their Greek neighbors. Others, however, did not hold the same optimistic worldview. One such text, known today as 3 Maccabees, presents a less rosy assessment of the Jews' Greek neighbors.[2]

The story begins in the period following the victory of the Ptolemaic king Ptolemy IV Philopator (r. 221–204 BCE) over the Seleucid king Antiochus III (r. 223–187 BCE) at the battle of Raphia. Ptolemy decides to celebrate his victory by entering the Jerusalem Temple's inner sanctum but is miraculously thwarted. Humiliated and furious, Ptolemy resolves to avenge the Judean Jews' insult by annihilating the Jews of Alexandria. He assembles these Jews into the city's hippodrome, where drunken elephants are to trample them to death. Ptolemy's plans, however, are thwarted once again, and he finally realizes that the Jewish people, wherever they live, are shielded from enemies by their loving and merciful god. The story closes with the Jews of Alexandria celebrating their survival by establishing a festival to commemorate the event (3 Macc 7:17–20).

The author's knowledge of Jewish life in Alexandria, interest in the welfare of the Alexandrian Jewish community, and familiarity with the workings of

---

1. Halpern-Amaru, "Land Theology," 65–93; Lieber, "Between Motherland and Fatherland," 193–210; Pearce, "Jerusalem as Mother-City," 19–36.
2. The work has little to do with the Hasmonean dynasty but bears the title "3 Maccabees" in the Alexandrinus and Venetus codices of the Bible. Perhaps the story was associated with Hasmonean heroes because Egyptian Jews viewed the novella, which recalls a plot to kill the Jews of Alexandria, as their version of the Hasmonean story.

the Ptolemaic government make Alexandria the most likely candidate for this story's place of composition. It is even possible that this story is a loose retelling of an actual crisis experienced by Alexandrian Jews. Josephus recounts a nearly identical story that took place under the rule of Ptolemy VIII Physcon, who governed Egypt intermittently between 170 and 116 BCE (*Ag. Ap.* 2.49–55). Dated papyri that record an amnesty decree produced by Physcon, and a royal inscription thanking soldiers for their support, point to the quelling of a civil conflict between Physcon and his siblings, Ptolemy VI and Cleopatra II.[3] Other evidence, such as allusions to crises in Egypt in the letters appended to 2 Maccabees, suggests that a clash took place in Egypt in around 145 BCE, when Physcon returned to Egypt from exile following his brother's death. While the author of 3 Maccabees set his story in the reign of Philopator, it is more likely that he drew from events that took place at this time.[4]

Some scholars suggest that 3 Maccabees was composed well after this crisis and perhaps even after the Roman invasion of Jerusalem in 63 BCE. This catastrophic invasion, which marked the beginning of Judea's Roman occupation, might have inspired an Alexandrian Jew to write a story that transferred the dangers endured by Judean Jews to Jews in Alexandria.[5] Other scholars suggest that the story can be traced to the period following anti-Jewish riots against Alexandrian Jews in 38 CE.[6] There is no need, however, to date 3 Maccabees by linking it to a catastrophic event.[7] The author could have composed his work many generations after any such incident, provided that it was well documented.

Given the political tensions in Egypt during the late second century BCE and first century BCE, and the dating of comparable Jewish texts, it is most likely that 3 Maccabees was written sometime around the turn of the second century BCE.[8] Jews living in Egypt at this time were under pressure to choose sides amid several civil clashes and more than once ended up supporting the

---

3. Material in this inscription overlaps with Physcon's edict recorded in 3 Maccabees. See Lenger, *Corpus des ordonnances des Ptolémées*; Capponi, "Martyrs and Apostates," 294–95.

4. Piotrkowski reviews how scholars have dated 3 Maccabees in "Re-Evaluating 3 Maccabees," 236–60.

5. According to Tcherikover, the reference to *laographia*, a mandatory poll tax (3 Macc 2:28), points to a compositional date following the introduction of the Roman poll tax in 24–23 BCE. See Tcherikover, "Third Book of Maccabees," 1–26; Barclay, *Jews in the Mediterranean Diaspora*, 448.

6. While some scholars suggest that Ptolemy IV Philopator may be a coded stand-in for Gaius Caligula, discrepancies between 3 Maccabees and the events of 38 CE call this theory into question. See Barclay, *Jews in the Mediterranean Diaspora*, 202–3.

7. The suggestions of Willrich and Collins that 3 Maccabees was written within a context of social conflict for the Jewish Alexandrian community are unconvincing. See Willrich, "Der historische Kern," 244–58; Collins, "3 Maccabees," 1752–67. Barclay rejects this position in *Jews in the Mediterranean Diaspora*, 203.

8. Hacham, "Sanctity," 155–79.

losing candidate, which nearly led to their ruin.[9] The author of 3 Maccabees might have also been influenced by the challenges that Judean Jews faced in the years following the Hasmonean victory over the Seleucid Greeks. Egyptian Jews were especially supportive of the Judean struggle to throw off the Seleucid yoke, since the Seleucids were bitter rivals of the Ptolemaic Kingdom in which they lived.

Some scholars suggest that the divergent attitudes toward Greeks in 3 Maccabees and the Letter of Aristeas indicate that the two works originated in distinct social contexts. As we will see, however, the stories share parallels that indicate that they may have derived from a common environment.[10] Third Maccabees also shares connections with 2 Maccabees, which opens with a vignette about an enemy general who intends to invade the Jerusalem Temple but is miraculously thwarted. The story even bears resonances with the Greek version of Esther, which was produced in the early first century BCE.[11] Based on the likelihood that Aristeas, 2 Maccabees, and Greek Esther were in circulation by the middle of the first century BCE, it is reasonable to surmise that 3 Maccabees was produced by this time as well.[12]

The Message of 3 Maccabees

Third Maccabees is sometimes read as a story about the hazardous relationship between Jews in Egypt and their Hellenistic rulers. Read through this lens, the book was written to dissuade Egyptian Jews from assimilating into Hellenistic culture. This objective, however, could have been easily accomplished without the book's opening vignette about the king's failed attempt to enter the Jerusalem Temple. The central role that Judean Jews play at the outset of the novella suggests that the author also wanted to convey a message about the relationship between Judean and Egyptian Jews. By linking the destinies of Judean Jews with the destinies of Egyptian Jews, the author makes the case that God protects all Jews, wherever they live.[13] This reading might explain why the author set his story during the rule of Ptolemy IV Philopator, even if he knew that the crisis that inspired him took place during the reign

---

9. Barclay, *Jews in the Mediterranean Diaspora*, 37–39.
10. Barclay, *Jews in the Mediterranean Diaspora*, 202–3; Johnson, *Historical Fictions*, 136. Hadas reads 3 Maccabees as a response to the Letter of Aristeas in *Letter of Aristeas*, 32–38.
11. Hacham, "3 Maccabees and Esther," 765–85.
12. Barclay, *Jews in the Mediterranean Diaspora*, 448; Hacham, "Sanctity," 177; Williams, "3 Maccabees," 23; D. Schwartz, *2 Maccabees*, 87; Kasher, *Jews in Hellenistic and Roman Egypt*, 212–13n16; Johnson, *Historical Fictions*, 32–35; Croy, *3 Maccabees*, xiii; Mélèze Modrzejewski, *Troisième livre des Maccabées*,123.
13. Williams, "3 Maccabees," 17–29.

of Ptolemy VIII Physcon. Philopator's triumph at the battle of Raphia placed him near Jerusalem and enabled the author to seamlessly incorporate Judean Jews into his story by adding a legend about Philopator wanting to celebrate his victory at the Jerusalem Temple.[14]

Third Maccabees's accounts of the Jerusalem Temple's near invasion and the Alexandrian Jews' near annihilation employ common phrases to describe the Jews of Judea and Egypt. The author referred to Jews as a "nation" (*ethnos*; 1:11; 2:27, 33) and as "fellow nationals" (*homoethneis*; 4:12; 7:14).[15] The notion that Jews comprise a single polity correlates with the idea that they are threatened by common enemies, who are identified as "those of another nation" (*alloethneis*; 4:6).[16] These designations reverse the standard social order. Rather than depicting Egyptian Jews as living on the margins of both Hellenistic and Jewish society, the author presented all Jews as united against a cultural outsider, the Ptolemaic Kingdom. In this framework, the fate of Alexandrian Jews functions as a stand-in for the fate of Jews everywhere.[17]

The author of 3 Maccabees had Judean and Egyptian Jews soften the boundaries around their ethnogeographic identities to enforce the idea that Jews were united in their devotion to Jerusalem. These Jews experienced the same crises and were equal beneficiaries of God's salvation. The author had a Jerusalem high priest affirm God's universal dominion, which diminished Judean exceptionalism, and he had an Egyptian Jewish elder bemoan the Jews' past suffering and highlight their reliance on God for salvation. By drawing comparisons between the fate of Jews in Judea and the fate of Jews in Alexandria, the author assured his Egyptian Jewish audience that all Jews experience the same existential threats at the hands of outsiders.

Some scholars read 3 Maccabees as a festival etiology that provides the backstory to an established Jewish holiday.[18] An etiological reading, however,

---

14. Williams, "3 Maccabees," 21.
15. Barclay, *Jews in the Mediterranean Diaspora*, 197–98.
16. Jews and Greeks are also identified according to race, with Jews being referred to as a *genos*. Those of the same race are *homophuloi* (3 Macc 3.21), and those of other races are *allophuloi* (3.6). The confusion over whether Jews are a race or a nation reflects the confusion about what precisely Jews actually were at this time. See Barclay, *Jews in the Mediterranean Diaspora*, 197–98.
17. While Williams posits that the author of 3 Maccabees sought to legitimize diasporic Judaism to an audience that included Judean Jews, Hacham goes further by arguing that the author's presentation of God's revelatory salvation in Alexandria was meant to surpass God's manifestation in the Jerusalem Temple. Hacham's claim that the author believed that God's presence is more apparent in the diaspora than in Judea, and thus the diasporic community is portrayed as superior to the Judean community, goes too far. See Hacham, "Sanctity," 161–65; Williams, "3 Maccabees," 17–29; White and Keddie, *Jewish Fictional Letters*, 344–45.
18. Esther and 2 Maccabees, for example, are etiological texts. See Bickerman, "Makkabäerbücher (III)," 797–800; Eissfeldt, *Old Testament*, 202–3. It is possible that the Letter of Aristeas was also written in part to clarify the origins of a festival celebrating the production of the Septuagint

does not explain all of 3 Maccabees's narrative features. Third Maccabees only mentions the Jews' celebration in two verses and does not mention a mandate that Jews celebrate this commemorative holiday for perpetuity (6:36; 7:19).[19] It is more likely that 3 Maccabees includes etiological features because its author drew from Esther and the Letter of Aristeas, which are more obviously etiological works. Like the authors of these novellas, the author of 3 Maccabees wrote in the voices of outsiders to affirm his belief in the legitimacy of Jewish life outside the land of Israel.

Aristeas and 3 Maccabees are sometimes contrasted with one another because of their opposing attitudes toward Hellenistic culture.[20] The author of Aristeas believed that Jewish values correlate with and even enhance Hellenistic ideas, while the author of 3 Maccabees maintained that adherence to Jewish laws was in tension with adherence to Greek customs and values. Both novellas feature a Ptolemaic king and a high priest of the Jerusalem Temple. But while Aristeas has the high priest express close friendship with the king, 3 Maccabees has the high priest plead with God to prevent the king's violation of the temple. Despite these differences, Aristeas and 3 Maccabees both argue that Egyptian and Judean Jews share a common history and an interconnected future. The authors of both works also understood that an Egyptian Jewish argument legitimizing Egyptian Jewry was less impactful than a Judean argument legitimizing Egyptian Jewry. They therefore counteracted Judean texts that use ventriloquy to denigrate Jewish life in Egypt by speaking in the voices of Judeans who embrace Egyptian Jewish life.

Unlike Aristeas and 3 Maccabees, which are often contrasted with one another, scholars compare the Greek version of Esther with 3 Maccabees because both books feature an antagonist who wants to annihilate the Jewish people.[21] Both books also suggest that Jewish life outside the land of Israel is inherently dangerous.[22] When it comes to the relationship between

---

that is mentioned in Philo, *Moses* 2.41–43, but the author clearly has broader interests that motivate him as well.

19. The verses that describe the Jews' celebrations make no mention of future annual observance, and refer to two distinct celebrations. Josephus's version of this story, however, includes a note that Alexandrian Jews celebrate their salvation with an annual festival (*Ag. Ap.* 2.55). The author of 3 Maccabees was either not aware of such a festival because it was not yet instituted and widespread, or he did not regard it as central to his story. See Cousland, "Reversal, Recidivism and Reward," 42.

20. White and Keddie, *Jewish Fictional Letters*, 344; Johnson, *Historical Fictions*, 141; Hadas, *Letter of Aristeas*, 11–12; Emmet, "Third Book of Maccabees," 1:156.

21. Hacham, "3 Maccabees and Esther," 765–85. White and Keddie, *Jewish Fictional Letters*, 342–44; Mogliano-Tromp, "Relations Between Egyptian Judaism," 57–76.

22. See Esther's claim that "Ever since I was born I have heard in the tribe of my family that you, O Lord, took Israel out of all the nations.... And now we have sinned before you, and you have handed us over to our enemies ... [T]hey are not satisfied that we are in bitter slavery, but

TABLE 2. Attitudes Toward Host Government and Judean Jewry in 3 Maccabees, the Letter of Aristeas, and Greek Esther

	3 Maccabees	Letter of Aristeas	Greek Esther
Host government (Persians and Greeks)	Negative	Positive	Negative
Judean Jewry	Positive: Judean-Egyptian Jewish unity	Positive: Judean-Egyptian Jewish unity	Positive: Judean authority over Egyptian Jewry

Jews within and without the land of Israel, however, Esther and 3 Maccabees diverge. Third Maccabees insists that all Jews, wherever they live, share a common destiny because they share a common existential threat. Jews in Egypt and Jews in Judea are thus fundamentally connected to one another. The Greek version of Esther, on the other hand, does not feature Judean Jews and Egyptian Jews as distinct populations. Yet its colophon indicates that the work was meant to be read by Egyptian Jews as a Judean tale that warns of the particular dangers of exile. The Judean author of this work believed that the suffering that Jews outside the land of Israel experienced was specific to life outside the homeland.

The contrasts that scholars have drawn between 3 Maccabees on the one hand and Aristeas and Greek Esther on the other are based on readings that address the relationship between Jews and non-Jews. A comparison of these texts through the lens of intra-Jewish relations, however, indicates that 3 Maccabees is aligned with Aristeas and contrasts with Greek Esther (see table 2). The differences between these texts correlate with their place of composition. The two Alexandrian works cite Judeans who express their concern for the integrity of Jewish life outside Judea. In these works, Judeans strive for global Jewish unity. The Greek version of Esther, however, features prayers that negatively refer to the exile and do not attempt to reconcile Judean and diasporic Jewish populations with one another. Greek Esther also advocates for the widespread observance of a Jewish holiday on the basis of its Judean derivation, while 3 Maccabees praises the establishment of a holiday that links the salvation of Alexandrian Jewry to the salvation of Judean Jewry. The observance of this holiday affirms rather than negates Egyptian Jewish life, even as the Jews who observe it are also committed to celebrating holidays that affirm the central role of Jerusalem and its temple.

---

they have covenanted with their idols to abolish what your mouth has ordained, and to destroy your inheritance, to stop the mouths of those who praise you and to quench your altar and the glory of your house" (Add Esth C 14:5a, 6, 8–9).

Third Maccabees is not framed as a letter, but its abrupt opening suggests that the story may be missing an introductory section. This section could have framed the text by attributing it to an authoritative figure and by addressing a particular audience.[23] Third Maccabees's conclusion, which notes that the Jews of Alexandria recorded the story of their salvation, may have once paralleled such an opening section. This framing would have brought the text in line with others that we have examined and would have paralleled the book's internal layering techniques that amplify the author's message. These techniques, which are found in the prayers for salvation attributed to the Judean high priest Simon and the Alexandrian elder Eleazar, make a case for the integrity of Egyptian Jewry and suggest that Egyptian and Judean Jews share a common destiny.

Simon's Prayer

When King Philopator decides to visit Jerusalem and enter the temple sanctuary at the outset of the story, local Jews become alarmed, and the high priest Simon utters a prayer that asks God to prevent the king's entry.[24] Simon's prayer shares thematic features with letters, speeches, and prayers that were written in Judea. Like the exhortatory letters appended to 2 Maccabees, which describe God's miraculous intervention in Judean affairs, and like the exiled Judahites' letter in Baruch, which asks Judahite leaders in Jerusalem to pray for God's salvation, Simon's prayer asks God to save the people as a demonstrative act that shows commitment to the covenantal relationship between God and Israel. Simon's prayer also parallels these Judean documents in the way that it highlights personal connections between the speaker and recipient to make its request more compelling. Most significantly, Simon's prayer, like these other letters and prayers, speaks in the voices of outsiders. And yet, unlike these Judean texts, Simon's prayer does not ask God to put an end to Jewish life outside the land of Israel.[25] It also does not suggest that Jews who live outside the land are embodiments of divine rejection.

Simon opens his prayer by praising God as a king whose power supersedes the human king that threatens the people. He praises God as the "king of the heavens, and sovereign of all creation" (3 Macc 2:2), the "creator of all things and the governor of all" (2:3), and the "Ruler over the whole creation" (2:7).

---

23. Contra Hacham, "3 Maccabees," 290.
24. This Simon would have been Simon II, son of Onias II, who held the position of high priest in 219–196 BCE. Cf. the Greek version of Sir 50:1–21; Josephus, *Ant.* 12:43, 157; Barclay, *Jews in the Mediterranean Diaspora*, 189.
25. Bar 1:15–3:8; cf. Ezra 9; Neh 9; Dan 9. See Collins, "3 Maccabees," 1756.

The keywords of his speech, *creator* and *creation* (*ktisas*; *ktisis*), unite the twin claims that God chose the people of Israel and is universally powerful. These juxtaposed themes imply that God's choosing Israel has universal stakes, and that the people's suffering, therefore, calls God's omnipotence into question:

> ¹Then the high priest Simon, facing the sanctuary, bending his knees and extending his hands with calm dignity, prayed as follows: ²"Lord, Lord, king of the heavens, and sovereign of all creation, holy among the holy ones, the only ruler, almighty, give attention to us who are suffering grievously from an impious and profane man, puffed up in his audacity and power. ³For you, the creator of all things and the governor of all, are a just Ruler, and you judge those who have done anything in insolence and arrogance." (3 Macc 2:1–3)

The prayer's first section (2:1–13) depicts God in constant action. God is the exclusive sovereign over the universe and the righteous ruler over all humanity who administers justice to those who are insubordinate (2:2–3). God's interest in protecting Israel, Simon continues, is active and perpetual:

> ⁴You destroyed those who in the past committed injustice, among whom were even giants who trusted in their strength and boldness, whom you destroyed by bringing on them a boundless flood. ⁵You consumed with fire and sulfur the people of Sodom who acted arrogantly, who were notorious for their vices; and you made them an example to those who should come afterward. ⁶You made known your mighty power by inflicting many and varied punishments on the audacious Pharaoh who had enslaved your holy people Israel. ⁷And when he pursued them with chariots and a mass of troops, you overwhelmed him in the depths of the sea, but carried through safely those who had put their confidence in you, the Ruler over the whole creation. ⁸And when they had seen works of your hands, they praised you, the Almighty. ⁹You, O King, when you had created the boundless and immeasurable earth, chose this city and sanctified this place for your name, though you have no need of anything; and when you had glorified it by your magnificent manifestation, you made it a firm foundation for the glory of your great and honored name. ¹⁰And because you love the house of Israel, you promised that if we should have reverses, and tribulation should overtake us, you would listen to our petition when we come to this place and pray. ¹¹And indeed you are faithful and true. ¹²And because oftentimes when our fathers were oppressed you helped them in their humiliation, and rescued them from great evils, ¹³see now, O holy King, that because of our many and

great sins we are crushed with suffering, subjected to our enemies, and overtaken by helplessness. (3 Macc 2:4–13)

As this section progresses, Simon develops an image of a bustling God who ensures the well-being of undeserving Israelites and protects them from their enemies (2:4–7). Though infinitely powerful, God nevertheless takes a particular interest in the people of Israel and the city of Jerusalem. The same God who created the cosmos chose and sanctified Jerusalem, making it "a firm foundation" upon which the people can celebrate God's glorious name (2:8–9). Because God's relationship with the people is motivated entirely by love, Simon argues, God must act on behalf of Israel's welfare once again (2:11–13). The prayer's next section homes in on the current crisis:

> [14] In our downfall this audacious and profane man undertakes to violate the holy place on earth dedicated to your glorious name. [15] For your dwelling is the heaven of heavens, unapproachable by human beings. [16] But because you graciously bestowed your glory on your people Israel, you sanctified this place. [17] Do not punish us for the defilement committed by these men, or call us to account for this profanation, otherwise the transgressors will boast in their wrath and exult in the arrogance of their tongue, saying, [18] "We have trampled down the house of the sanctuary as the houses of the abominations are trampled down." [19] Wipe away our sins and disperse our errors, and reveal your mercy at this hour. [20] Speedily let your mercies overtake us, and put praises in the mouth of those who are downcast and broken in spirit, and give us peace. (3 Macc 2:14–20)

Simon's closing petition appeals to God on three counts: the defilement of the temple will violate God's honor ("you sanctified this place," 2:16); the defilement of the temple will provide a victory to God's enemies, who will "boast in their wrath and exult in the arrogance of their tongue" (2:17); and the defilement of the temple will be unjust in light of the people's desire to repent ("wipe away our sins and disperse our errors"; 2:19). Simon admits that this repentance has yet to fully take place. Still, Philopator's violation would tarnish God's reputation among the nations and would threaten the potential for universal recognition of God's dominion. Through this petition, the Egyptian Jewish author speaks in the voice of a Judean high priest—who in turn speaks in the voices of Greek enemies—to affirm a connection between all Jews and a binary between Jews and enemy outsiders.

Simon's prayer clarifies that in the past, God punished the people not with exile but with increased susceptibility to their enemies, who threaten Jews wherever they may be. His prayer, therefore, makes no distinction between how God treats Jews who live in Judea versus how God treats Jews who live elsewhere. Rather than recalling specific experiences of exile, as Judean prayers do, Simon describes general Jewish suffering and God's providential rescue (2:12). Along with the rest of the incident concerning Ptolemy's near invasion of the temple, Simon's prayer functions as a complement to the rest of 3 Maccabees. Without this subplot, the reader might treat the text as an exclusively Egyptian Jewish story.

Ptolemy IV Philopator's Edict

After Philopator's attempt to enter the temple is thwarted (3 Macc 2:21–24), he implements a plan to take revenge on Jews who live in the heart of his empire (2:25–30). The decision to transfer culpability from one community of Jews to another suggests that all Jews are interconnected. This transference recalls the story of Esther, in which Haman responds to Mordecai's insolence by seeking vengeance against all Jews in the Persian Kingdom. Whereas Esther's story does not acknowledge the presence of Jews in the land of Israel, 3 Maccabees makes a point of distinguishing between the Jews of Egypt and Judea and noting the connections that bring them together. Philopator's edict, which complains about the Judean Jews' offenses and announces the decision to annihilate the Jews of Alexandria, demonstrates this dynamic. The edict opens by describing Philopator's clash with the Jews of Jerusalem:

> [12] King Ptolemy Philopator to his generals and soldiers in Egypt and all its districts, greetings and good health: [13] I myself and our government are faring well. [14] When our expedition took place in Asia, as you yourselves know, it was brought to conclusion, according to plan, by the gods' deliberate alliance with us in battle, [15] and we considered that we should not rule the nations inhabiting Coele Syria and Phoenicia by the power of the spear, but should cherish them with clemency and great benevolence, gladly treating them well. [16] And when we had granted very great revenues to the temples in the cities, we came on to Jerusalem also, and went up to honor the temple of those wicked people, who never cease from their folly. [17] They accepted our presence by word, but insincerely by deed, because when we proposed to enter their inner temple and honor it with magnificent and most beautiful offerings, [18] they were carried away by their traditional arrogance, and excluded us from entering; but they were spared the exercise of our power because of the benevolence that we have towards all. [19] By maintaining their manifest ill will

towards us, they become the only people among all nations who hold their heads high in defiance of kings and their own benefactors, and are unwilling to regard any action as sincere. (3 Macc 3:12–19)

Philopator declares that he had once intended to govern the regions of Coele Syria and Phoenicia with generosity. The "wicked people" of Jerusalem, however, initially welcomed Philopator with words of loyalty and then shocked him with their refusal to allow him entry into their temple. Philopator interprets the Judean Jews' resistance to his entry as proof of their deceitfulness and arrogance. Philopator then recalls a parallel incident with the Alexandrian Jewish community:

> [20] But we, when we arrived in Egypt victorious, accommodated ourselves to their folly and did as was proper, since we treat all nations with benevolence. [21] Among other things, we made known to all our amnesty toward their compatriots here, both because of their alliance with us and the myriad affairs liberally entrusted to them from the beginning; and we ventured to make a change, by deciding both to deem them worthy of Alexandrian citizenship and to make them participants in our regular religious rites. [22] But in their innate malice they took this in a contrary spirit, and disdained what is good. Since they incline constantly to evil, [23] they not only spurn the priceless citizenship, but also both by speech and by silence they abominate those few among them who are sincerely disposed towards us; in every situation, in accordance with their infamous way of life, they secretly suspect that we may soon alter our policy. (3 Macc 3:20–23)

Philopator declares that he sought to make Alexandrian Jews "worthy of Alexandrian citizenship" by including them in his religious rites. The Alexandrian Jews' rejection of this honor, however, has further proven to Philopator that all Jews are irreparably misanthropic. Like the Judean Jews who incurred the king's wrath, Egyptian Jews possess irredeemable qualities. They bear "innate malice," a "contrary spirit," "disdained what is good," and "incline constantly to evil." These Jews, however, are not quite like the two-faced Jews of Judea, who welcomed Philopator into Jerusalem but resisted his entry into the temple. The Jews of Egypt are consistent. They spurn citizenship "both by speech and by silence … in every situation." By characterizing all Jews as separatists but depicting some as explicitly separatist and others as privately separatist, Philopator's letter sows suspicion of every Jew in his empire, even those who were not involved in these incidents. Philopator then declares that all Jews should be rounded up and handed over to his government:

²⁴"Therefore, fully convinced by these indications that they are ill disposed towards us in every way, we have taken precautions so that, if a sudden disorder later arises against us, we shall not have these impious people behind our backs as traitors and barbarous enemies. ²⁵Therefore we have given orders that, as soon as this letter arrives, you are to send to us those who live among you, together with their wives and children, with insulting and harsh treatment, and bound securely with iron fetters, to suffer the sure and shameful death that befits enemies. ²⁶For when all of these have been punished, we are sure that for the remaining time the government will be established for ourselves in good order and in the best state. ²⁷But those who shelter any of the Jews, whether old people or children or even infants, will be tortured to death with the most hateful torments, together with their families. ²⁸Any who are willing to give information will receive the property of those who incur the punishment, and also two thousand drachmas from the royal treasury, and will be awarded their freedom. ²⁹Every place detected sheltering a Jew is to be made unapproachable and burned with fire, and shall become useless for all time to any mortal creature. (3 Macc 3:24–29)

The author of 3 Maccabees speaks in the voice of an enemy king who imagines how the Jews of his kingdom speak about his own people.[26] This ventriloquy suggests that outsiders perceive Judean Jews and Egyptian Jews as equally impious and ill disposed toward their Greek neighbors (3:19, 22–23). In Philopator's edict, the Jews of Alexandria are not mere substitutes for the Jewish community in Judea. They are guilty of the same crimes committed by their Judean brethren. By suggesting that Jews in Egypt and Judea are equally prone to persecution, the author undermines the Judean claim that Egyptian Jewish suffering signifies God's particular dissatisfaction with Jews outside the land of Israel.

Eleazar's Prayer

An Alexandrian elder named Eleazar responds to Philopator's edict with a prayer that parallels the prayer of Simon. Like Simon, Eleazar does not distinguish between the suffering of Jews in Judea and the suffering of Jews who live

---

26. Ptolemy's letter parallels the letter of Artaxerxes in Greek Esther that announces his decision to kill the Jews of the Persian Kingdom (Addition B). Like Ptolemy's letter, the edict opens with references to the king's prior conquests that brought the kingdom peace and presents the Jewish people as misanthropic and insular, qualities that threaten to destabilize the kingdom's fragile tranquility.

elsewhere. He also affirms that the Jerusalem Temple is the holiest spot for all Jewish people but indicates that God's relationship with the Jews is unaffected by a diasporic divide:

> ²King of great power, Almighty God Most High, governing all creation with mercy, ³look upon the descendants of Abraham, O Father, upon the children of the sainted Jacob, a people of your consecrated portion who are perishing as foreigners in a foreign land. ⁴Pharaoh with his abundance of chariots, the former ruler of this Egypt, exalted with lawless insolence and boastful tongue, you destroyed together with his arrogant army by drowning them in the sea, manifesting the light of your mercy on the nation of Israel. ⁵Sennacherib exulting in his countless forces, oppressive king of the Assyrians, who had already gained control of the whole world by the spear and was lifted up against your holy city, speaking grievous words with boasting and insolence, you, O Lord, broke in pieces, showing your power to many nations. ⁶The three companions in Babylon who had voluntarily surrendered their lives to the flames so as not to serve vain things, you rescued unharmed, even to a hair, moistening the fiery furnace with dew and turning the flame against all their enemies. ⁷Daniel, who through envious slanders was thrown down into the ground to lions as food for wild animals, you brought up to the light unharmed. ⁸And Jonah, wasting away in the belly of a huge, sea-born monster, you, Father, watched over and restored unharmed to all his family. (3 Macc 6:2–8)

Eleazar opens his prayer by highlighting four examples of God's special care for the people of Israel. The first two, which describe God's defeat of Pharaoh and the Neo-Assyrian king Sennacherib, concentrate on God's triumphs over Israel's enemies. The second two, which recount God's salvation of Daniel and Jonah, focus on God's protection of righteous heroes. God's concern for Israel in this prayer extends well beyond the region of Judea. The prayer's geographic scope ranges from Egypt to Babylon and from Judea to the sea. Its chronological scope, moreover, ranges from Assyrian to Persian rule. The defeat of these kingdoms suggests that God's control over creation traverses space and time. Whereas Sennacherib merely "gained control of the whole world by the spear," God can defeat all of humanity on a whim and yet governs "all creation with mercy" (6:2, 5). While Eleazar is not at home in Egypt, he believes that Jews who live there enjoy the same divine love and protection as Jews in Judea. Eleazar then turns to the present crisis:

> ⁹And now, you who hate insolence, all-merciful and protector of all, reveal yourself quickly to those of the nation of Israel—who are being

outrageously treated by the abominable and lawless Gentiles. ¹⁰If our lives have become entangled in impieties in our exile, rescue us from the hand of the enemy, and destroy us, Lord, by whatever fate you choose. ¹¹Let not the vain-minded praise their vanities at the destruction of your beloved people, saying, "Not even their god has rescued them." ¹²But you, O Eternal One, who have all might and all power, watch over us now and have mercy on us who by the senseless insolence of the lawless are being deprived of life in the manner of traitors. ¹³And let the Gentiles cower today in fear of your invincible might, O honored One, who have power to save the nation of Jacob. ¹⁴The whole throng of infants and their parents entreat you with tears. ¹⁵Let it be shown to all the Gentiles that you are with us, O Lord, and have not turned your face from us; but just as you have said, "Not even when they were in the land of their enemies did I neglect them," so accomplish it, O Lord. (3 Macc 6:9–15)[27]

Both halves of Eleazar's prayer open with statements that seem to denigrate Jewish life outside Judea. Eleazar begins by asking God to "look upon the descendants of Abraham ... who are perishing as foreigners in a foreign land" (6:3). The second half of his prayer similarly begins with a request that God show mercy to those who have been oppressed by their enemies due to "impieties in our exile" (6:10). For Eleazar, however, exile is not worrisome because it symbolizes divine rejection, but rather because it endangers Jewish people through increased exposure to outsiders and temptations that lead to sin. Such temptations are more widespread outside the homeland, though Jews can nevertheless achieve piety and enjoy divine protection wherever they are. What matters to Eleazar is not where the people are, but whether they are protected by God.

It is perhaps for this reason that Eleazar addresses God as a father (*pater*). Just as a father protects his child wherever the child is, Eleazar asks God to intervene on behalf of all Jews, who are entitled to this protection. *Pater*, moreover, is related to *patris*, "fatherland," a term that Jews in Alexandria might have used in reference to the land of Israel.[28] Perhaps Eleazar uses *pater* to suggest that the Father, not the fatherland, will save the Jewish people by restoring them to their peaceful lives in Egypt. Unlike the exitled people in Judean texts,

---

27. In verse 10 I have modified the NRSV's translation of the Greek conjunction *ei* from "even if" to "if." "Even if" gives too much weight to the conjunction. By suggesting a close correlation between this phrase and the previous verse, the NRSV's rendering implies that the people's exilic circumstances are a sign of their negative standing with God. The phrase is better rendered as "If our lives have become entangled in our exile."

28. *Patris* appears in Greek Esther and 2 Maccabees, which both share cultural influences with 3 Maccabees (Esth 2:10, 20; 8:6; 2 Macc 4:1; 8:21, 33; 13:1, 10, 14; 14:18).

who beg God to restore them to the land of Israel, Eleazar never asks God to uproot his people and bring them to Judea.

The author of 3 Maccabees embedded multiple layers of ventriloquy into Eleazar's speech that affirm God's unique connection with all Jews. Eleazar imagines that if God does not rescue the Jews, other nations will mockingly declare that "not even their god has rescued them" (6:11). Eleazar also cites God's past promises of protection to the Israelite people, noting that God has boasted, "not even when they were in the land of their enemies did I neglect them" (6:15).[29] Eleazar quotes God and the nations to make the case that outsiders view the Jewish people as unique. The foreign nations view the Jews as abject and contemptible, but God views the Jews as precious children.

The prayers of Simon and Eleazar are nearly identical. Both associate exile with increased opportunity for sin but not with divine rejection.[30] Both speeches also present Jerusalem as a holy city but insist that God protects all Jews, regardless of where they live.[31] The complementary messages of these prayers are evident in their identical structure. The author sets the stage for both prayers by introducing the speaker with praiseworthy language (2:1; 6:1). Both prayers open by extolling God's control over creation (2:2; 6:2). They move on to describe the present crisis (2:2–3; 6:3) and God's past interventions to save the people (2:4–8; 6:4–8). They then request salvation from God (2:9–12; 6:9), express regret for the sins that have led to the people's suffering (2:13; 6:10), and close by making a case for why God should save the people (2:14–20; 6:11–15).

The only significant difference between these prayers is that the Judean Simon, far more than the Alexandrian Eleazar, underscores God's universal power and protection of all Jews. Like the author of Aristeas, the author of 3 Maccabees avoided having an Egyptian Jewish character make a case for the legitimacy of Egyptian Jewry. Both authors knew that their readers would hear their message differently depending on who was conveying their message.

Ptolemy IV Philopator's Second Edict

At the moment that the Jews of Alexandria are about to be trampled to death by elephants in the city's hippodrome, two angels appear and terrorize the

---

29. 3 Macc 6:15 paraphrases Lev 26:44: "Yet for all that, when they are in the land of their enemies, I will not spurn them, or abhor them so as to destroy them utterly and break my covenant with them; for I am the Lord their God."
30. Contrast this description with the prayer in Baruch, which has exiled Judahites attributing their circumstances to communal sin (Bar 1:15–3:8).
31. Barclay highlights the similarities of these prayers without noting their differences in *Jews in the Mediterranean Diaspora*, 198.

Greek enemy. Amid this confusion, the elephants retreat and trample the Greeks' own army. Witnessing this chaos, Philopator has a change of heart and accuses his friends of misleading him. He then issues a decree that repeals his first edict:

> ¹King Ptolemy Philopator to the generals in Egypt and all in authority in his government, greetings and good health: ²We ourselves and our children are faring well, the great God guiding our affairs according to our desire. ³Certain of our friends, frequently urging us with malicious intent, persuaded us to gather together the Jews of the kingdom in a body and to punish them with barbarous penalties as traitors; ⁴for they declared that our government would never be firmly established until this was accomplished, because of the ill will that these people had towards all nations. ⁵They also led them out with harsh treatment as slaves, or rather as traitors, and, girding themselves with a cruelty more savage than that of Scythian custom, they tried without any inquiry or examination to put them to death. ⁶ᵃBut we very severely threatened them for these acts, and in accordance with the clemency that we have towards all people we barely spared their lives. (3 Macc 7:1–6a)

As in his first edict, Philopator speaks of the Jews as a single polity that exists outside Hellenistic society. While he initially treats Jews as guilty of misanthropic behaviors, Philopator now presents them as innocent of wrongdoing. The Jews are still a cohesive group but one that deserves admiration. Philopator's second edict transforms the Jewish people from being outsiders who introduce conflict into Greek society into emblems of social unity who embody the values that Greeks cherish. The Jews' unity contrasts with Philopator's own court, which by the end of this story is fractured by infighting. His edict closes with a recognition of the universal God:

> ⁶ᵇSince we have come to realize that the God of heaven surely defends the Jews, always taking their part as a father does for his children, ⁷and since we have taken into account the friendly and firm goodwill that they had towards us and our ancestors, we justly have acquitted them of every charge of whatever kind. ⁸We also have ordered all people to return to their own homes, with no one in any place doing them harm at all or reproaching them for the irrational things that have happened. ⁹For you should know that if we devise any evil against them or cause them any grief at all, we always shall have not a mortal but the Ruler over every power, the Most High God, in everything and inescapably as an antagonist to avenge such acts. Farewell. (3 Macc 7:6b–9)

Like the prayers of Simon and Eleazar, Philopator speaks of God as a protective caretaker by using paternal language ("always taking their part as a father does for his children"; 7:6) and he couples this language with descriptions of God's universal power. The Egyptian Jewish writer thus has all of his main characters—an Egyptian Jew, a Judean Jew, and a foreign king—affirm his belief that, just as a parent does not constrain care for their child to the home, God's care for the Jewish people is not limited to the land of Israel.

The Festival Celebration

The Jews of Alexandria joyfully celebrate their miraculous salvation with two festivals. The first is a public celebration that establishes "a public rite for these things in their whole community and for their descendants" (6:36). Once the Jews receive formal permission to be dismissed to their homes, they travel to Ptolemais, where they celebrate again for another seven days. This longer celebration may have been motivated by a cautious desire to wait for the king's edict to spread throughout the kingdom:[32]

> [17]When they had arrived at Ptolemais, called "rose-bearing" because of a characteristic of the place, the fleet waited for them, in accordance with the common desire, for seven days. [18]There they celebrated their deliverance, for the king had generously provided all things to them for their journey until all of them arrived at their own houses. [19]And when they had all landed in peace with appropriate thanksgiving, there too in like manner they decided to observe these days as a joyous festival during the time of their stay. [20]Then, after inscribing them as holy on a pillar and dedicating a place of prayer at the site of the festival, they departed unharmed, free, and overjoyed, since at the king's command they had all of them been brought safely by land and sea and river to their own homes. (3 Macc 7:17–20)

In the midst of their celebrating, the Jews produce a written record that describes the story of their near annihilation.[33] The image of Jews establishing

---

32. The king issues a public letter after the first festival declaring that no one should harm the Jews (3 Macc 7:1–9), and the Jews petition the king to execute "those of the Jewish nation who had wilfully transgressed against the holy God and the law of God" (7:10). This incident contrasts with Esther, which ends with a conflict that results in the deaths of five hundred Persians in the citadel of Susa, three hundred others in the city, and seventy-five thousand more across the entire kingdom (Esth 9:6, 15–16). It is also reminiscent of the civil conflict in Exod 32:27–28, wherein three thousand Israelites are killed in the wake of the golden calf episode.

33. Barclay suggests that the detail concerning how the Jews "decided to observe these days as a joyous festival during the time of their stay" (3 Macc 7:19) suggests that the author

a holiday and certifying it with an act of writing evokes scenes in other Egyptian and Judean Jewish texts that treat writing and public reading as sacred acts that unite Jewish people by linking them to a common past.[34] In the Letter of Aristeas, Judean translators celebrate the production of the Septuagint by having Demetrius, head of the Alexandrian library, read the work before an assembly of Jews (Let. Aris. 302, 308). The book of Baruch, likewise, opens with a description of the scribe in exile reading a letter to leaders in Jerusalem before an assembly of Judahites (Bar 1:1, 3). Actual correspondence between Judean and Egyptian Jews also anchor their arguments in earlier acts of writing. Jedaniah's letter to officials in Judea, the Judean letters to Egyptian Jews appended to 2 Maccabees, the prologue of Ben Sira's Greek translation, and the colophon of Greek Esther all reference older documents that were read, copied, and recited.[35]

Jewish writers in the Hellenistic era believed that writing stories was a safeguard to ensure that Jews would properly celebrate their festivals. But the importance of writing and circulating these stories went far beyond the observance of Jewish festivals. Writing was a significant and sacred act in itself, a bridge between the ancient past and an uncertain future. The Jews who produced, preserved, and transmitted their written stories were admired for imitating the actions of ancestors who, centuries earlier, worked to preserve these same stories. As sacred stories were disseminated, the events they commemorated were continually reexperienced by new generations of Jews who transmitted them. These reexperiences, then, took place not only in the observance of holidays that were connected to significant events in Jewish history. They also took place in the process of reading stories that recounted their origins.

The common threats that Egyptian and Judean Jews encounter in 3 Maccabees, along with their shared access to divine protection, transform Egyptian Jewish life from being a doubly liminal experience to being paradigmatic of an authentic Jewish identity. The result of this transformation reminded Egyptian Jewish readers that they could attain piety and benefit from divine love, even outside the land of Israel.

Third Maccabees was written at a time when Jews living in Egypt were navigating a delicate relationship with their host empire. These Jews paid close attention to events in Judea, where their Jewish kin were navigating similarly

---

perceives the diaspora as temporary (*Jews in the Mediterranean Diaspora*, 198). Yet this phrase is not about the diaspora; it is about the Jews' time at Ptolemais.

34. 3 Maccabees's closing benediction, "Blessed be the Deliverer of Israel through all times! Amen," suggests that the text was meant for public recitation (7:23).

35. See Jedaniah's letter preserved at Elephantine: B19 TAD A4.7 Cowley 30 (Sachau Plates 1–2); 2 Macc 1:7–8; 2:1, 4, 13–15; Esth 9:20–29, and the colophon of Greek Esther.

fragile relationships with Seleucid Greeks, Ptolemaic Greeks, and the Republic of Rome. The author of 3 Maccabees was probably aware that Judean Jews wanted Egyptian Jews to show fealty to Judea. He was glad to acquiesce to such requests, but on his terms. Rather than merely presenting the Jerusalem Temple as the locus of Jewish life, the author wanted to show that Judean and Egyptian Jews stand on equal footing before God. He therefore wrote a story about an enemy king who makes no distinction between Egyptian Jews and Judean Jews. The king substitutes all Jews for one another and marginalizes them in ways that force Jews into a state of interconnectedness. Only the Jews who recognize this interconnectedness can strengthen themselves by invoking their collective right to divine protection.

The Letter of Aristeas and 3 Maccabees include letters and speeches in which Judean Jews and Egyptian Greeks express their love for Egyptian Jews. These outsiders do not acknowledge Judean exceptionalism or Judean authority. Nor do they express hope that Egyptian Jews will soon return to the land of Israel. Instead, they share a conviction that Egyptian Jews play a key role in bringing knowledge of the universal God to all the world's nations. They also underscore the themes of Egyptian Jewish piety and divine universality. Taken together, these ideas respond to Judean accusations that Jews in Egypt observed an inauthentic form of their ancestral practices. They also respond to Greek accusations that Jews in Egypt made no contributions to their broader society.

Above all, the writers of Aristeas and 3 Maccabees dismantled the ancient association between God's scriptural curses and Jewish life outside Judea. They did not ignore the Jerusalem Temple or express disinterest in Judean affairs.[36] Instead, they coupled their devotion to Judea with the confidence that God lovingly protects all Jews regardless of their location. Their stories helped to produce a radically new set of ideas about how Jews outside the land of Israel can cultivate relationships with God, their homeland, and the Jews who live there.

---

36. Contra Tuval, "Doing Without the Temple," 181–239; Hacham, "Sanctity," 178–79.

Conclusion

THE SUCCESSFUL ESTABLISHMENT OF JEWISH communities outside the land of Israel was the single biggest theological problem for Jews in the Hellenistic era. Far from being liminal to the practice of Judaism (or Judean-ism), the Jews who lived in these communities observed the main identifying markers of Jewish practice at the time. They observed the Sabbath and other Jewish holidays, practiced circumcision on their baby boys, and observed dietary laws. They also assembled regularly in synagogues, where they read and interpreted their scriptural traditions. These Jews were enthusiastically involved in building successful Jewish communities outside Judea. But they were also loyal to their homeland and to the Jerusalem Temple. By the end of the second century BCE, outsiders to these communities might have wondered whether these Jews were more pious than Jews who lived in Judea, where bitter infighting was taking place over whether to abandon the Jews' ancestral practices in favor of a more Hellenized way of life.

Political instability in Judea called the future of the Hasmonean monarchy into question. It also brought questions about identity and geography into the public sphere that had been lingering in the minds of Jews for centuries. Did the presence of Jews outside the land of Israel mean that Jews were still living in a state of exile and that a restoration awaited them in the distant future, even though Jews in Judea had already established political independence? How was the astonishing success of Jews outside the land of Israel meant to be understood? Was God going to put an end to Jewish life outside the land, as the prophets had long ago promised? And if God was planning to allow these communities to thrive, what did Jewish life outside the land of Israel *mean*?

This book suggests that Jews never reached a consensus regarding how to answer these questions. Sometime in the late Second Temple period, a misalignment emerged between Jews who lived in Judea and Jews who lived elsewhere. Judean writers, eager to maintain the notions of Judean exceptionalism and authority, responded to questions about exile by enforcing the idea that Jewish life outside the land of Israel was an extension of the biblical *gōlâ* and was linked to continuous misbehavior that resulted in God's anger and rejection. According to these writers, Judean leadership was a channel that fed currents of authentic tradition to its thirsty tributaries. Jews outside the land of Israel who received this tradition became embodiments of monolithic theological meaning that signified God's displeasure with the Jewish people. These Jews, who were destined to one day return to their homeland, occupied a space that became known as *diaspora*.[1]

There is little evidence that suggests that Jews outside Judea accepted this approach. Instead, these Jews wrote texts that present the family of world Jewry as united in values and bound by a common history.[2] They also emphasized the idea that the universal God is equally accessible anywhere and cares for all humankind. They even established their own holidays, which commemorated events that took place outside Judea and signified God's protection. The absence of the Greek word *diaspora* in literature produced by these Jews suggests that they did not think with the category of diaspora or with the concept that Jews outside Judea occupy a theologically meaningful space that signifies divine rejection.

Nowhere is the misalignment between these populations of Jews more apparent than in documents produced by Judean and Egyptian Jews. The uniquely close connections that bound these Jews to one another highlight the force of their misalignment. Beginning in the late seventh century BCE, Jews in the land of Israel were streaming to Egypt for a variety of reasons. In some cases, they were taken by force from the land of Israel as political captives and transplanted to Egypt. In other cases, Egypt offered them a safe haven from local dangers and unrest. In most cases, however, Jews left their homeland of their own accord. They perceived Egypt not through the lens of biblical warnings that depict it as a place where their God could not be worshiped, but as a cosmopolitan center that tolerated the Jews' observance of ancestral law and offered them exciting cultural opportunities.

While there is substantial evidence that many Jews left the land of Israel for Egypt during the Second Temple era, we have less evidence that Jews migrated from Egypt to the land of Israel at this same time. It is no wonder that Judean

---

1. This Judean understanding of the diaspora contrasts with modern homelands, which expect their diaspora communities to show loyalty by adhering to ancestral customs but rarely express the wish for them to return. See Sheffer, *Diaspora Politics*, 123; Safran, "Diasporas in Modern Societies," 95.

2. The Third Sibylline Oracle, which may have been composed by an Egyptian Jew sometime in the late Second Temple period, does express a hope to return to the land of Israel (Sib. Or. 3.265–290). Its prediction, however, appears in the context of an end-time event and does not mandate that Jews outside the land of Israel return to the land on their own.

leaders were concerned about talented Jews investing resources into building Jewish communities in Egypt. By the first century BCE, these communities boasted independent systems of Jewish leadership, and their connection to Judea derived from choice rather than need. Judean Jews might have hoped that, following the establishment of the Hasmonean monarchy, the Jews of Egypt would finally return to the land of Israel. There is no evidence that any such migrations took place.

Still, it is clear that Jews in both regions felt deeply connected to one another, even if they perceived their relationship differently. They expressed support for one another's political and social well-being and practiced their ancestral laws in similar ways. The factor that singularly differentiated them was their attitude toward the concept of diaspora. Most Jews hoped for a time when all people would live in harmonious coexistence, when foreign nations would embrace the Jewish people and recognize their God, and when Jews would embrace one another and unite in common worship. For Judean Jews, the image of this common worship was shaped by scriptural depictions of Jews returning from exile to worship alongside one another at the Jerusalem Temple. For Jews in Egypt, it rested on the critical role that Jews outside the land of Israel would play in bringing the knowledge of the one true God to the foreign nations. The texts produced by Jews who lived in these regions express these fantasies about the future by imagining a radically different past.

The strongest evidence for cultural interaction between the Jews of Egypt and the Jews of Judea is that they used the same strategies to make opposing arguments about the category of diaspora. Whether they wrote personal correspondences to one another or documents for their own communities, Jews in both regions spoke in the voices of outsiders to live out their fantasies of an idealized relationship between Judean and Egyptian Jews. By speaking in one another's voices, Jewish writers produced a surround-sound system of diverse but harmonious voices that amplified their own opinions. These writers presented themselves as participants in an unbroken chain of scriptural transmission that contained messages that legitimized their own outlooks about life outside the land of Israel.

The Roman destruction of the Jerusalem Temple in 70 CE animated intra-Jewish debates about the meaning of diaspora. Ancient disputes about whether Jewish life outside the land of Israel held theological meaning evolved into discussions about the meaning of diaspora (or in rabbinic parlance, *gālût*) in the absence of a temple.[3] One fact was not disputed: without a temple, it was no longer possible to argue that the exile had come to an end. The question now was no longer whether Jews outside Judea were living in

---

3. Klawans, "Josephus," 278–309; Gregerman, *Building on the Ruins*.

exile, but whether this exile encompassed all Jews, even those in the land of Israel. The difficulty in determining what these conversations looked like is compounded by the fact that, after 70 CE, the range of Jewish literature that was produced and successfully conserved narrowed in scope. Whereas Jewish writings produced in the Second Temple era reflect a vast spectrum of practices, cultures, and perspectives, most of our information about Jewish life after 70 CE comes from rabbinic documents produced in Babylonia and the land of Israel.[4] We know little about how most Jews at this time lived and what they thought about the diaspora as a theological category. Yet there is no reason to doubt that Jews outside the land of Israel continued to practice and develop their ancestral traditions.

The Jews' religious practices probably did not undergo significant changes immediately after the fall of the temple, even as Jews debated the meaning of *gālût*. Responses to the fall of the temple and discourses about exile slowly developed over centuries.[5] The various texts that rabbinic writers produced that engage with the subject of exile, therefore, should not be read as components of one harmonized and monolithic rabbinic attitude toward the diaspora. Within the expansive corpus of rabbinic literature are textured differences that reflect opinions that were produced in divergent cultural contexts. Still, some generalizations can be made about trends within rabbinic literature concerning the exile.

The early rabbis understood that the presence of Jewish life outside the land of Israel was a demographic reality that required practical attention. They therefore embarked upon the daunting project of producing a normative and practicable way of life that accommodated the absence of the temple. The rabbis expanded on a system that was already emerging in the Second Temple period that centered on scriptural study and synagogue attendance. Any Jew, regardless of whether they lived in proximity to one of the great centers of rabbinic learning, could engage in these activities.[6] Paradoxically, the rabbis also produced legal texts that explore the minutiae of laws concerning temple sacrifices and ritual purity that seem to presume the existence of a temple. This tension parallels an older tension that emerged in the Second Temple period between temple-centric worship and text-centric worship. As Jews began to gather in synagogues to read and interpret scriptural texts, most of them

---

4. The material that survives from this period represents a rabbinic community that comprised just a tiny percentage of the global Jewish population. See S. Schwartz, *Imperialism and Jewish Society*. Cf. Fine's important response to Schwartz in the 2004 summer edition of *Biblical Archaeology Review*.

5. D. Schwartz and Weiss, *Was 70 CE a Watershed*.

6. Much of rabbinic literature seems to ignore the fact that the temple had fallen. See N. Cohn, *Memory of the Temple*; N. Cohn, "Sacred Space in the Mishnah," 85–121.

continued to show devotion to the temple regardless of where they lived. Such Jews lived with an unresolved tension. While the *modality* of their written scriptures served to legitimize Jewish communities outside the land of Israel by enabling them to thrive, the *content* of these scriptures presented Jerusalem and its temple as the spiritual center of Jewish life. By studying these texts, Jews outside the land of Israel enforced the notion that Jerusalem remained at the center of their spiritual lives, and they affirmed the idea that they could properly worship God right where they were.

The rabbis did not shy from this tension. Instead, they located a middle ground by adding new dimensions to existent concepts about the land of Israel that were already in development in the Second Temple period. Rather than building exclusively upon the older Judean Jewish position that only Jews outside the land of Israel live in a state of divine disfavor, or building exclusively upon the older Egyptian Jewish position that all pious Jews live in a state of divine favor, most rabbinic writers opted for a moderate attitude that recognized a concept of *gālût* that mitigated the concept of Judean exceptionalism. The rabbis' moderate approach helped to alleviate the messianic zealotry that culminated in the temple's destruction in 70 CE and the catastrophic rebellion of Simon bar Kokhba that followed in 132–135 CE.

The rabbis distinguished their conception of *gālût* by adding two novel features that are not found in Second Temple discourses about life outside the Jewish homeland. First, they depicted God as entering exile and suffering with the people of Israel. Whereas some Egyptian Jewish texts insist that God has jurisdiction over the entire universe and protects Jews outside the land of Israel, rabbinic texts present God not only as a guardian but as a fellow sufferer. Rabbinic texts also privilege a temporal dimension of exile that is less interested in *gālût* as a demarcated space outside the land of Israel than in *gālût* as a time period that Jews must live through to reach the messianic age. These features soften the experience of exile by moving God's reconciliation with the people from taking place in the far future to taking place within *gālût* itself. The image of God suffering alongside the people as they endured foreign occupation alleviated the power of the people's eschatological expectations.[7] It accommodated life under occupation but still allowed Jews to anticipate an ultimate restoration.

The rabbis knew that shaping a legal system around the expectation that Jews who lived abroad would soon return to their homeland en masse could

---

7. This shift may reflect a response to early Christian thinkers who argued that the temple's destruction, and the Jews' scattering, was evidence that a reconciliation between God and the Jews would never take place. See Marmorstein, "Essays in Anthropomorphism," 170; Abelson, *Immanence of God*, 126; Urbach, *Sages*, 56.

result in a disastrous schism that divided world Jewry. They therefore accommodated the reality of *gālût* by focusing on the sanctification of time over space, even while acknowledging the unique and sacred role that the land of Israel played in the lives of all Jews.[8] By developing a calendar with uniform practices and liturgies, the rabbis ensured that Jews across the globe remained interconnected. In this system, all Jews could live a life of sanctity, though all Jews lived in a state of *gālût*. The rabbis' successful establishment of normative Jewish practices in the absence of a temple became a powerful safeguard against the threat of rupture among Jewish communities that had spread across the world. Their innovations allowed Jews, wherever they lived, to embrace sacred space and sacred time as twin pillars of Jewish faith. Even today, these features form a tension that cannot not—and need not—be resolved.

---

8. Gribetz, *Time and Difference*; Kaye, *Time in the Babylonian Talmud*; Stern, *Time and Process in Ancient Judaism*; Kimelman, "Rabbinic Theology of the Physical," 946–76; Heschel, *Sabbath*.

ACKNOWLEDGMENTS

One of my favorite college professors, David Glaser, once shared with me a story that took place in his Introduction to Music class at Columbia University. A student in his class who was a newcomer to the world of music composition raised her hand and asked him a question: What is a beat? Glaser had been composing music for decades but found himself speechless, unable to describe one of music's most basic elements. He furrowed his brow, struggling to think like someone who was encountering music for the very first time. After a few moments of contemplation, Glaser provided a definition of a beat for the first time in his life.

The sources I studied while working on this book solicited questions that sometimes made me feel like a musician struggling to define a beat. These sources invite readers to reconsider elemental categories that scholars who study the development of Jewish identity often take for granted. I feel fortunate for the many colleagues and mentors who helped me to discern how to understand and define these categories.

Steven Fine and Larry Wills provided invaluable feedback regarding how to organize the material in this book and frame it as a cohesive story. I also received advice from friends and colleagues at meetings convened by the Association for Jewish Studies, the Society of Biblical Literature, and the World Jewish Congress, where I delivered papers on the subject of Judea-diaspora relations in antiquity. A session at the Midwest Regional Meeting for Biblical Studies at St. Mary's College in South Bend, Indiana, convened by Olivia Stewart Lester and Scott Harris, provided a priceless opportunity to engage with colleagues who graciously read and responded to a paper that articulated the main ideas of this book. I am deeply grateful to Olivia and Scott, as well as to David Lincicum, whose generous response helped me to reframe some of the guiding questions in this book. A writing accountability group with Rebecca Wollenberg, Alice Miller, Isabel Cranz, Chontel Syfox,

Megan Nutzman, and Monika Amsler provided friendship and morale building that pushed me, at an early stage of research, to reach my goal of writing a page a day. Shayna Sheinfeld diligently edited proposal chapters at the earliest stages of the project's inception. Gillian Steinberg and Michael Bernstein pored through the manuscript and provided vital editorial support, as did Jonathan Abbett and my father, Allen Zeiger. Yehiel Poupko provided advice that expanded my understanding of early Judaism and its relationship to rabbinic thought in dozens of conversations over the past three years. My friend and colleague Emily Filler, with whom I often find myself in loving disagreement about homeland and diaspora, shared a joke with me while I was wrapping up research for this book that, to my delight, encapsulates the findings of my project. It now serves as the epigraph of this book. Two anonymous reviewers provided detailed suggestions that prompted me to make crucial adjustments to the manuscript. I cannot repay my debt to these colleagues, who selflessly undertook the thankless but vital task of peer review.

Many other friends listened, in various states of enthusiasm, as I consulted with them about ideas that found their way into this project. I edited the final version of the manuscript over a summer at the idyllic Jerusalem campus of the Shalom Hartman Institute, where I have been a Kogod Fellow since 2021. Among the friendships I have made at Hartman, I am especially grateful for time well spent with Yedidah Koren. In one of our conversations, Yedidah referenced the image in Ezekiel 10 of God leaving Jerusalem, which she noted is a reflection of Judean anxiety about whether God would ever return to the temple. I do not analyze Ezekiel in this book, but this image has guided me in the last stages of editing as a clarifying expression of the worries that Judean Jewish writers held in their hearts as they penned their texts.

I have lost count of the many questions and requests that I have sent to my extraordinary editors, Maria Metzler and Alex Ramos. Whether it related to content, style, formatting, or one of the other countless details that require attention when producing a book like this, Maria and Alex thoroughly responded to each question and closed each email with an offer to speak further. Maria and Alex are the editors that every author hopes for, and their personal care for this project is evident on every page. I also want to thank Blake Jurgens and Jennifer Norton and the rest of the staff at Eisenbrauns for their endless patience and the attentive care that they have shown this project.

This book could not have been produced without the generous support of a grant provided by the Catholic Biblical Association, which enabled me to take a year-long sabbatical from teaching at Catholic Theological Union. I am proud to be a member of the CBA, which has done tremendous work in the past few decades to combat theological anti-Judaism in Catholic scholarship. I am especially grateful for the privilege of being a member of the CBA's task force that addresses representations of Jews and Judaism, and I am in awe of my fellow task force members, who have invested their time and energy into rectifying anti-Jewish teachings in the Catholic Church.

I dedicate this book to my grandfather, Aaron Sabghir, who passed away at the age of one hundred as I was writing this book. My grandfather was an economist who directed the United States' first HMO, the Group Health Association. He was born in 1922 in Brooklyn, where he worked as a "seltzer boy" who schlepped cases of seltzer up and down Jewish tenement houses every day before he went to school. It was on one of these delivery runs, at the age of nine or ten, that he first came across the Brooklyn Jewish Center. He walked inside the Center to deliver a box of seltzer during morning services, heard congregants singing cantorial music, and fell in love. For the rest of his life, my grandfather enveloped himself in music. He married a pianist, Beatrice Simmons, and sang in his synagogue choir. He encouraged his children, including my mother Naomi, to join him each Sunday afternoon as he played recordings of Brahms and Rachmaninoff, mime-conducted symphonies, and listened to different versions of the same Beethoven piano sonata while producing hand-written notes that compared their differences. My grandfather was also a passionate letter writer. One of his proudest moments was when, after being unable to obtain tickets to hear a string quartet scheduled to perform at the Library of Congress's concert series, he wrote a lamentful ode to an employee of the Library, who was so charmed by his poem that she sent him season passes.

My grandfather enthusiastically supported his children's and grandchildren's interests. He took me to concerts when I was a child and sent me his personal set of Adin Steinsaltz's edition of the Talmud when I began my doctoral program. I first encountered Daniel Schwartz's commentary to 2 Maccabees, which has served as a major influence on this project, on his coffee table twenty-five years ago (that book, he told me when I inquired about it, he was not quite ready to part with). My grandfather's love for Judaism and the musicality of written words is the beating heart of this book, which studies the pulses and patterns of ancient Jewish letters. He might not have taught me how to define a beat, but he certainly taught me how to feel one.

This project could not have been completed—or started—without my husband Aaron, whose natural brilliance, gentle humility, and constant loyalty are an inspiration to me, our children, and all those who know him. It's no wonder that my grandfather loved Aaron the moment they first met, and it is no surprise that when we visited him a few weeks before his passing, he took Aaron's hand and clasped it between his own as we sang the Yiddish songs of my grandfather's childhood.

Like many of our ancestors, my grandfather spent his life cultivating a spiritual and intellectual legacy to leave his children. I have endless gratitude to

Aaron for being my partner in honoring his life's work by trying to ensure that our children, wherever they are, feel at home in our love.

I write these words just a few weeks after the worst attack against the Jewish people since the destruction of European Jewry in World War II. I write them with the hope that all Jewish people, wherever they are, can live in peace alongside their neighbors as proud Jews who are unafraid to honor the legacy of their ancestors, ancestors who embraced the idea that they have much to offer the world, and have much to learn from the world, but who never surrendered their tender love for the land that had been their home.

November 2023
Chicago, IL

BIBLIOGRAPHY

Abelson, Joshua. *The Immanence of God in Rabbinic Literature*. New York: Macmillan, 1912.
Adler, Yonatan. *The Origins of Judaism: An Archaeological-Historical Reappraisal*. Anchor Yale Bible Reference Library. New Haven: Yale University Press, 2022.
Ahlström, Gosta W. *History of Ancient Palestine*. Minneapolis: Fortress, 1993.
Aitken, James A. "The Ptolemaic Setting for the Translation of the Greek Pentateuch." *Hebrew Bible and Ancient Israel* 9.4 (2020): 398–414.
Alexander, Elizabeth Shanks, and Beth A. Berkowitz, eds. *Religious Studies and Rabbinics: A Conversation*. London: Routledge, 2018.
Alon, Gedalyahu. *The Jews in Their Land in the Talmudic Age (70–640 C.E.)*. 2 vols. Jerusalem: Magnes, 1980, 1984.
Amzallag, Nissim. "The Authorship of Ezra and Nehemiah in Light of Differences in Their Ideological Background." *JBL* 137.2 (2018): 271–97.
Askin, Lindsey A. "Beyond Encomium or Eulogy: The Role of Simon the High Priest in Ben Sira." *JAJ* 9.3 (2018): 344–65.
Aune, David E. *The New Testament in Its Literary Environment*. Library of Early Christianity. Philadelphia: Westminster, 1987.
Barclay, John M. G. *Jews in the Mediterranean Diaspora: From Alexander to Trajan (323 BCE–117 CE)*. Berkeley: University of California Press, 1996.
———, ed. *Negotiating Diaspora: Jewish Strategies in the Roman Empire*. London: T&T Clark, 2004.
———. "Paul Among Diaspora Jews: Anomaly or Apostate?" *Journal for the Study of the New Testament* 60 (1995): 89–120.
Bar-Kochva, Bezalel. "On the Festival of Purim and Some of the Sukkot Practices in the Period of the Second Temple and Afterward" [Hebrew]. *Zion* 62 (1997): 387–407.
Bayme, Steven, Leonard Fein, Samuel Freedman, and Eric Yoffie, eds. *The A. B. Yehoshua Controversy: An Israel-Diaspora Dialogue on Jewishness, Israeliness, and Identity*. New York: American Jewish Committee, 2006.
Becking, Bob. "'We Are All Returned As One!' Critical Notes on the Myth of Mass Return." Pages 1–18 in *Judah and Judeans in the Persian Period*. Edited by Oded Lipschits and Manfred Oeming. University Park: Penn State University Press 2006.

———. "Yehudite Identity in Elephantine." Pages 403–19 in *Judea and the Judeans in the Achaemenid Period*. Edited by Oded Lipschits, Gary N. Knoppers, and Manfred Oeming. Winona Lake, IN: Eisenbrauns, 2011.

Ben-Eliyahu, Eyal. *Identity and Territory: Jewish Perceptions of Space in Antiquity*. Oakland: University of California Press, 2019.

Ben Zvi, Ehud, and Sylvie Honigman, eds. "*Tōrâ*-Centred Israel: When a Yehudite Concept Met Ptolemaic Egypt." Special issue of *Hebrew Bible and Ancient Israel* 9.4 (2020).

Bergren, Theodore A. "Nehemiah in 2 Maccabees 1:10–2:18." *JSJ* 28.3 (1997): 247–70.

Bhabha, Homi K. *The Location of Culture*. London: Routledge, 2004.

Bickerman, Elias J. "The Colophon of the Greek Book of Esther." *JBL* 63 (1944): 339–62.

———. "The Date of the Testaments of the Twelve Patriarchs." *JBL* 69.3 (1950): 245–60.

———. "Notes on the Greek Book of Esther." *Proceedings of the American Academy for Jewish Research* 20 (1950): 101–33.

———. *Studies in Jewish and Christian History: A New Edition in English Including "The God of the Maccabees"*. Edited by Amram Tropper. 2 vols. Leiden: Brill, 2007.

Biezunska-Malowist, Iza. *Période ptolémeïque*. Vol. 1 of *L'esclavage dans l'Égypte gréco-romaine*. Wroclaw: Akademii Nauk, 1974.

Boda, Mark J., and Paul L. Redditt, eds. *Unity and Disunity in Ezra-Nehemiah: Redaction, Rhetoric, and Reader*. Sheffield: Sheffield Academic Press, 2008.

Bohak, Gideon. *Joseph and Aseneth and the Jewish Temple in Heliopolis*. Early Judaism and Its Literature 10. Atlanta: Scholars Press, 1996.

Bousset, Wilhelm. "Die Bedeutung der Person Jesu für den Glauben. Historische und rationale Grundlagen des Glaubens." Pages 291–305 in *Fünfter Weltkongress für Freies Christentum und Religiösen Fortschritt, Berlin 5. Bis 10. August 1910: Protokoll der Verhandlungen*. Edited by M. Fischer and M. Schiele. Berlin: Protestantischer Schriftenvertrieb, 1911.

Boyarin, Daniel. *Judaism: The Genealogy of a Modern Notion*. New Brunswick: Rutgers University Press, 2019.

———. "Placing Reading: Ancient Israel and Medieval Europe." Pages 10–37 in *The Ethnography of Reading*. Edited by Jonathan Boyarin. Berkeley: University of California Press, 1993.

Brueggemann, Walter. *The Prophetic Imagination*. Minneapolis: Fortress, 1978.

Brutti, Maria. *The Development of the High Priesthood During the Pre-Hasmonean Period: History, Ideology, Theology*. Leiden: Brill, 2006.

Bultmann, Rudolf. *Primitive Christianity in Its Contemporary Setting*. Translated by R. H. Fuller. London: Thames & Hudson, 1956.

Bunge, Jochen G. "Untersuchungen zum zweiten Makkabäerbuch: Quellenkritische, literarische, chronologische und historische Untersuchungen zum zweiten Makkabäerbuch als Quelle syrisch-palästinensischer Geschichte im 2. Jh. v. Chr." PhD diss., Rheinische Friedrich-Wilhelms-Universität Bonn, 1971.

Burns, Joshua Ezra. "The Special Purim and the Reception of the Book of Esther in the Hellenistic and Early Roman Eras." *JSJ* 37 (2006): 1–34.

Capponi, Livia. "Martyrs and Apostates: 3 Maccabees and the Temple of Leontopolis." *Henoch* 29 (2007): 288–306.

Carr, David M. *The Formation of the Hebrew Bible: A New Reconstruction*. Oxford: Oxford University Press, 2011.

———. *Writing on the Tablet of the Heart: Origins of Scripture and Literature*. Oxford: Oxford University Press, 2005.
Carroll, Robert P. "Deportation and Diasporic Discourses in the Prophetic Literature." Pages 63–88 in *Exile: Old Testament, Jewish, and Christian Conceptions*. Edited by James M. Scott. JSJSup 56. Brill: Leiden, 1997.
———. "Exile! What Exile? Deportation and the Discourses of Diaspora." Pages 62–79 in *Leading Captivity Captive: "The Exile" as History and Ideology*. Edited by Lester Grabbe. Journal for the Study of the Old Testament Supplement Series 278. Sheffield: Sheffield Academic Press, 1998.
Charles, Ronald. "Hybridity and the Letter of Aristeas." *JSJ* 40.2 (2009): 242–59.
Childs, Brevard S. *Introduction to the Old Testament as Scripture*. Philadelphia: Fortress, 1979.
Chomsky, Noam. *New Horizons in the Study of Language and Mind*: Cambridge: Cambridge University Press, 2000.
———. *Reflections on Language*. New York: Pantheon, 1975.
———. "A Review of B. F. Skinner's Verbal Behavior." *Language* 35 (1959): 26–58.
Clines, David J. A. *Esther Scroll: The Story of the Story*. London: Bloomsbury, 1984.
Cohen, Shaye J. D. *The Beginnings of Jewishness: Boundaries, Varieties, Uncertainties*. Berkeley: University of California Press, 1999.
———. *Josephus in Galilee and Rome: His Vita and Development as a Historian*. Leiden: Brill, 1979.
Cohen, Shaye J. D., and Ernest S. Frerichs, eds. *Diasporas in Antiquity*. BJS 288. Atlanta: Scholars Press, 1993.
Cohn, Dorrit. "Metalepsis and Mise en Abyme." *Narrative* 20.1 (2012): 105–14.
Cohn, Naftali. *The Memory of the Temple and the Making of the Rabbis*. Philadelphia: University of Pennsylvania Press, 2012.
———. "Sacred Space in the Mishnah: From Temple to Synagogue and … City." Pages 85–121 in *La question de la "sacerdotalisation" dans le judaïsme synagogal, le christianisme et le rabbinisme*. Edited by Simone C. Mimouni and Louis Painchaud. Turnhout: Brepols, 2018.
Collins, John J. "3 Maccabees, Introductory Essay and Notes." Pages 1752–67 in *HarperCollins Study Bible with the Apocryphal/Deuterocanonical Books*. Edited by Wayne A. Meeks. New York: HarperCollins, 1993.
———. *Between Athens and Jerusalem: Jewish Identity in the Hellenistic Diaspora*. 2nd ed. Grand Rapids: Eerdmans, 2000.
———. *Daniel: A Commentary on the Book of Daniel*. Hermeneia. Minneapolis: Fortress, 1993.
———. "Ecclesiasticus, or the Wisdom of Jesus Son of Sirach." Pages 68–111 in *The Apocrypha*. Edited by Martin Goodman. Oxford Bible Commentary Series. Oxford: Oxford University Press, 2012.
———. "Epilogue: Genre Analysis and the Dead Sea Scrolls." *Dead Sea Discoveries* 17.3 (2010): 418–30.
———. *The Invention of Judaism: Torah and Jewish Identity from Deuteronomy to Paul*. Oakland: University of California Press, 2017.
Corley, Jeremy. "Searching for Structure and Redaction in Ben Sira: An Investigation of Beginnings and Endings." Pages 21–47 in *The Wisdom of Ben Sira: Studies on Tradition, Redaction, and Theology*. Edited by A. Passaro and G. Bellia. DCLS 1. Berlin: de Gruyter, 2008.

Cousland, J. R. C. "Reversal, Recidivism and Reward in 3 Maccabees: Structure and Purpose." *JSJ* 34.1 (2003): 39–51.
Cowley, A. E. *Aramaic Papyri of the Fifth Century B.C.* Ancient Texts and Translations. Oxford: Clarendon, 1923. Repr., Eugene, OR: Wipf & Stock, 2005.
Crawford, Sidnie White. "Additions to Esther." Pages 426–27 in *Eerdman's Dictionary of the Bible.* Edited by David Noel Freedman, Allen C. Myers, and Astrid B. Beck. Grand Rapids: Eerdmans, 2000.
Cribiore, Raffaella. *Gymnastics of the Mind: Greek Education in Hellenistic and Roman Egypt.* Princeton: Princeton University Press, 2001.
Croy, N. Clayton. *3 Maccabees.* Septuagint Commentary Series. Leiden: Brill, 2006.
Dällenbach, Lucien. *The Mirror in the Text.* Chicago: University of Chicago Press, 1977.
Davis, Todd F., and Kenneth Womack. *Formalist Criticism and Reader-Response Theory.* London: Palgrave, 2002.
Dell'Acqua, Anna Passoni. "The Liberation Decree of 'Addition' E in Esther LXX: Some Lexical Observations Starting From a New Papyrus (POxy LXVI, 4443)." *Admantius* 10 (2004): 72–88.
Deissman, G. A. "Prolegomena to the Biblical Letters and Epistles." Pages 1–59 in *Bible Studies: Contributions, Chiefly from Papyri and Inscriptions, to the History of the Language, the Literature, and the Religion of Hellenistic Judaism and Primitive Christianity.* Edited by G. A. Deissman. Translated by A. Grieve. Edinburgh. T&T Clark, 1903.
Delcor, Matthias. "Le temple d'Onias en Égypte." *Revue Biblique* 75 (1968): 188–205.
Dickmann, Iddo. *The Little Crystalline Seed: The Ontological Significance of Mise en Abyme in Post-Heideggerian Thought.* Intersections: Philosophy and Critical Theory. Albany: State University of New York Press, 2010.
Doering, Lutz. *Ancient Jewish Letters and the Beginnings of Christian Epistolography.* WUNT 298. Tübingen: Mohr Siebeck, 2012.
Doran, Robert. *Temple Propaganda: The Purpose and Character of 2 Maccabees.* Catholic Biblical Quarterly Monograph Series 12. Washington, DC: Catholic Biblical Association of America.
Droge, Arthur J., and James D. Tabor. *A Noble Death: Suicide and Martyrdom Among Christians and Jews in Antiquity.* San Francisco: HarperCollins, 1992.
Dufoix, Stéphane. "Diaspora Before It Became a Concept." Pages 13–21 in *Routledge Handbook of Diaspora Studies.* Edited by Robin Cohen and Carolin Fischer. New York: Routledge, 2019.
———. *The Dispersion: A History of the Word Diaspora.* Leiden: Brill, 2017.
Eckhardt, Benedikt, ed. *Jewish Identity and Politics Between the Maccabees and Bar Kokhba: Groups, Normativity, and Rituals.* JSJSup 155. Leiden: Brill, 2012.
———. "The Psalms of Solomon as a Historical Source for the Late Hasmonean Period." Pages 7–30 in *The Psalms of Solomon: Language, History, Theology.* Edited by Eberhard Bons and Patrick Pouchelle. Atlanta: Scholars Press, 2015.
Edrei, Arye, and Doron Mendels. "A Split Jewish Diaspora Again—A Response to Fergus Millar." *JSP* 21.3 (2012): 305–11.
———. "A Split Jewish Diaspora: Its Dramatic Consequences." *JSP* 16 (2007): 91–137.
Eichhorn, J. G. "Bemerkungen über den Text des Propheten Jeremias." *Repertorium für Biblische und Morgenländische Litteratur* 1 (1777): 167–68.

Eissfeldt, Otto. *The Old Testament: An Introduction.* Oxford: Blackwell, 1965.
Emmet, Cyril W. "The Third Book of Maccabees." Pages 1:155–73 in *Apocrypha and Pseudepigrapha of the Old Testament.* Edited by Robert H. Charles. 2 vols. Oxford: Clarendon, 1913.
Evans, Craig A., and H. Daniel Zacharias. *Old Testament Pseudepigrapha: Greek and English.* Grand Rapids: Eerdmans, 2015.
Exler, Francis. "The Form of the Ancient Greek Letter." PhD diss., Catholic University of America, 1923.
Faust, Avraham. *Judah in the Neo-Babylonian Period: The Archaeology of Desolation.* Atlanta: Society of Biblical Literature, 2012.
Feldman, Louis. "The Orthodoxy of the Jews in Hellenistic Egypt." *Jewish Social Studies* 22 (1960): 215–37.
Fine, Steven. Review of *Imperialism and Jewish Society*, by Seth Schwartz. *Biblical Archaeology Review* 30.2 (2004): 56–58.
Fishbane, Michael. *The Garments of Torah: Essays in Biblical Hermeneutics.* Bloomington: Indiana University Press, 1989.
Fitzmyer, Joseph A. "Some Notes on Aramaic Epistolography." *JBL* 93 (1974): 201–25.
———. *A Wandering Aramean: Collected Aramaic Essays.* Atlanta: Scholars Press, 1979.
Floyd, Michael H. "Penitential Prayer in the Second Temple Period from the Perspective of Baruch." Pages 51–81 in *The Development of Penitential Prayer in Second Temple Judaism*, vol. 2 of *Seeking the Favor of God*. Edited by Mark J. Boda, Daniel K. Falk, and Rodney A. Werline. Early Judaism and Its Literature 22. Atlanta: Society of Biblical Literature, 2007.
Fox, Marvin V. *Character and Ideology in the Book of Esther.* Studies on Personalities of the Old Testament. Columbia: University of South Carolina Press, 1991.
———. "Three Esthers." Pages 50–59 in *The Book of Esther in Modern Research.* Edited by Sidnie White Crawford and Leonard J. Greenspoon. Journal for the Study of the Old Testament Supplement Series 380. London: T&T Clark, 2003.
Frey, Jörg. "Temple and Rival Temple—The Cases of Elephantine, Mt. Gerizim, and Leontopolis." Pages 171–205 in *Gemeinde ohne Tempel: Zur Substituierung und Transformation des Jerusalemer Tempels und seines Kults im Alten Testament, antiken Judentum und frühen Christentum.* Edited by Beate Ego, Armin Lange, and Peter Pilhofer. WUNT 118. Tübingen: Mohr Siebeck, 1999.
Gadot, Yuval. "In the Valley of the King: Jerusalem's Rural Hinterland in the 8th–4th Centuries BCE." *Journal of the Institute of Archaeology of Tel Aviv University* 42 (2015): 3–26.
Gafni, Isaiah. *Land, Center, and Diaspora: Jewish Constructs in Late Antiquity.* Journal for the Study of the Pseudepigrapha Supplement Series 21. Sheffield: Sheffield Academic Press, 1997.
Genette, Gerard. *Narrative Discourse: An Essay in Method.* Ithaca, NY: Cornell University Press, 1980.
Glick, Edward Bernard. "America, Israel and American Jews: The Triangular Connection Revisited." Pages 229–42 in *Eretz Israel, Israel, and the Jewish Diaspora: Mutual Relations: Proceedings of the First Annual Symposium of the Philip M. and Ethel Klutznick Chair.* Edited by Menachem Mor. Studies in Jewish Civilization. Lanham, MD: University Press of America 1988.

Goldstein, Jonathan A. "The Apocryphal Book of 1 Baruch." *Proceedings of the American Academy for Jewish Research* 46/47 (1979–1980): 179–99.

———. *I Maccabees*. AB 41. New Haven: Yale University Press, 1976.

———. *II Maccabees*. AB 41A. New Haven: Yale University Press, 1995.

Goswell, Greg. "The Order of the Books in the Greek Old Testament." *Journal of the Evangelical Theological Society* 52.3 (2009): 449–66.

Grabbe, Lester L. *An Introduction to Second Temple Judaism: History and Religion of the Jews in the Time of Nehemiah, the Maccabees, Hillel, and Jesus*. London: Bloomsbury, 2010.

———. "Israel's Reality After the Exile." Pages 9–32 in *The Crisis of Israelite Religion: Transformation of Religious Traditions in Exilic and Post-Exilic Times*. Edited by Bob Becking and M. C. A. Korpel. Old Testament Studies 42. Leiden: Brill 1999.

———. *Yehud: A History of the Persian Province of Judah*. Vol. 1 of *A History of the Jews and Judaism in the Second Temple Period*. Library of Second Temple Series 47. London: T&T Clark, 2004.

Graham, William. *Beyond the Written Word: Oral Aspects of Scripture in the History of Religion*. Cambridge: Cambridge University Press, 1993.

Grant, Deena E. "Fire and the Body of Yhwh." *Journal for the Study of the Old Testament* (2015): 139–61.

Gregerman, Adam. *Building on the Ruins of the Temple: Apologetics and Polemics in Early Christianity and Rabbinic Judaism*. TSAJ 165. Tübingen: Mohr Siebeck, 2016.

Gregg, J. A. F. "The Additions to Esther." Pages 1:665–84 in *The Apocrypha and Pseudepigrapha of the Old Testament*. Edited by Robert H. Charles. 2 vols. Oxford: Clarendon, 1913.

Grelot, Pierre. *Documents araméens d'Égypte: Introduction, traduction, présentation*. Littératures anciennes du Proche-Orient 5. Paris: Cerf, 1972.

Gribetz, Sarit Kattan. *Time and Difference in Rabbinic Judaism*. Princeton: Princeton University Press, 2022.

Gruen, Erich S. "Diaspora and Homeland." Pages 18–46 in *Diasporas and Exiles: Varieties of Jewish Identity*. Edited by Howard Wettstein. Berkeley: University of California Press, 2002.

———. *Diaspora: Jews Amidst Greeks and Romans*. Cambridge: Harvard University Press, 2012.

———. *Heritage and Hellenism: The Reinvention of Jewish Tradition*. Berkeley: University of California Press, 1998.

———. "The Letter of Aristeas and the Cultural Context of the Septuagint." Pages 413–36 in Gruen, *The Construct of Identity in Hellenistic Judaism: Essays on Early Jewish Literature and History*. DCLS 29. Berlin: de Gruyter, 2016.

———. "The Origins and Objectives of Onias' Temple." *Scripta Classica Israelica* 16 (1997): 47–70.

Hacham, Noam. "3 Maccabees." Pages 289–308 in *Jewish Annotated Apocrypha*. Edited by Jonathan Klawans and Lawrence Wills. Oxford: Oxford University Press, 2020.

———. "3 Maccabees and Esther: Parallels, Intertextuality, and Diaspora Identity." *JBL* 126.4 (2007): 765–85.

———. "Sanctity and the Attitude Towards the Temple in Hellenistic Judaism." Pages 155–79 in *Was 70 CE a Watershed in Jewish History?: On Jews and Judaism Before and After the Destruction of the Second Temple*. Edited by Daniel R. Schwartz and Zeev Weiss. AJEC 78. Leiden: Brill, 2012.

Hadas, Moses. *Aristeas to Philocrates (Letter of Aristeas)*. New York: Harper & Brothers, 1951. Repr., Eugene, OR: Wipf & Stock, 2007.

Hall, Stuart. "Cultural Identity and Diaspora." Pages 392–404 in *Colonial Discourse and Post-Colonial Theory: A Reader*. Edited by Patrick Williams and Laura Chrisman. New York: Columbia University Press, 1994.

Halpern-Amaru, Betsy. "Land Theology in Philo and Josephus." Pages 65–93 in *The Land of Israel: Jewish Perspectives*. Edited by Lawrence Hoffman. Notre Dame: University of Notre Dame Press, 1986.

Hanson, Paul D. *The Dawn of Apocalyptic: The Historical and Sociological Roots of Jewish Apocalyptic Eschatology*. Philadelphia: Fortress, 1975.

Haran, Menahem. "Archives, Libraries, and the Order of the Biblical Books." *Journal of the Ancient Near Eastern Society* 22 (1993): 51–61.

Harnack, Adolf von. *New Testament Studies*. Translated by J. R. Wilkinson. London: Williams & Norgate, 1908.

Harrington, Daniel J. *The Maccabean Revolt: Anatomy of a Biblical Revolution*. Old Testament Studies 1. Wilmington: Glazier, 1988.

Hart, J. H. A. "The Prologue to Ecclesiasticus." *JQR* 19 (1907): 284–97.

Hayes, Christine. *Between the Babylonian and Palestinian Talmuds: Accounting for Halakhic Difference in Selected Sugyot from Tractate Avodah Zarah*. Oxford: Oxford University Press, 1997.

Hays, Nathan. "Yedaniah's Identity as Priest or Lay Person and the Rhetoric of the Letter from the Judean Garrison of Elephantine to Bagavahya." *JBL* 139.3 (2020): 521–41.

Henderson, Ruth. "Baruch's Jerusalem: The Conception of Jerusalem in 1 Baruch 4:5–5:9." *JBL* 135.3 (2016): 543–56.

———. *Second Temple Songs of Zion: A Literary and Generic Analysis of the Apostrophe to Zion (11QPs^a XXII 1–15); Tobit 13:9–18 and 1 Baruch 4:30–5:9*. DCLS 17. Berlin: de Gruyter, 2014.

Hengel, Martin. *Judentum und Hellenismus: Studien zu ihrer Begegnung unter besonderer Berücksichtigung Palästinas bis zur Mitte des 2. Jahrhunderts vor Christus*. 3rd ed. WUNT 10. Tübingen: Mohr, 1988.

Heschel, Abraham Joshua. *The Sabbath: Its Meaning for Modern Man*. New York: Farrar, Straus and Giroux, 1951.

Hicks-Keeton, Jill. "Putting Paul in His Place: Diverse Diasporas and Sideways Spaces in Hellenistic Judaism." *Journal of the Jesus Movement in Its Jewish Setting* 6 (2019): 1–21.

Himmelfarb, Martha. "The Wisdom of the Scribe, the Wisdom of the Priest, and the Wisdom of the King According to Ben Sira." Pages 65–76 in *For a Later Generation: The Transformation of Tradition in Israel, Early Judaism, and Early Christianity*. Edited by Randal A. Argall, Beverly A. Bow, and Rodney A. Werline. Harrisburg, PA: Trinity Press International, 2000.

Hirschhorn, Sara Yael, *City on a Hilltop: American Jews and the Israeli Settler Movement*. Cambridge: Harvard University Press, 2017.

Hogan, Karina Martin. "Baruch." Pages 1027–34 in *The Apocrypha*. Edited by Matthew J. M. Coomber, Hugh R. Page Jr., and Gale A. Yee. Fortress Commentary on the Bible. Philadelphia: Fortress, 2016.

Honigman, Sylvie. "The Birth of a Diaspora: The Emergence of a Jewish Self-Definition in Ptolemaic Egypt in the Light of Onomastics." Pages 93–128 in

Diasporas in Antiquity. Edited by Shaye J. D. Cohen and Ernest S. Frerichs. BJS 288. Atlanta: Scholars Press, 1993.

Ilan, Tal. *Integrating Women into the Second Temple History*. TSAJ 76. Tübingen: Mohr Siebeck, 1991.

Jaffee, Martin S. *Torah in the Mouth: Writing and Oral Tradition in Palestinian Judaism, 200 BCE–400 CE*. Oxford: Oxford University Press, 2001.

Japhet, Sara. "The Expulsion of the Foreign Women (Ezra 9–10): The Legal Basis, Precedents, and Consequences for the Definition of Jewish Identity." Pages 141–61 in *"Sieben Augen auf einem Stein" (Sach 3,9): Studien zur Literatur des Zweiten Tempels: Festschrift für Ina Willi-Plein zum 65. Geburtstag*. Edited by Friedhelm Hartenstein and Michael Pietsch. Neukirchen-Vluyn: Neukirchener, 2007.

Jellicoe, Sidney. "The Occasion and Purpose of the Letter of Aristeas: A Re-Examination." *New Testament Studies* 12.2 (1966): 158–9.

Jeremias, Joachim. *Jesus and the Message of the New Testament*. Translated by K. C. Hanson. Minneapolis: Fortress, 2002.

———. *Jesus' Promise to the Nations*. Translated by S. H. Hooke. Naperville, IL: Allenson, 1958.

Johnson, Sara Raup. *Historical Fictions and Hellenistic Jewish Identity: Third Maccabees in its Cultural Context*. Oakland: University of California Press, 2005.

Jonge, Marinus de. *The Testaments of the Twelve Patriarchs: A Study of Their Text, Composition, and Origin*. Assen: Van Gorcum, 1975.

Kahn, Dan'el. "Judean Auxiliaries in Egypt's Wars Against Kush." *JAOS* 127.4 (2007): 507–16.

Kasher, Aryeh. *The Jews in Hellenistic and Roman Egypt: The Struggle for Equal Rights*. TSAJ 7. Tübingen: Mohr Siebeck, 1985.

———. "Political and National Connections Between the Jews of Ptolemaic Egypt and Their Brethren in Eretz Israel." Pages 24–41 in *Eretz Israel, Israel, and the Jewish Diaspora: Mutual Relations: Proceedings of the First Annual Symposium of the Philip M. and Ethel Klutznick Chair*. Edited by Menachem Mor. Studies in Jewish Civilization. Lanham, MD: University Press of America 1988.

Kaye, Lynn. *Time in the Babylonian Talmud: Natural and Imagined Times in Jewish Law and Narrative*. Cambridge: Cambridge University Press, 2018.

Kee, H. C. "Testaments of the Twelve Patriarchs." Pages 1:775–828 in *The Old Testament Pseudepigrapha*. Edited by James H. Charlesworth. 2 vols. New York: Doubleday, 1983.

Kimelman, Reuven. "The Rabbinic Theology of the Physical: Blessings, Body and Soul, Resurrection, and Covenant and Election." Pages 946–76 in *The Late Rabbinic Period*. Edited by Steven T. Katz. Vol. 4 of *The Cambridge History of Judaism*. Cambridge: Cambridge University Press, 2006.

Klausner, Samuel A. "Diaspora in Comparative Perspective." Pages 194–221 in *Eretz Israel, Israel, and the Jewish Diaspora: Mutual Relations: Proceedings of the First Annual Symposium of the Philip M. and Ethel Klutznick Chair*. Edited by Menachem Mor. Studies in Jewish Civilization. Lanham, MD: University Press of America 1988.

Klawans, Jonathan. "Josephus, the Rabbis, and Responses to Catastrophes Ancient and Modern." *JQR* 100.2 (2010): 278–309.

Klawans, Jonathan, and Lawrence M. Wills, eds. *Jewish Annotated Apocrypha*. Oxford: Oxford University Press, 2020.

Klutznick, Philip M. "The Relations Between Diaspora Jewry and the State of Israel, 1948–1988: An American Jewish Leader's Perspective." Pages 93–101 in *Eretz Israel, Israel, and the Jewish Diaspora: Mutual Relations: Proceedings of the First Annual Symposium of the Philip M. and Ethel Klutznick Chair*. Edited by Menachem Mor. Studies in Jewish Civilization. Lanham, MD: University Press of America 1988.

Knoppers, Gary R., and Bernard M. Levinson, eds. *The Pentateuch as Torah: New Models for Understanding its Promulgation and Acceptance*. Winona Lake, IN: Eisenbrauns, 2007.

Koller, Aaron. *Esther in Ancient Jewish Thought*. Cambridge: Cambridge University Press, 2014.

———. "The Self-Referential Coda to *Avot* and the Egyptian-Israelite Literary Tradition of Wisdom." *JAJ* 8.1 (2017): 2–25.

Kraabel, A. Thomas. "The Roman Diaspora: Six Questionable Assumptions." *Journal of Jewish Studies* 33.1–2 (1982): 445–64.

———. "Unity and Diversity Among Diaspora Synagogues." Pages 49–60 in *The Synagogue in Late Antiquity*. Edited by Lee I. Levine. Philadelphia: American Schools of Oriental Research, 1987.

Kraeling, Emil G. "New Light on the Elephantine Colony." Pages 1:49–67 in *The Biblical Archaeologist Reader*. Edited by George Ernest Wright and David Noel Friedman. 3 vols. Garden City, NY: Doubleday, 1961.

Kugel, James L. *In Potiphar's House: The Interpretive Life of Biblical Texts*. Cambridge: Harvard University Press, 1994.

Leith, Mary Joan Winn. "New Perspectives on the Return from Exile and Persian-Period Yehud." Pages 147–69 in *The Oxford Handbook of the Historical Books of the Hebrew Bible*. Edited by Brad E. Kelle and Brent A. Shawn. Oxford: Oxford University Press, 2020.

Lenger, Marie-Thérèse. *Corpus des ordonnances des Ptolémées*. Bruxelles: Palais des Académies, 1964.

Levenson, Jon D. *Esther*. Old Testament Library. Louisville, KY: Westminster John Knox, 1997.

———. "The Scroll of Esther in Ecumenical Perspective." *Journal of Ecumenical Studies* 13 (1976): 440–51.

Lieber, Andrea. "Between Motherland and Fatherland: Diaspora, Pilgrimage, and the Spiritualization of Sacrifice in Philo of Alexandria." Pages 193–210 in *Heavenly Tablets: Interpretation, Identity and Tradition in Ancient Judaism*. Edited by Lynn LiDonnici and Andrea Lieber. JSJSup 119. Leiden: Brill, 2007.

Lindenberger, James M. *Ancient Aramaic and Hebrew Letters*. 2nd ed. Writings from the Ancient World 14. Atlanta: Society of Biblical Literature, 2003.

Lipschits, Oded. "Demographic Changes in Judah Between the 7th and the 5th Centuries BCE." Pages 323–76 in *Judah and the Judeans in the Neo-Babylonian Period*. Edited by Oded Lipschits and Joseph Blenkinsopp. Winona Lake, IN: Eisenbrauns, 2003.

———. "Persian-Period Judah: A New Perspective." Pages 187–211 in *Texts, Contents, and Readings in Postexilic Literature: Explorations into Historiography and Identity Negotiation in Hebrew Bible and Related Texts*. Edited by Louis Jonker. Forschungen zum Alten Testament 2.53. Tübingen, Mohr Siebeck, 2011.

Lowe, Malcolm. "Concepts and Words." *Marginalia*, August 26, 2014. https://themarginaliareview.com/concepts-words-malcolm-lowe/.

———. "Ἰουδαῖοι of the Apocrypha: A Fresh Approach to the Gospels of James, Pseudo-Thomas, Peter and Nicodemus." *Novum Testamentum* 23.1 (1981): 56–90.
———. "Who Were the ΙΟΥΔΑΙΟΙ?" *Novum Testamentum* 18.2 (1976): 101–30.
Lundbom, J. R. "Baruch, Seraiah, and Expanded Colophons in the Book of Jeremiah." *Journal for the Study of the Old Testament* 36 (1986): 89–114.
MacRae, Duncan. *Legible Religion: Books, Gods, and Rituals in Roman Culture.* Cambridge: Harvard University Press, 2016.
Mandel, Paul D. *The Origins of Midrash: From Teaching to Text.* JSJSup 180. Leiden: Brill, 2017.
Marmorstein, Arthur. *The Old Rabbinic Doctrine of God.* Oxford: Oxford University Press, 1927.
Martin, Raymond A. "Syntax Criticism of the LXX Additions to Esther." *JBL* 94 (1975): 65–72.
Mason, Steve. "Jews, Judaeans, Judaizing, Judaism: Problems of Categorization in Ancient History." *JSJ* 38.4–5 (2007): 457–512.
McDowell, Markus. *Prayers of Jewish Women: Studies of Patterns of Prayer in the Second Temple Period.* WUNT 211. Tübingen: Mohr Siebeck, 2006.
Mélèze Modrzejewski, Joseph. "How to Be a Jew in Hellenistic Egypt?" Pages 65–92 in *Diasporas in Antiquity.* Edited by Shaye J. D. Cohen and Ernest S. Frerichs. BJS 288. Atlanta: Scholars Press, 1993.
———. *The Jews of Egypt: Ramses II to Emperor Hadrian.* Princeton: Princeton University Press, 1995.
———. *Troisième livre des Maccabées.* Paris: Cerf, 2008.
Millar, Fergus. "A Rural Jewish Community in Late Roman Mesopotamia, and the Question of a 'Split' Jewish Diaspora." *JSJ* 42.3 (2011): 351–74.
Mogliano-Tromp, Johannes. "The Relations Between Egyptian Judaism and Jerusalem in Light of 3 Maccabees and the Greek Book of Esther." Pages 57–76 in *Feasts and Festivals.* Edited by Christopher Tuckett. Leuven: Peeters, 2009.
Moore, Carey A. *Daniel, Esther, and Jeremiah: The Additions.* AB 44. Garden City, NY: Doubleday, 1977.
———. *Esther.* AB 7. Garden City, NY: Doubleday, 1971.
———. *Tobit.* AB 40A. Garden City, NY: Doubleday, 1996.
———. "Toward the Dating of the Book of Baruch." *Catholic Biblical Quarterly* 36.3 (1974): 312–20.
Moore, George Foot. "Simon the Righteous." Pages 348–64 in *Jewish Studies in Memory of Israel Abrahams.* Edited by G. A. Kohut. New York: Jewish Institute of Religion, 1927.
Morgan, Teresa Jean. *Literate Education in the Hellenistic and Roman Worlds.* Cambridge, Cambridge University Press, 1998.
Moss, Candida. *The Myth of Persecution: How Early Christians Invented a Story of Martyrdom.* New York: HarperOne, 2014.
Mroczek, Eva. "The Hegemony of the Biblical in the Study of Second Temple Literature." *JAJ* 6 (2015): 2–35.
———. *The Literary Imagination in Jewish Antiquity.* Oxford: Oxford University Press, 2016.
Najman, Hindy. *Destruction, Mourning and Renewal in 4 Ezra and its Precursors.* Cambridge: Cambridge University Press, 2011.

———. "The Idea of Biblical Genre: From Discourse to Constellation." Pages 307–23 in *Prayer and Poetry in the Dead Sea Scrolls and Related Literature: Essays in Honor of Eileen Schuller on the Occasion of her 65th Birthday*. Edited by Jeremy Penner, Ken M. Penner, and Cecilia Wassen. Studies on the Texts of the Desert of Judah 98. Leiden: Brill, 2012.

———. "Torah of Moses: Pseudonymous Attribution in Second Temple Writings." Pages 202–16 in *The Interpretation of Scripture in Early Judaism and Christianity: Studies in Language and Tradition*. Edited by Craig A. Evans. Journal for the Study of the Pseudepigrapha Supplement Series 33. Sheffield: Sheffield Academic Press, 2000.

Najman, Hindy, Itamar Manoff, and Eva Mroczek. "How to Make Sense of Pseudonymous Attribution: The Cases of 4 Ezra and 2 Baruch." Pages 308–36 in *A Companion to Biblical Interpretation in Early Judaism*. Edited by Matthias Henze. Grand Rapids: Eerdmans, 2012.

Newman, Judith H. *Praying by the Book: The Scripturalization of Prayer in Second Temple Judaism*. Atlanta: Society of Biblical Literature, 1999.

Newsom, Carol A. "Spying Out the Land: A Report from Genealogy." Pages 19–30 in *Bakhtin and Genre Theory in Biblical Studies*. Edited by Roland Boer. Semeia Studies 63: Atlanta: SBL, 2007.

Nickelsburg, George W. E. "The Bible Rewritten and Expanded." Pages 89–156 in *Jewish Writings of the Second Temple Period: Apocrypha, Pseudepigrapha, Qumran Sectarian Writings, Philo, Josephus*. Vol. 2 of *The Literature of the Jewish People in the Period of the Second Temple and the Talmud*. Edited by Michael Stone. Compendia Rerum Iudaicarum ad Novum Testamentum 2.2. Leiden: Brill, 1984.

Niditch, Susan. *Oral World and Written Word: Ancient Israelite Literature*. Library of Ancient Israel. Louisville, KY: Westminster John Knox, 1996.

Niehoff, Maren R. "Why Compare Homer's Readers to Biblical Readers?" Pages 3–14 in *Homer and the Bible in the Eyes of Ancient Interpreters*. Edited by Maren R. Niehoff. Leiden: Brill, 2012.

Nongbri, Brett. *Before Religion: A History of a Modern Concept*. New Haven: Yale University Press, 2013.

Noy, David. "The Jewish Communities of Leontopolis and Venosa." Pages 162–82 in *Studies in Early Epigraphy*. Edited by Jan W. van Henten and Pieter W. van der Horst. Arbeiten zur Geschichte des antiken Judentums und des Urchistentums 21. Leiden: Brill 1994.

Olyan, Saul. "Ben Sira's Relationship to the Priesthood." *Harvard Theological Review* 80 (1987): 264–66.

Ong, Walter. *Orality and Literacy: The Technologizing of the World*. London: Routledge, 1989.

Ophir, Adi, and Ishay Rosen-Zvi. *Goy: Israel's Multiple Others and the Birth of the Gentile*. Oxford Studies in the Abrahamic Religions. Oxford: Oxford University Press, 2018.

Overman, J. Andrew, and Robert S. McLennan, eds. *Diaspora and Judaism: Essays in Honor of, and in Dialogue with, A. Thomas Kraabel*. South Florida Studies in the History of Judaism 41. Atlanta, Scholars Press, 1992.

Parente, Fausto. "Le témoignage de Théodore de Mopsueste sur le sort d'Onias III et la fondation du temple de Léontopolis." *Revue des études juives* 154 (1995): 429–36.

Pearce, Sarah. "Jerusalem as Mother-City in the Writings of Philo of Alexandria." Pages 19–36 in *Negotiating Diaspora: Jewish Strategies in the Roman Empire*. Edited by John M. G. Barclay. Library of Second Temple Studies 45. London: T&T Clark, 2004.

Peirano, Irene. *The Rhetoric of the Roman Fake: Latin Pseudepigrapha in Context*. Cambridge: Cambridge University Press, 2012.

Person, Raymond F., Jr. "The Problem of 'Literary Unity' from the Perspective of the Study of Oral Traditions." Pages 217–38 in *Empirical Models Challenging Biblical Criticism*. Edited by Raymond F. Person Jr. and Robert Rezetko. Ancient Israel and its Literature. Atlanta: Society of Biblical Literature, 2015.

———. "Text Criticism as a Lens for Understanding the Transmission of Ancient Texts in Their Oral Environments. Pages 197–215 in *Contextualizing Israel's Sacred Writings: Ancient Literacy, Orality, and Literary Production*. Edited by Brian Schmidt. Atlanta: SBL Press, 2015.

Petrie, Flinders W. M. *Hyksos and Israelites Cities*. London: British School of Archaeology, 1906.

Peursen, W. T. van. "Sirach 51:13–30 in Hebrew and Syriac." Pages 357–74 in *Hamlet on a Hill: Semitic and Greek Studies Presented to Professor T. Muraoka on the Occasion of His Sixty-Fifth Birthday*. Edited by M. F. J. Baasten and W. T. van Peursen. Leuven: Peeters, 2003.

Pfeiffer, Robert H. *History of New Testament Times with an Introduction to the Apocrypha*. New York: Harper & Brothers, 1949.

Piaget, Jean. *Le Langage et la pesée chez l'enfant*. Paris: Delachaux & Niestlé, 1923.

Pietersma, Albert, and Benjamin G. Wright. *A New English Translation of the Septuagint*. Oxford: Oxford University Press, 2007.

Pilgrim, Cornelius von. "Tempel des Jahu und 'Straße des Königs': Ein Konflikt in der späten Perserzeit auf Elephantine." Pages 303–17 in *Egypt, Temple of the Whole World: Studies in Honour of Jan Assmann*. Edited by Sibylle Meyer. Leiden: Brill, 2003.

Pinker, Steve. *The Language Instinct: How the Mind Creates Language*. New York: HarperCollins, 1994.Piotrkowski, Meron M. "Re-Evaluating 3 Maccabees: An Oniad Composition?" Pages 117–42 in *Jüdisch-hellenistische Literatur in ihrem interkulturellen Kontext*. Edited by Martina Hirschberger. Frankfurt am Main: Lang, 2012.

Porten, Bezalel. *The Elephantine Papyri in English: Three Millennia of Cross-Cultural Continuity and Change*. 2nd rev. ed. Studies in Near Eastern Archaeology and Civilization 22. Atlanta: SBL Press, 2011.

———. "The Structure and Orientation of the Jewish Temple at Elephantine: A Revised Plan of the Jewish District." *JAOS* 81 (1961): 38–42.

Rajak, Tessa. "The Jewish Diaspora." Pages 53–68 in *Origins to Constantine*. Edited by Margaret M. Mitchell and Frances M. Young. Vol. 1 of *Cambridge History of Christianity*. Cambridge: Cambridge University Press, 2006.

———. "The Jewish Diaspora in Greco-Roman Antiquity." *Interpretation: A Journal of Bible and Theology* 72.2 (2018): 146–62.

———. "Synagogue and Community in the Graeco-Roman Diaspora." Pages 22–38 in *The Jews in the Hellenistic and Roman Cities*. Edited by John R. Bartlett. London: Routledge, 2002.

Ready, Jonathan. *Orality, Textuality, and the Homeric Epics: An Interdisciplinary Study of Oral Texts, Dictated Texts, and Wild Texts*. Oxford: Oxford University Press, 2019.

Reed, Annette Yoshiko. "'Ancient Jewish Sciences' and the Historiography of Judaism." Pages 195–253 in *Ancient Jewish Sciences and the History of Knowledge in Second Temple Literature*. Edited by Jonathan Ben-Dov and Seth Sanders. New York: New York University Press, 2013.

———. *Demons, Angels, and Writing in Ancient Judaism*. Cambridge: Cambridge University Press, 2020.

Reymond, Eric D. "Sirach 51:13–30 and 11Q5 (=11QPs^a) 21:11–22:1." *Revue de Qumran* 90 (2007): 207–31.

Rosenberg, Stephen G. "The Jewish Temple at Elephantine." *Near Eastern Archaeology* 67.1 (2004): 4–13.

Rosenmeyer, Patricia A. *Ancient Greek Literary Letters: Selections in Translation*. London: Routledge, 2006.

Rutgers, Leonard Victor. *The Hidden Heritage of Diaspora Judaism*. Contributions to Biblical Exegesis and Theology 20. Leuven: Peeters, 1998.

Safran, William. "Diasporas in Modern Societies: Myths of Homeland and Return." *Journal of Transnational Studies* 1.1 (1991): 83–99.

Saldarini, Anthony J. *The Book of Baruch*. Vol. 6 of *The New Interpreter's Study Bible*. Nashville: Abingdon, 2001.

Sanders, Edward P. *Jewish Law from Jesus to the Mishnah: Five Studies*. Philadelphia: Trinity Press International, 1990.

Satlow, Michael L. "Ben Sira." Pages 427–28 in *Jewish Annotated Apocrypha*. Edited by Jonathan Klawans and Lawrence Wills. Oxford: Oxford University Press, 2020.

Schäfer, Peter. "'From Jerusalem the Great to Alexandria the Small:' The Relationship Between Palestine and Egypt in the Graeco-Roman Period." Pages 1:129–40 in *The Talmud Yerushalmi and Graeco-Roman Culture*. Edited by Peter Schäfer. 3 vols. TSAJ 71. Tübingen: Mohr Siebeck, 1998.

Schmidt, Karl Ludwig, "διασπορά." Pages 2:98–104 in *Theological Dictionary of the New Testament*. Edited by Gerhard Kittle and Gerhard Friedrich. Translated by Geoffrey W. Bromiley. 10 vols. Grand Rapids: Eerdmans, 1964.

Schniedewind, William M. *How the Bible Became a Book: The Textualization of Ancient Israel*. Cambridge: Cambridge University Press, 2004.

Schürer, Emil. "The Book of Baruch (1 Baruch)." Pages 3.2:733–43 in *The History of the Jewish People in the Age of Jesus Christ (175 B.C.E.–135 C.E.)*. Revised and edited by Geza Vermes, Fergus Millar, Martin Goodman, Matthew Black, and Pamela Vermes. 3 vols. Edinburgh: T&T Clark, 1973–1987.

Schwartz, Daniel R. *2 Maccabees*. Commentaries on Early Jewish Literature. Berlin: de Gruyter, 2008.

———. *Judeans and Jews: Four Faces of Dichotomy in Ancient Jewish History*. Toronto: University of Toronto Press, 2014.

Schwartz, Daniel R., and Zeev Weiss, eds. *Was 70 CE a Watershed in Jewish History?: On Jews and Judaism Before and After the Destruction of the Second Temple*. AJEC 78. Leiden: Brill, 2012.

Schwartz, Seth. *Imperialism and Jewish Society, 200 BCE–640 CE*. Princeton: Princeton University Press, 2001.

———. "Law in Jewish Society in the Second Temple Period." Pages 48–75 in *The Cambridge Companion to Judaism and Law*. Edited by Christine Hayes. Cambridge: Cambridge University Press, 2017.

Scott, James M. "Exile and the Self-Understanding of Diaspora Jews." Pages 173–220 in *Exile: Old Testament, Jewish, and Christian Conceptions*. Edited by James M. Scott. JSJSup 56. Leiden: Brill, 1997.

———. "Philo and the Restoration of Israel." Pages 553–75 in *SBL 1995 Seminar Papers*. Edited by Eugene H. Lovering Jr. Atlanta: Scholars Press, 1995.

Segal, Michael. *Dreams, Riddles, and Visions: Textual, Contextual, and Intertextual Approaches to the Book of Daniel*. BZAW 455. Berlin: de Gruyter, 2016.

Sharon, Nadav. "The Title Ethnarch in Second Temple Period Judea." *JSJ* 41.4–5 (2010): 472–93.

Sheffer, Gabriel. *Diaspora Politics: At Home Abroad*. Cambridge: Cambridge University Press, 2003.

Siljanen, Esko. "Judeans of Egypt in the Persian Period (539–332 BCE) in Light of the Aramaic Documents." PhD diss., University of Helsinki, 2017.

Silverman, Michael H. "The Religion of the Elephantine Jews: A New Approach." Pages 377–88 in *Proceedings of the World Congress of Jewish Studies, 1973*. Edited by A. Shin'an. Jerusalem: World Union of Jewish Studies, 1975.

Simkovich, Malka Z. "The Diaspora as a Word and Concept in Early Judaism." Pages 153–70 in *Forget Not God's Benefits (Psalm 103:2): A Festschrift in Honor of Leslie J. Hoppe, OFM*. Edited by Barbara E. Reid. Catholic Biblical Quarterly Imprints 3. Washington, DC: Catholic University of America Press, 2022.

———. "Greek Influence on the Composition of 2 Maccabees." *JSJ* 42.3 (2011): 293–310.

Simone, Michael R. *"Your God Is a Devouring Fire": Fire as a Motif of Divine Presence and Agency in the Hebrew Bible*. Catholic Biblical Quarterly Monograph Series 57. Washington, DC: Catholic Biblical Association of America, 2019.

Simon-Shoshan, Moshe. "Past Continuous: The Yerushalmi's Account of Honi's Long Sleep and its Roots in Second Temple Era Literature." *JSJ* 51 (2020): 398–431.

Ska, Jean-Louis. "From History Writing to Library Building: The End of History and the Birth of the Book." Pages 145–69 in *The Pentateuch as Torah: New Models for Understanding its Promulgation and Acceptance*. Edited by Gary R. Knoppers and Bernard M. Levinson. Winona Lake, IN: Eisenbrauns, 2007.

Skehan, Patrick W., and Alexander A. Di Lella. *The Wisdom of Ben Sira*. AB 39. New York: Doubleday, 1987.

Skinner, Burrhus F. *Verbal Behavior*. New York: Appleton-Century-Crofts. 1957.

Smallwood, Mary E. *The Jews Under Roman Rule from Pompey to Diocletian: A Study in Political Relations*. Studies in Judaism in Late Antiquity 20. Leiden: Brill, 1981.

Smith, Jonathan Z. "Religion, Religions, Religious." Pages 269–84 in *Critical Terms for Religious Studies*. Edited by Mark C. Taylor. Chicago: University of Chicago Press, 1998.

Soll, William. "Tobit and Folklore Studies, with Emphasis on Propp's Morphology." Pages 39–53 in *Society of Biblical Literature 1988 Seminar Papers*. Edited by David J. Lull. Atlanta, Scholars Press, 1988.

Southwood, Katherine. *Ethnicity and the Mixed Marriage Crisis in Ezra 9–10: An Anthropological Approach*. Oxford: Oxford University Press, 2012.

Sprengling, Martin. "The Aramaic Papyri of Elephantine in English." *American Journal of Theology* 21.3 (1917): 411–52.

Staples, Jason. *The Idea of Israel in Second Temple Judaism: A New Theory of People, Exile, and Israelite Identity*. Cambridge: Cambridge University Press, 2021.

Steck, Odil H., Reinhold G. Kratz, and Ingo Kottsieper. *Das Buch Baruch. Der Brief des Jeremiah. Zusätze zu Esther und Daniel*. Das Alte Testament Deutsch, Apokryphen 5. Göttingen: Vandenhoeck & Ruprecht, 1998.

Steiner, Richard C. "The Two Sons of Neriah and the Two Editions of Jeremiah in the Light of Two *Atbash* Code-Words for Babylon." *Vetus Testamentum* 46.1 (1996): 74–84.

Stern, Menahem. "Judaea and Her Neighbors in the Days of Alexander Jannaeus." *Jerusalem Cathedra* 1 (1982): 22–46.

———. "The Relations Between the Hasmonean Kingdom and Ptolemaic Egypt in View of International Relations during the Second and First Centuries BCE" [Hebrew]. *Zion* 50 (1985): 81–196.

Stern, Sacha. *Time and Process in Ancient Judaism*. Littman Library of Jewish Civilization. Liverpool: Liverpool University Press, 2007.

Stowers, Stanley K. *Letter Writing in Greco-Roman Antiquity*. Louisville, KY: Westminster John Knox, 1986.

Taylor, Joan E. "A Second Temple in Egypt: The Evidence for the Zadokite Temple of Onias." *JSJ* 29.3 (1998): 297–321.

Tcherikover, Victor A. *Hellenistic Civilization and the Jews*. Translated by S. Applebaum. Philadelphia: Jewish Publication Society of America, 1959.

———. "The Third Book of Maccabees as a Historical Source of Augustus's Time." *Scripta Hierosolymitana* 7 (1961): 1–26.

Thackeray, H. St. J. "Translation of the Letter of Aristeas." *JQR* 15.3 (1903): 337–91.

Tölölyan, Khachig. "Rethinking Diaspora(s): Stateless Power in the Transnational Moment." *Diasporas* 5 (1996): 3–36.

Toorn, Karel van der. "Anat-Yahu, Some Other Deities, and the Jews of Elephantine." *Numen* 39 (1992): 80–101.

———. *Becoming Diaspora Jews: Behind the Story of Elephantine*. Anchor Bible Reference Library. New Haven: Yale University Press, 2019.

———. "Previously, at Elephantine." *JAOS* 138.2 (2018): 255–70.

Torrey, Charles Cutler. "The Letters Prefixed to Second Maccabees." *JAOS* 60 (1940): 119–50.

———. "The Older Book of Esther." *Harvard Theological Review* 37.1 (1944): 1–40.

Toury, Gideon. *Descriptive Translation Studies and Beyond*. Benjamins Translation Library 4. Amsterdam: Benjamins, 1995.

Tov, Emanuel. *The Book of Baruch: Also Called 1 Baruch (Greek and Hebrew)*. Atlanta: Scholars Press, 1975.

———. "The Literary History of the Book of Jeremiah in the Light of Its Textual History." Pages 211–37 in *Empirical Models for Biblical Criticism*. Edited by J. H. Tigay. Philadelphia: University of Pennsylvania Press, 1985.

———. *The Septuagint Translation of Jeremiah and Baruch: A Discussion of an Early Revision of the LXX of Jeremiah 29–52 and Bar 1:1–3:8*. Harvard Semitic Monographs 8. Missoula, MT: Scholars Press, 1976.

Trotter, Jonathan R. "The Homeland and the Legitimation of the Diaspora: Egyptian Jewish Origin Stories in the Hellenistic and Roman Periods." *JSP* 28.2 (2018): 93–124.

———. *The Jerusalem Temple in Diaspora: Jewish Practice and Thought During the Second Temple Period.* JSJSup 192. Leiden: Brill, 2019.

Tuval, Michael. "Doing Without the Temple: Paradigms in Judaic Literature of the Diaspora." Pages 181–239 in *Was 70 CE a Watershed in Jewish History? On Jews and Judaism Before and After the Destruction of the Second Temple.* Edited by Daniel R. Schwartz and Zeev Weiss. AJEC 78. Brill: Leiden, 2012.

———. *From Jerusalem Priest to Roman Jew: On Josephus and the Paradigms of Ancient Judaism.* WUNT 2.357. Tübingen: Mohr Siebeck, 2013.

Unnik, Willem Cornelis van. *Das Selbstverständnis der jüdischen Diaspora in der hellenistisch-römischen Zeit: Aus dem Nachlaß herausgegeben und bearbeitet von P. W. van der Horst.* Arbeiten zur Geschichte des Antiken Judentums und des Urchristentums 17. Leiden: Brill, 1993.

Urbach, Ephraim E. *The Sages: Their Concepts and Beliefs.* Translated by Israel Abrahams. Jerusalem: Magnes, 1975.

Venter, P. M. "Penitential Prayers in the Books of Baruch and Daniel." *Old Testament Essays* 18.2 (2005): 406–25.

Vincent, Albert. *La religion des judéo-araméens d'Éléphantine.* Paris: Librairie Orientaliste Geuthner, 1937.

Vygotsky, Lev S. *Thought and Language.* Edited and translated by Eugenia Hanfmann, Gertrude Vakar, and Alex Koxulin. Rev. ed. Cambridge: MIT Press, 2012.

Wacholder, Ben Zion. "The Letter from Judah Maccabee to Aristobulus: Is 2 Maccabees 1:10b–2:18 Authentic?" *Hebrew Union College Annual* 49 (1978): 89–133.

Waxman, Chaim I. *American Aliya: Portrait of an Innovative Migration Movement.* Detroit: Wayne State University Press, 2017.

White, L. Michael, and G. Anthony Keddie. *Jewish Fictional Letters from Hellenistic Egypt: The Epistle of Aristeas and Related Literature.* Writings from the Greco-Roman World 37. Atlanta: SBL Press, 2018.

Whitters, Mark F. *The Epistle of Second Baruch: A Study in Form and Message.* London: Bloomsbury, 2003.

———. "Some New Observations About Jewish Festal Letters." *JSJ* 32.3 (2001): 272–88.

Williams, David S. "3 Maccabees: A Defense of Diaspora Judaism?" *JSP* 7.13 (1995): 17–29.

Willrich, Hugo. "Der historische Kern des III Makkabäerbuches." *Hermes* 39 (1904): 244–58.

Wills, Lawrence M. "Challenged Boundaries: Gender and the Other in Periods of Crisis." Pages 41–51 in *Women and Exilic Identity in the Hebrew Bible.* Edited by Martien A. Halvorsen-Taylor and Katherine E. Southwood. London: Bloomsbury, 2018.

———. *The Jewish Novel in the Ancient World.* Eugene, OR: Wipf and Stock, 2015.

Wollenberg, Rebecca. *The Closed Book: How the Rabbis Taught the Jews (Not) to Read the Bible.* Princeton: Princeton University Press, 2023.

Wright, Benjamin G., III. "Fear the Lord and Honor the Priest: Ben Sira as Defender of the Jerusalem Priesthood." Pages 9–29 in *The Book of Ben Sira in Modern Research.* Edited by Pancratius C. Beentjes. BZAW 255. Berlin: de Gruyter, 1997.

———. "Joining the Club: A Suggestion about Genre in Early Jewish Texts." *Dead Sea Discoveries* 17.3 (2010): 289–314.

———. *The Letter of Aristeas: "Aristeas to Philocrates" or "On the Translation of the Law of the Jews"*. Commentaries on Early Jewish Literature 8. Berlin: de Gruyter, 2015.

———. *No Small Difference: Sirach's Relationship to Its Hebrew Parent Text*. Society of Biblical Literature Septuagint and Cognate Studies 26. Atlanta: Scholars Press, 1989.

———. "Translation Greek in Sirach in Light of the Grandson's Prologue." Pages 75–94 in *The Texts and Versions of the Book of Ben Sira*. Edited by Jean-Sébastien Rey and Jan Joosten. JSJSup 150. Leiden: Brill, 2011.

Zahn, Molly M. "Talking About Rewritten Texts: Some Reflections on Terminology." Pages 93–119 in *Changes in Scripture: Rewriting and Interpreting Authoritative Traditions in the Second Temple Period*. Edited by Hanne von Weissenberg, Juha Pakkala, and Marko Marttila. BZAW 419. Berlin: de Gruyter, 2011.

SUBJECT INDEX

Aaron, 94, 99–100
Abraham, 78, 107–108, 165–66
Achior, 57
Ahaseurus, 22
Alcimus, 58, 72, 99, 111
Alexander Jannaeus, 74, 131
Alexander the Great, 44, 92, 139
Alexandria, 50, 73n6, 94, 129, 131, 133,
    153–54, 156, 159, 162, 164, 166–67, 169
  Philo of, 51
  Clement of, 52n20
Ananias, 74, 131
Andreas, 138, 143, 145, 148
Antioch, 48
Antiochus III, 153
Antiochus IV Epiphanes, 7n19, 58n36,
    72n2, 76–77, 81–83, 92n1, 132
Antiochus VII Sidetes, 3, 73–74
Antipater, 132
Aramaeans, 35n8
Aramaic, 30, 35, 35n8, 38–39, 46, 76, 79,
    80, 111
Aristeas, courtier of Ptolemy II Philadel-
    phus, 142–45, 150–51
Aristeas the Exegete, 137
Aristobulus, son of John Hyrcanus, 74
Aristobulus, tutor of King Ptolemy, 81–83
Arsames, 36, 38, 41, 43
Artaxerxes II, 36n11
Assyria, 17n1, 20, 35, 46, 57, 165

Babylon, 2, 18, 23, 28, 43n29, 111n4, 116–
    18, 165

Babylonia, 2, 17, 20, 87, 110, 116, 175
  Babylonian Empire, 26, 35, 111
  Babylonian exile, see exile
  Babylonian kings, 23
  Babylonian royal family, 118
Bagavahya, 36, 39–43, 80
Baruch, Ezra's scribe, 26–27, 110–12, 114–
    17, 121–22
Belshazzar, 32n30, 111n3, 117–18

Cairo Genizah, 95n8, 100n15
calendar, 177
Cambyses, 37, 40–41, 140
Canaan, 17, 73n5
canon, 9, 24, 62, 65n18, 93
  canonical authority, 105n35
captivity, 47, 51–52, 56, 60n42, 139, 142
Chaldeans, 116
Chelkias, 74, 131
circumcision, 2, 18, 45–46, 172
Cleopatra II, 72, 78, 80, 131, 154
Cleopatra III, 3, 74–75
Cleopatra V, 104–5
Cleopatra VII, 132
Coele Syria, 139, 162–63
covenant, 7, 25n23, 53, 78, 99, 167n29
  covenantal confession, 122n19
  covenantal promises, 5–6, 17, 111
  covenantal people, 4, 18
  covenantal relationship, 30, 59n39, 108,
    125, 159
  covenantal laws, 53, 57
  covenantal love, 107

Cyrene, 76n9, 76n12, 45n33
Cyrus, 18, 21, 23, 40

Daniel, 23, 32, 119n17, 165
Daphne, 72n2
Darius, 36–38, 41
David, 20, 74, 88
decalogue, 25n22
Demetrius, Alexandrian librarian, 133, 170
Demetrius I, 58n36, 139
Demetrius II, 76, 78
Demetrius of Phalerum, 63n8
dietary laws, 2, 18, 45–46, 151, 92n1, 93, 172
Dis, 141
displacement, 21, 47–48, 52, 54n26, 123
  displacement theory, 5
Dositheus, 105, 131

Eleazar, 129, 136, 138, 142–49, 159, 164–67, 169
Elephantine, 11, 35–39, 41–42
Esther, 22n11, 23, 33, 92–93, 102–9, 162
Ethnarch, 59
Eumenes II, 89
Euergetes II, 131
exile, 10–13, 19–20, 23–25, 33, 44–45, 47–49, 52–56, 75, 100–103, 105, 107, 109, 112–13, 119, 123, 125, 158, 161–62, 166–67, 172, 174–76
  Babylonian, 7–8, 10, 12, 17–25, 27–30, 32–33, 35, 46, 66, 68, 82–88, 90, 110–25, 145, 159, 170
  theology, 5
  of Ptolemy VIII Physcon, 154
  Neo-Assyrian, 102, 143
exodus, 24n15, 107, 120
Ezekiel, 180, 56n31
Ezra, 21, 28–31, 85n33, 117, 121–22, 145n30

fasting, 37, 39, 121
fatherland, 153, 166
festal letters, 64, 82n29, 103n26
Flavius Josephus, *see* Josephus

gālût, 49n11, 52, 174–77
Gemariah, 26
Gerousia, 59n40, 83n30

gōlâ, 7–8, 20, 22, 52, 64, 173
grief, 123, 168

Hades, 120
Haman, 162
Hanukkah, *see* Purification
Hasmonean
  era, 8, 11–12, 18n2
  family, 76–77
  kingdom, 3, 57, 73–77, 80–81, 90, 112, 131, 172, 174
  rebellion, 94, 111, 113, 125, 132, 155
Heliopolis, 73nn5–6
Herodotus, 45, 133
Hezekiah, 20, 54n26
Hilkiah, 26, 116–17
hippodrome, 153, 167
holidays, 12, 46, 60, 63–64, 71, 75, 77–78, 158, 170, 172–73
Holofernes, 57
holy of holies, 86n37
Hyrcanus, Judean leader in 55 BCE, 132
Hyrcanus, Judean King, *see* John Hyrcanus

idols, 107–8, 158n22
Ioudaiois, 47n7
Ioudaismos, 7

Jacob, 55, 78, 101–2, 165–66
Jedaniah, 1, 36–37, 39–43, 78, 80, 170
Jeconiah, 116–17
Jehoiakim, 26, 116–17
Jeremiah, 12, 26–27, 58, 83, 86–88, 90–91, 110–11, 113, 115, 117, 121, 122n19, 140n26
Jerusalem, 1, 8, 11–12, 17, 20–23, 28–29, 31–32, 37, 39–41, 44, 46, 48, 51, 55, 58–59, 63, 68, 71, 74, 78, 81–83, 89, 93–94, 100–101, 102n22, 104–5, 109–10, 111n4, 113–14, 116–19, 123–25, 138, 140, 142, 154, 156, 158–59, 161–63, 167, 176, 180
  leaders of, 1, 11–12, 26, 39–42, 44, 59–60, 71, 77, 80, 110, 112–13, 116–18, 122, 124–25, 133, 135, 145, 170
Jerusalem Temple, *see* Temple
Jesus, 25n23, 51

Subject Index

Jesus, author of Ben Sira, 96
Jesus followers, 51, 63n11
Johanan, 36n11
John Hyrcanus, 3, 74–75
Jonah, 165
Jonathan, high priest, 84–5, 87–88, 90
Joseph, 99
Josephus, 7, 14, 36n11, 48n10, 52nn20–21, 58, 72–74, 81, 122n19, 130–31, 140, 154, 157n19
Josiah, 26–27, 40n21, 117, 121n18
Jubilee year, 54
Judaism, 2, 5–7, 9, 25n23, 49n12, 97, 130n1, 172, 180–81
 anti-Judaism, 103n26, 180
 diaspora Judaism, 156n17
Judah, kingdom of, 17n1, 20, 36, 54n26, 58, 78, 116–19
Judah, son of Mattathias, 91
Judah, son of Simon, 74
Judith, 92n1, 48n10, 52n23, 57
Julius Caesar, 132

Khnum, 36, 38, 39n17, 40, 43

Lady Wisdom, 101
land of Israel, 1–6, 8, 10–11, 14, 17–19, 22–24, 27–28, 32–34, 45–49, 59–61, 63–64, 66–68, 71, 75, 85, 87, 89, 93–94, 97, 100–107, 110, 112–16, 119–25, 135, 140–41, 145, 157–59, 162, 164, 166–67, 169–177
Leontopolis, 59, 71–72, 73n6, 73n7, 77, 98n13, 99, 129n1, 131n5
Levites, 30–31, 100, 105, 122n19, 125n24
literacy, 62
Lysimachus, 104–5

Manasseh, 26, 35, 54n26
martyrdom, 7, 92n1
Masada, 93, 95n8
Mattathias, 74
Menedemus of Eritrea, 148
mercenary soldiers, 35, 71, 140
Micaiah, 26
military campaigns, 3, 35n6, 71–72, 74–75, 139–40
mirroring, 4, 11–12, 14, 65, 67, 71

mise en abyme, 4, 14, 65, 67–68, 91, 140, 145, 151
Mordecai, 23, 33, 92–93, 103–9, 162
motherland, 112–52
Moses, 87–88, 91, 118–20
Mount Nebo, 87
Mount Sinai, 8, 61

Nanaia, 82–83
Nebuchadnezzar, 87n38, 111n3, 117–18
Nehemiah, 85, 91n46
Neo-Assyrian Empire, 102
 neo-Assyrian king, 143
Nile River, 1, 33, 35
Nubia, 35

Onias III, 72n2, 99, 131n5, 140n26
Onias IV, 71, 72nn2–3, 74, 99, 131n5, 140

Palmyra, 35
Paraenetic writing, 64
Parthian Empire, 74
Patris, *see* fatherland
Pergamum, 89
Persia, 81, 83–84
 Persian Empire, 1, 21, 44, 92, 105n36, 106
Pharaoh, 22n11, 160, 165
Pharos, 50, 129
Philo of Alexandria, 51
Philocrates, 129, 136–38, 144–45, 147, 150–51
Phinehas, 99–100
Phoenicia, 139, 162–63
pilgrimage, 48
pilgrims, 46
Potiphar, 22n11
prayer, 4, 32, 45, 54, 66, 78–79, 84–85, 87–88, 90–91, 98, 100–104, 106–9, 110n2, 114, 118–20, 153, 158–62, 164–67, 169
priesthood, 29, 72, 89, 94, 99, 100n17, 117
priests
 Egyptian priests of Yeb, 1, 36, 38–40, 43
 high priest in Jerusalem, 26, 37, 58, 72, 88, 98–99, 129, 131n5, 136, 138, 142, 144, 146, 156–57, 159–61

priests (*continued*)
  in Jerusalem, 37, 39, 83–86, 93–94, 99–100, 105, 117–18, 122
  Jewish priests in Egypt, 81, 83
  Judean priests of Yeb, 36, 38–39, 42
  of Nanaia, 82
  returnees from Babylonian exile, 28–31
prophets, 19–21, 25, 27, 31–32, 34, 47, 61, 87–88, 96, 101, 114n10, 116, 118, 120, 122, 172
  false, 87
protreptic writing, 64
Psammetichus I, 35, 72n1, 139–140
Psammetichus II, 35, 72n1, 139–140
Pseudepigraphy, 4, 11, 13–14, 65–66, 68, 113, 129
Ptolemais, 169, 170n33
Ptolemy I Soter, 71n1, 89, 139–40
Ptolemy II Philadelphus, 50, 129–30, 133–34, 139, 149n24, 141–50
Ptolemy IV Philopator, 59, 98n13, 153, 154n6, 155, 162, 167–68
Ptolemy VI Philometor, 58, 72, 130, 154
Ptolemy VII Euergetes, 97
Ptolemy VIII Physcon, 72n3, 78, 131, 154, 156
Ptolemy IX Soter, 74, 131
Ptolemy XII Auletes, 103–4, 132
Ptolemy son of Abubus, 73–74
Ptolemy, son of Dositheus, 105
Ptolemy, father of Lysimachus, 105
Purification Holiday, 64, 67–68, 75, 77, 81–85, 88–91

Qumran, 21n6, 93

repentance, 77, 112–13, 119, 121–22, 145n30, 161
restoration, 1, 18–19, 21, 27–29, 55, 57, 59, 76, 87, 90, 102, 111–15, 117, 120–24, 172, 176
Rome, 132, 171
Roman Empire, 5, 46
royal edicts, 18, 21, 34, 103, 104n28, 154n3, 162, 164, 167–69

Sabbath, 2, 18, 45–46, 151, 172

sacrifice, 1, 7, 29, 38, 41–43, 79, 83–85, 88, 91, 95n3, 110, 116–18, 144–46, 175
Samaria, 35, 38, 42
Sanballat, 38, 42
scribes, 1, 21, 27, 61, 75, 95n7
Scythopolis, 74
Seleucid Kingdom, 3, 11–12, 72–76, 80–81, 94, 109, 111, 113, 132, 153, 155, 171
Sennacherib, 20, 165
Septuagint, 8, 11, 13, 46–58, 60, 77n15, 115n13, 122n20, 129, 138, 156n18, 170
Seraiah, 115, 115n13
Shalmaneser V, 143
shame, 11–12, 19, 32, 53–54, 56–57, 60, 68, 94, 110, 115, 118–120, 122–23, 125, 141, 149, 164
Shaphan, 26–27
Shelemiah, 38
Simon II, 98, 99, 159n24
Simon, high priest in *3 Maccabees*, 159–62, 164, 167, 169
Simon bar Kokhba, 176
Six Syrian Wars, 72
slavery, 17, 52n20, 107, 139, 141, 157
Solomon, 17n1, 20, 39, 83, 86–91, 102, 121n18
Sosibius of Tarentum, 138
Susa, 93–94, 105, 169n32
Syene, 37, 43
symposium, 129, 148–49
Syria, 51, 72, 139

Tabernacles Holiday, 31, 77, 79–81, 83, 90, 122
tax, 48, 154n5
Temple
  of Jerusalem, 3, 6–8, 10, 12–14, 17, 18n3, 20–22, 24–30, 32–33, 39, 41–42, 44, 46, 48–49, 58–61, 71–72, 75–77, 79, 81–83, 85–91, 93–94, 98–101, 110, 113, 117, 125, 129, 134, 143, 145, 153, 155–59, 161–63, 165, 171–72, 174–77, 180
  of Egyptian gods, 40
  of Elephantine, 1, 36–44, 71, 80
  of Nanaia, 83
  of Onias, 58–59, 72–73, 77, 99, 131n5
  First Temple period, 17, 19–20, 22, 74, 102

Second Temple period, 2, 4, 6–9, 11, 22n11, 23–24, 47, 58, 72, 92, 172–73, 175–76
Theodotion, 57n32
Twelve tribes of Jacob, 55, 101–2, 143, 146
Torah, 6, 8, 10–11, 13, 18–19, 21, 24–34, 45–46, 50, 60–62, 68, 78, 86–87, 89, 114, 121, 129–130, 135, 138, 142–47, 149–52

Universality, 45, 63, 138, 171

Ventriloquy, 4, 11, 13–14, 65–66, 68, 75, 81–82, 91–92, 109, 113, 122, 124, 129, 134–35, 157, 164, 167
Vidranga, 36–38, 41

Yeb, *see* Elephantine
Yehud, 11, 18, 21–22, 33–34, 36, 40, 42–44, 55, 83, 85

Zadokite priesthood, 72
Zedekiah, 87, 116–17
Zion, 87, 98, 100–102, 113–14, 123
Zeus, 141

ANCIENT SOURCE INDEX

Hebrew Bible
Exodus
   3:1–2   61n2
   5:2,   24n15
   6:2–9   24n15
   9:4   24n15
   9:9–11   61n2
   9:24   24n15
   10:2   24n15
   11:7   24n15
   14:1   24n15
   14:18   24n15
   19:4   24n15
   31:16–18   25n21, 61n2
   32:15–16   25n21, 61n2
   32:27–28   169n32
   34:1–2   25n21

Leviticus
   9:24   85n34
   10:16   28
   23   31
   23:40–42   31
   25:10   54
   26:44   167n29

Numbers
   5:22   30n27
   25:1–18   99
   31:25–26   52n20

Deuteronomy
   1:11   38n15
   1:21   125n24
   3:2   125n24
   4:26–28   47
   9:9–11   25n21
   17:18–20   29, 61n3
   17:16   72
   27:3   25
   27:15–26   30n27
   28   56
   28:15–68   119
   28:25   45, 53, 54n26
   25:36   53
   28:15–30:4   19
   28:63–65   47
   28:67   19
   28:68   59n39
   29:20   25
   30   55
   30:4   54–55
   30:4–5   53
   30:10   25
   32   123n22

Joshua
   8:1   125n24
   8:31   25n19
   10:8   125n24
   11:6   125n24
   23:6   25n19

   24:26   25n19

1 Kings
   6:2   39n19
   8   121n18
   8:2   90
   18:36–39   85n34
   22:8   28

2 Kings
   14:6   25n19
   19:14–35   20
   22–23   121n18
   22:1–20   26, 61n3
   22:11   121n18
   23:1–3   121n18
   23:5   40n21
   24:14   52n20
   24:14–16   20n6, 52n21
   25:8–9   110

Isaiah
   3.13–17   47n3
   19:18–19   73n5
   49:6   55
   49:12   43n29
   61:1   54n25

Jeremiah
   2:27–28   78n17
   7:34   118n15

Jeremiah (*continued*)
- 9:16   118n15
- 11:12   78n17
- 13:9   52n21
- 15:2   56
- 15:4   54n26
- 15:7   55
- 17:1–10   47n3
- 24:9   54n26
- 27:9–12   118n15
- 27:9–15   115n13
- 28:6   20n6, 52n21
- 29:1   20n6, 52n21
- 29:4   20n6, 52n21
- 29:16   20n6, 52n21
- 29:18   54n26
- 29:20   20n6, 52n21
- 29:22   87
- 29:31   20n6, 52n21
- 30:19   52n21
- 31:7   52n21
- 32:40   118n15
- 34:8   54n25
- 34:17   53, 54n24
- 35:4   52n21
- 35:6   52n21
- 36   32n30
- 36:1   52n21
- 36:1–4   26
- 36:1–32   61n3
- 36:4   52n21, 117
- 36:5–8   26
- 36:9–13   26
- 36:14–19   27
- 36:17   27
- 36:20–26   27
- 36:22   52n21
- 36:26–32   122n19
- 36:27–28   117
- 36:27–32   27
- 36:31   52n21
- 37:3   52n21
- 39:44   52n21
- 40:7   52n21
- 40:11   52n21
- 41:17   51n16, 54
- 42:4   118n15
- 43:1–7   110n2
- 43:5–7   35
- 43:6   110n2
- 44,   72
- 44:1–30   58, 140n26
- 44:12   58
- 46:19   20n6, 52n21
- 47:11   52n11
- 48:7   20n6, 52n21
- 48:9   118n15
- 48:11   20n6, 52n21
- 49:3   20n6, 52n21
- 52:24   115n13

Ezekiel
- 1:1   20n6
- 3:11   20n6
- 3:15   20n6
- 11:24–25   21n6
- 12:3–4   21n6
- 12:7   21n6
- 12:11   21n6
- 23:46   54n26
- 25:3   21n6
- 29:10   43n29, 59n39
- 29:18–20   43n29
- 30:10–11   43n29
- 30:15–16   43n29, 59n39
- 30:24–25   43n29
- 37:1–14   56n31
- 46:17   54n25

Joel
- 1:8–13   39n18

Amos
- 1:15   21n6

Zechariah
- 6:10   21n6
- 14:2   21n6

Malachi
- 3:13–24   61n2

Proverbs
- 26:2   54n25

Lamentations
- 1:12–22   123n22
- 2–3   123n22

Esther
- 2:10   166n28
- 2:20   166n28
- 3:12–13   103n27
- 4:17   104n29
- 5:1   104n29
- 8:6   166n28
- 8:9–12   104n28
- 8:9–10   104n28
- 8:13   104n28
- 9:1–19   105n36
- 9:1–10:3   105n36
- 9:6   169n32
- 9:15–16   169n32
- 9:20   106n39
- 9:20–29   170n35
- 9:20–32   33, 105n36
- 9:27   106n39
- 9:28   106n39
- 10:1–3   105n36

Ezra
- 1:1–4   117
- 1:11   21n6, 52n21
- 2:1   21n6, 52n21
- 2:2   36n11
- 2:64–65   21
- 4:1   21n6, 52n21
- 6:19–21   21n6, 52n21
- 7:7   36n11
- 7:9–10   28
- 8:1–32   21n8
- 8:24–30   117
- 8:35   21n6
- 9   159n25
- 9:4   21n6, 52n21
- 9:7   60n42, 119n17
- 10:6   52n21
- 10:6–8   21n6, 52n21
- 10:16   21n6, 52n21
- 10:1–44   22

Nehemiah
- 1   55n28

1:8–9 55n27	30:22 30n28	Ezekiel
1:9 54	34 121n18	1:1 52n20
7:6 21n6, 52n21	34:14 25n19	3:11 52n20
7:64–65 29		3:15 52n20
8 29, 31, 121–22	Psalms	11:24–5 52n20
8–9 25	37:18–19 78n17	12:3–4 52n20
8:1 25n20, 30, 121, 122n19	41:13 30n27	12:7 52n20
8:1–12 145n30	72:19 30n27	12:11 52n20
8:2 122n19	84:4 54n25	25:3 52n20
8:4 122n19	89:52 30n27	
8:6–8 30	114 24n15	Amos
8:9 122n19, 125n24	136 99	1:15 52n20
8:11 125n24	147:2 53–54, 55n29	
8:13 122n19		Zechariah
8:13–16 31	**Septuagint**	6:10 52n20
8:14 30	Deuteronomy	14:2 52n20
8:14–15 25	28:25 51n16, 53	
8:15 31	30:4 51n16, 52, 54	Psalms
8:18 25n20, 30		146:2 51n16, 55, 55n29, 57n33
9 159n25	Jeremiah	
9:3 25n20	13:9 52n21	Daniel
10:7 122n19	15:1–2 56	12:2 51n16, 56–57
23:31 22	15:4 56	
	15:7 51n16, 56	**Apocrypha**
	26:19 20n6, 52n21	Baruch
Daniel	30:19 20n6, 52n21	1:1 170
1–6 23	31:7 20n6, 52n21	1:1–9 114
3:19–23 87n38	31:33 20n6, 52n21	1:1–3:8 110, 112, 114, 115n12, 116
5:2 111n3	34 53	1:1–4 116
5:5–9 32n30, 111n3	35:4 52n21	1:2 110
6:10 23	35:6 20n6, 52n21	1:3 121, 170
9 32, 119n17, 159n25	36:1 20n6, 52n21	1:3–4 121
9:5–19 111n3	36:4 20n6, 52n21	1:5 116
9:7–8 111n3	36:22 52n21	1:5–9 116–17
9:7–14 119n17	36:31 20n6, 52n21	1:8 110n1
9:8–13a 32	37:3 52n21	1:10 110
9:11 60n42, 119n17	39:44 52n21	1:10–14 117–18
12:2 57n32	40:7 52n21	1:10–3:8 114
	40:11 52n21	1:15–16 111n3
1 Chronicles	41:17 51n16, 54	1:15–22 60n42, 118
28:7–10 80n25	43:4 117	1:15–3:8 111n3, 159n25, 167n30
	43:27–28 117	
2 Chronicles	47:11 52n21	2:1–5 121
7:1–3 85n34	51:31–35 115n13	2:1–10 119
17:9 25n19		2:6–3:8 121
29:8 54n26	Isaiah	2:11–18 114n11, 120
30:1–9 64n15	41:16 56n30	
30:6–9 80n25	49:6 51n16, 55	

Baruch (continued)
2:12   120
2:14–15   122n21
2:19–26   120
2:27–35   120
3:7–8   52n21
3:1–8   120
3:9–4:4   114
3:9–5:9   114
4:4–5:9   114
4:5   123n22, 124–25
4:5–9   123n22
4:5–5:9   122
4:9–16   123n22
4:9b–29   123
4:17–29   123n22
4:21   123n22, 124–25
4:21–23   111n4
4:21–24   122n21, 123
4:25   123
4:27   123n22, 124–25
4:28   123
4:30   123n22, 123–25, 125n24
4:30–5:9   123
4:36–37   111n4, 122n21, 124
5:1   123n22
5:5   123n22, 124
5:5–9   111n4, 122n21, 124

Esther
9:20   105
9:20–32   33
Addition A   103
Addition B   103–4, 164n26
Addition C   104, 106
Addition C   13:8–17, 106–7
Addition C   14:3–11, 107–8
Addition C   14:5a, 158n22
Addition C   14:6, 158n22
Addition C   14:8–9, 158n22

Addition C   14:12–19, 108
Addition D   104
Addition E   103–4
Addition F   103–6, 170n35
Addition F   11:1, 105

Judith
5:19   51n16, 57

1 Maccabees
10:46–56   58n36

2 Maccabees
1:1   79n23
1:1–9   76, 78–79
1:1–2:18   12, 71
1:2–6   77
1:5   79
1:6   78n17
1:7   79
1:7–8   170n35
1:9   80
1:10   83
1:10–18   82–3
1:10–2:18   76, 81, 121–22, 151
1:10b–17   82
1:17–18   90
1:17–2:18   91
1:18   77, 83
1:18–2:15   82
1:19–36   83–84
1:20   91
1:22   91
1:24–30   91
1:26–28   78n17
1:27   51n16, 85
1:27–29   91
1:29   86n36, 91
1:32   91
1:36   91
2:1   86, 88, 91, 170n35
2:1–3   77
2:1–8   86, 121
2:2–2   91
2:3   87
2:4   87–88, 170n35

2:4–6   91
2:8, 87, 91
2:9   91
2:9–12   88, 121
2:10   91
2:10–11   91
2:13   91
2:13–15   88, 121, 151, 170n35
2:14   89, 91
2:15   89
2:16   77, 91
2:16–17   91
2:16–18   82, 89, 121
2:18   90–91
2:19   45n33, 83
2:21   7
2:22   45n33, 48n8
3:2   45n33
3:4   45n33
3:12   45n33, 48n8
3:30   45n33
4:1   166n28
4:4–34   72n2
4:15   45n33
4:34   45n33
4:42   45n33
5:15   45n33
5:21   45n33
6:2   45n33
6:4   45n33
7   92n1
7:1–42   7n19
8:1   7
8:2   45n33
8:21   166n28
8:33   166n28
9:1–9   83n31
9:16   45n33
10:1–5   45n33
10:6   90
11:3   45n33
11:25   45n33
13:1   166n28
13:10   166n28
13:14   166n28
13:15   45n33
13:23   45n33
14:4   45n33

Ancient Source Index

14:18   166n28
14:31–3   45n33
14:38   7
15:17–18   45n33
15:33   45n33
15:36   105n38

3 Maccabees
1:8   59n40, 83n30
1:11   156
2:1   167
2:1–3   160
2:1–12   160
2:1–20   98n13
2:2   159
2:2–3   160, 167
2:3   159
2:4–7   161
2:4–8   167
2:4–13   160–61
2:7   159
2:8–9   161
2:9–12   167
2:11–12   161
2:13   167
2:14–20   161, 167
2:16   161
2:17   161
2:19   161
2:21–24   162
2:23   162
2:25–30   162
2:27   156
2:28   154n5
2:33   156
3:6   156n16
3:12–19   162–63
3:19   164
3:20–23   163
3:21   156n16
3:22–23   164
3:24–29   164
4:6   156
4:12   156
7:1   167
7:14   156
6:2   165
6:2–8   165
6:3   166–67

6:4–8   166–67
6:9   167
6:9–15   166
6:10   52n21, 167
6:11–15   167
6:15   167
6:15   167n29
6:36   157, 169
7:1–6a   168
7:1–9   169n32
7:6b–9   168
7:7   169
7:10   169n32
7:14   156
7:17–20   77, 153, 169
7:19   157, 169n33
7:23   170n34

4 Maccabees
4:26   7

1 Esdras
1:11   52n21
2:1   52nn20–21
4:1   52n21
8:35   52n20
8:74   119n17
8:74–77   60n42
8:77   119n17
9:4   52n21
10:6   52n21
10:16   52n21

2 Esdras
7:6   52nn20–21
11   55n28
11:8–9   54–55n28
20:6   122n19

Ben Sira
Prologue   95–98,
   129n1, 151
0:1–14   96
0:5   97
0:10   96
0:13–14   137
0:15–26   96
0:20   97
0:21–22   138

0:23–26   138
0:27   97
0:27–36   97
0:29   97
0:34   97
0:34–36   97
1:1–23:27   100n15
6:23–26   100
7:31   95n3
10:1–5   95
10:14–17   95
11:5–6   95
16:17–21   101
17:1–17   101n19
24:8–12   101
24:10   101n18
24:11   101n18
34:21–33   95n2
35:1–13   95n2
36:1–4   101
36:10   102
36:12–22   101
36:13–16   102
36:16   102
36:19   98, 101n18, 102
45:6–22   93, 100
45:19   101n18
45:23–26   99
47:24   100n18
48:15   100n18
48:18   101n18
48:24   101n18
49:12   101n18
49:15   99
50:1   98–99
50:1–2   101n18
50:1–21   93, 100,
   159n24
50:7   101n18
50:22–24   99
51:12   100n15, 101n18
51:14   101n18
51:13–30   100n15

Tobit
14:4–6   102n22

Wisdom of Solomon
12:7   52n21

Pseudepigrapha
Joseph and Aseneth
  15:6–8 45n35

The Letter of Aristeas
  1–2 137n19
  1–8 136–37
  3 138
  5 137n19
  12–14 138–39
  13 35n6, 71n1, 139–40
  15–16 141
  35–37 142
  38 142–43
  39 143
  40 143–44
  41 144
  42–43 144–45
  44 146n31
  44–46 146
  84 48n8
  120b–123 147–48
  190 45n35, 149–50
  195 45n35, 150
  197 45n35
  197–98 150
  201 148–49
  206 148n33
  207 45n35, 148n33
  210 45n35, 148n33
  224 148n33
  249 149
  293 150
  302 170
  307–308 170
  310–311 77
  322 150–51

2 Baruch
  6:4–8 86n37
  78–86 64n11

3 Baruch
  0:2–3 52n20

4 Baruch
  6:19 52n20

Psalms of Solomon
  2:6 52n20
  8:28 51, 102n22
  8:33 102n22
  9:2 51

Testaments of the Twelve Patriarchs

T. Levi
  13:6–7 52n20

T. Judah
  4:3 52n20
  5:6 52n20
  6:3 52n20
  7:8 52n20
  23:5 52n20

T. Dan
  5:7–8 52n20
  5:11 52n20

T. Naphtali
  4:2 52n20
  5:8 52n20

T. Asher
  7:2 51
  7:3 51

T. Joseph
  1:5 52n20

T. Benjamin
  7:2 52n20

Sibylline Oracle
  3.274–302 48n8
  3.265–290 173n2

Elephantine
TAD A4.5

TAD A4.7 36–38, 170n35
  l.3 40
  ll.4–13 38
  ll. 13–14 39
  l. 19 40
  ll. 20–21 39
  l. 26 40

TAD A4.7–8 48

TAD A.4.9 41

TAD A4.10 42–3
  ll.5–7 44

Qumran
1QM I, 2–3 21n6
4Q169 3–4 IV, 1 21n6
4Q385a 17a–e II, 7 21n6
4Q391 77 2 21n6
6Q9 1 2 21n6
11 Q5 XXI, 11– XXII, 1 100n15

Josephus
Antiquities
1.110–112 52n21
1.120 52n21
1.216 52n21
1.255 52n21
4.186 59n40
4.218 59n40
4.220 59n40
4.222 59n40
4.255–256 59n40
4.324–325 59n40
5.15 59n40
5.23 59n40
5.55 59n40
5.57 59n40
5.80 59n40
5.103 59n40
5.115 59n40
5.135 59n40
5.151 59n40
5.170 59n40
5.332 59n40
5.335 59n40
5.353 59n40

7.294 59n40	94 45n35	77 52n21
10.155–158 122n19	74–80 59n40, 83n30	85 52n21
10.223 52n21		
12.43 72n2, 140n26, 159n24	*Allegorical Interpretation*	*On the Life of Moses*
	2.35 52n20	1.71 52n21
12.157 72n2, 140n26, 159n24	161 45n35	1.103 52n21
	306 45n35	1.163 52n21
12.224 131		1.170 52n21
13.62–63 73n5	*Hypothetica*	1.195 52n21
13.64 73n5	7.1–9 45n35	1.222 52n21
13.65–67 72–3		1.233 52n21
13.240, 74 81	*On the Cherubim*	1.236 52n21
13.240–245 73	109 45n35	1.239 52n21
13.249 74		1.254–255 52n21
13.287 131	*On the Confusion of Tongues*	2.41–43 157n18
13.349 131		2.232 52n21
13.354 131	77–78 52n21	2.246 52n21
13.352–55 131–32	197 51	2.288 52n21
14.73 59n40		
14.184 59n40	*On the Contemplative Life*	*On the Migration of Abraham*
14.194 59n40	22 52n21	
14.208–210 59n40		176 52n21
18.312, 48n8	*On the Creation of the World*	
		On the Preliminary Studies
The Jewish War	135 52n21	84 52n21
1.31–33 72n2, 131, 140n26	*On the Decalogue*	*On Rewards and Punishments*
1.61 73	41 45n35	
1.153 59n40	64 45n35	9 45n35
1:175 131n7	99 45n35	16 52n21
1.194 59n40	178 45n35	80 52n21
7.407–419 83n30		115 51
7.421–436 72n2	*On Drunkenness*	
7.423–424 73	85 48n8	*On the Special Laws*
7.431 73n6		1.97 45n35
	On the Embassy to Gaius	1.169 45n35
Against Apion	229 59n40, 83n30	1.304–5 45n35
1.183–186 140	281 52n21	1.327 45n35
2.38 52n21		2.25 52n21
2.49–55 59n38, 154	*On Flight and Finding*	2.146 52n21
2.49–56 131	36 52n21	2.150 52n21
2.55 157n19	95 52n21	2.158 52n21
2.60 132		3.111 52n21
	On the Life of Abraham	4.178 52n21
Philo of Alexandria	66 52n21	
Against Flaccus	68 52n21	*On the Virtues*
46–47 52n21, 153	72 52n21	77 52n21

Ancient Source Index   213

On the Virtues (continued)
  102   52n21
  109–24   45n35
  141   45n35
  147   45n35
  219   52n21

Questions and Answers on Genesis
  1.27   52n21

Who Is the Heir?
  75   48n8
  38:186
  98   52n21

Papyrus Fragments
  P. Amherst 63   35n8
  P. Valençay
    1.2–6   38n15

New Testament
Matthew
  17:24   48n8

John
  7:35   51

Acts of the Apostles
  2:5–11   46n1
  15:23–29   63n11

Galatians
  1:13–14   7

Greek and Roman Writers
Aristotle, *Rhetoric*
  1402a 24   66n21

Cicero, *Brutus*
  30   66n21

Polybius, *The Histories*
  3:19   83n31

Diodorus Siculus, *Bibliotheca Historica*
  1.28.1–3   52n21

Appian, *Syrian War*
  66   83n31

Herodotus, *The Histories*
  3.68   45n34
  8:44   133

Diogenes Laertius, *Lives and Opinions of Eminent Philosophers*
  10.65   45n34

Plutarch, *Moralia*
  1105a   45n34
  1109f   45n34
  1110f–1111a   45n34

Plato, *Laws*
  3.699d   45n34

Thucydides, *Peloponnesian War*
  2.27   50n14

Church Fathers
Clement of Alexandria, *Miscellanies*
  1.141   52n20

Eusebius, *Praeparatio evangelica*
  9.25.1–4   137n18

Rabbinic Sources
Babylonian Talmud

Yoma
  39a   72n2

Menahot
  109b   72n2

Sanhedrin
  11a–b   64n15
  38a

Megillah
  15b   23n12

Jerusalem Talmud
Yoma
  6:3   72n2

Tosefta
Sotah
  13:6–8   72n2

Sanhedrin
  2:5–6   64n15

Midrash
Tanhuma VaYeshev
  5   99n14

Gen Rabbah
  87:5–7   99n14

Esther Rabbah
  1:15   23n12
  2:1   23n12
  2:11   23n12

Mekilta de-Rabbi Ishmael
  14:21   24n15

Seder 'Olam Rabbah
  26   122n19

Targum Sheni to Esther
  9:26   105n37
  9:29   105n37